Julieanna Preston

Performing Matter
interior surface and feminist actions

The Deutsche Nationalbibliothek lists this publication in the Deutsche Nationalbibliografie; detailed bibliographic data are available in the Internet at http://dnb.dnb.de.

Cover Images:
BALE, 2011 © Julieanna Preston
~~in~~ertia: OF interiors, surface, matter, 2013 © Julieanna Preston

Julieanna Preston
Performing Matter
Interior Surface and Feminist Actions

ISBN 978-3-88778-412-6

Publication © by Spurbuchverlag 1. print run 2014
Am Eichenhügel 4, 96148 Baunach, Germany

AADR – Art, Architecture and Design Research publishes research with an emphasis on the relationship between critical theory and creative practice.

AADR Curatorial Editor: Rochus Urban Hinkel, Stockholm

Production: pth-mediaberatung GmbH, Würzburg

For further information on Spurbuchverlag and AADR visit
www.aadr.info / www.spurbuch.de.

Performing Matter: interior surface and feminist actions asks: What can an interior surface do?

This seemingly simple and open-ended question set in motion a series of creative works that inquired about an interior's material constitution as a site of political protest and everyday demonstration, a surface of resistance and compliance, and a space of ethical exchange and engagement. Dwelling primarily in the domains of interior design, spatial design and architecture, the creative practice-led project liberally migrated amongst other bodies of knowledge such as continental feminist philosophy, fine art practice, contemporary social science theory, building construction and material science as a means to disrespect, to cross out, or to cross over artificial divides separating theory and practice, interior and exterior, art and design, making and philosophy. Incited by an transdisciplinary material feminist ethos, I found myself working at full scale, using common materials and technologies, testing the limits of my own labouring (female) body and creating sculptural objects, performative installations, site-specific exhibitions, videos and spatial writing practice essays to liberate interior surfaces from an oppression of supposed inertia. These creative works and the accompanying critical reflection attest to interior surfaces as affective and affirmative assemblages of live, politically-charged matter and as such, they highlight a research trajectory focused on the advocacy of a sustaining ethical engagement with matter developed at the synapse of art, design and philosophy.

Acknowledgements

Thank you, Hélène Frichot, Charles Anderson and Laurene Vaughan for your collegiality, keen sensibilities and critical observations.

This book and research project it presents advanced with the skill and intelligence of numerous research and technical assistants: Jane Apthorp, David Carleton, Kevin Cook, Meagan Frauenstein, John Hawkins, Paul Hillier, Tristan Maxwell, Wendy Neale, Phil Nelson, Luz Savinón, Karna Sigurðardóttir, Lauren Skogstad, Lorna Smith, Nick Sorensen, and Uli Thie. A special note of gratitude goes to Klaus Kremer for his graphic expertise.

Every researcher relies on other creative people to talk things through or make things with. I am grateful to Suzie Attiwill, Caroline Campbell, Rachel Carley, Bronwyn Labrum, Gini Lee, Warwick McLeod, Michael Ostwald, Jessica Payne, Jane Rendell, Paulette Singley, Michael Spooner, Mark Southcombe and Marcus Williams for their probing questions, generosity of time and open minds.

The project featured in this book developed as a Doctor of Philosophy at RMIT School of Architecture and Design in Melbourne, Australia 2008-2013. It was an amazing experience well worth all the turmoil and joy it brought to my life and the energy it still fosters in my current practice. One of the virtues of the twice-yearly RMIT Graduate Research Conference is that each candidate gets exposed to some of the best thinkers, makers, writers and critics in the world who are knowledgeable on one's topic or method. The collection of critics on my panels acted with due diligence to spur me on, offer direction and expose the gnarly issues I could not see myself. Thank you to Esther Anatolitis, Karen Burns, Marion Campbell, Robert Cook, Peter Downtown, Pia Ednie-Brown, Bianca Hester, Gini Lee, Stephen Loo, Antonia Pont, Elizabeth Pressa, Jane Rendell, Bruce Russell, Udine Sellbach, Teresa Stoppani and Michael Trudgeon.

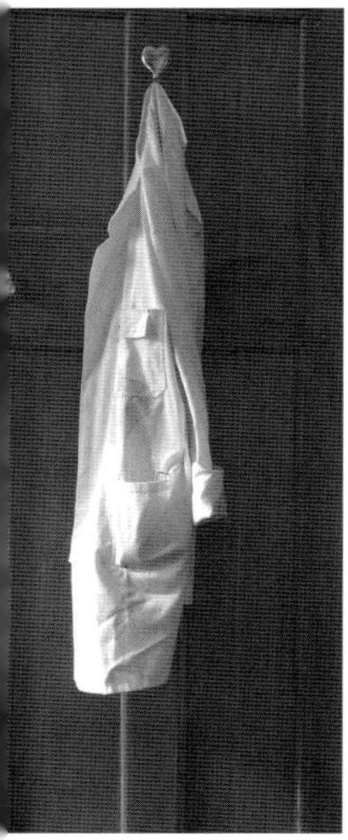

This book is dedicated to Chora Luz Carleton.
E kore e ea i te kupu taku aroha mōu.

Fig 1. J. Preston (2012). Throughout this project I have worn lab coats as a signifier of working with factual knowledge, the scientific properties of materials, and as a practical garment worn while creating art works, a process that is often messy.

Table of Contents

Videos associated with this book can be accessed using this QR code.

Fig 3: J. Preston, *all that matters* (2012). An array of common and ordinary devices that served as metaphoric and literal tools in the research project.

Foreword

Lori A. Brown

The obvious connection between the domestic realm, a woman's space and interior design has been historically and culturally connected for centuries. Of most influential to contemporary domestic ideas and spatial practices stems from Western domestic identities during the late 19th and early 20th centuries. As geographer Linda McDowell has noted, an "important influence in constructing the identity of home has been its separation from developing capitalist economies during the nineteenth century. During industrialization, the idea of the home as this haven, separate and safe from the city, became inscribed into Western ideology. The home's religiosity and sacredness became ever more apparent throughout the late eighteenth and nineteenth century. As the centre of love, nurturance, and family, the home as overseen by the mother was a place of peace and a constant refuge from the competitive city.[1] McDowell cites the Victorian critic John Ruskin who espoused and reinforced these views in Sesame and Lilies where he wrote the "...very true nature of home – it is the place of peace – the shelter not only from all injury, but from all terror, doubt and division. In so far as it is not this, it is not home..."[2]

Women were relegated to the interior of the home, as it was improper to be seen alone in public. A woman's moral and ethical character was constructed in such a way that required her to be spatially isolated within the domestic realm in order to remain socially acceptable. It was specifically during this time period that designing of interiors became a pastime for many women of means. Enhancing the surfaces of the interior was a creative practice and she became the arbiter of domestic aesthetics.[3] This anesthetising of interior surfaces, decorating and enhancing the spaces of domesticity became a social norm and expectation.[4]

Preston's creative practice acknowledges this history of the interior and uses it as a catalyst for her critical research. Through interdisciplinary avenues of material, political, and feminist research, she seeks to upend a discipline that has been inherently gendered female, and deconstructs and constructs differently spatial possibilities that have been quite limited and prescriptive. Through her nuanced alterations of material surfaces, she demonstrates how generic and banal interior building materials can be dramatically transformed. Her work requires the viewer to question some of the most common 20th century assumptions about domestic interiors and their surfaces.

Preston's research provokes me to think about the role surface plays in our lived experiences: be those at work, at home or out in the public realm. How often does one actually observe a room's surface? What appears to be seamless has seams; what appears structural can be superficial. From something as common as light entering through a window to the manipulation of banal sheetrock lining our interiors, her 'minor' interventions dramatically alter one's way of inhabiting a space. Often these subtle interplays have some of the most profound affects. As the alteration of her office window inadvertently works to keep most visitors out during the performance *Neutral, not so*, one begins to recognize how space can so easily influence one's daily encounters.

methodologies + feminism

The use of feminist methods seeks to both disrupt power structures and reveal power inequalities.[5] Feminist scholarship is interested in issues of subjectivity, identity and the body and how sexual difference reflects power relations.[6] "The philosopher Sandra Harding has written that an important component of feminist research is that it is generated from the experiences of women. These experiences are critical for the larger concerns of "social life in general."[7] Asking, "[h]ow can politicized inquiry be increasing the objectivity of inquiry?"[8] She responds that these "social values and political agendas" are believed to expand the scope and breadth of research and provoke "greater care in the conduct of inquiry … "[9]

Preston clearly articulates her position as a feminist designer and how, over the duration of her research, her attitude evolved from one of resistance, fighting the vast systems of culturally and institutionally embedded patriarchy, to one using a feminist lens engaging materials and objects connected with interior construction. Through this transformation she has opened up possibilities of occupation, affect and intimacy. I think it is important to acknowledge her employment of feminism. She is broadening feminism's influence on our built environment through questioning and intervening upon generic building materials and their typical applications. Her inquiries place pressure on how our building materials perform and undermine their historical applications.

Preston's research, as she herself asserts, is indebted to the feminist philosopher Elizabeth Grosz. Framing larger theoretical questions about architecture's potential, Grosz asks [h]ow to think architecture differently? How to think in architecture, or of architecture, without conforming to the standard assumptions, the doxa, the apparent naturalness, or rather the evolutionary fit assumed to hold between being and building? … How to see dwelling as something other than the containment or protection of subjects? In short, how to think architecture beyond complementarity and binarization, beyond subjectivity and signification?[10]

If the hope for architecture is to not just rely on its given modes of production but to create something outside architecture's typical sets of responses, what enables this to happen? What other ways can architecture be conceived and produced? As Grosz writes, "[i]nsofar as architecture is seeking not so much "innovation," not simply "the latest fad," but to produce differently, to engender the new, to risk creating otherwise … How to keep architecture open to its outside, how to force architecture to think?"[11] Through asking architects and by extension interior designers to think beyond how we know or expect these disciplines to operate is critical to dismantling the patriarchal structures they still operate within.

I find most fascinating Preston's ability to move her feminist ideas into material exploration. What we thought we understood about such generic materials of sheetrock, glass, and even wool is turned upside down and inside out. Literally, she is testing Grosz's theories through material investigations at the scale of the interior. She is urging us to reconsider certain material realities and posits potentials for quite a radical reconsidering of these everyday materials and their applications within the discipline of interiors.

futures: interiors, architecture and interdisciplinarities

If in feminism, as feminist activist bell hooks posits, "we are compelled to examine systems of domination and our role in their maintenance and perpetuation…" we as designers begin from a place questioning normative design relations and their expected outcomes."[12] Situated within a feminist critique, her work challenges and upends traditional ideas about interiors and domesticity. Her work moves the discipline of interior design beyond it's historically narrow application of decorating within the woman's realm into a 21st century material practice that is experimental, engages digital technologies and destabilizes gender spatial expectations. Her work radically recalibrates the way interiors are researched and practiced. She has discovered power within, literally underneath, interior surface materials and mines their potential. Her creative practice is a new trajectory for design and I look forward to continue following her on-going feminist material explorations, installations and textual inquiries.

[1] Linda McDowell, *Gender, Identity & Place Understanding Feminist Geographies* (Minneapolis: University of Minnesota Press, 1999), 75.
[2] Lori A. Brown, "Social and Spatial Practices," *Contested Spaces Abortion Clinics, Women's Shelters and Hospitals: Politicizing the Female Body* (Surrey, England: Ashgate Publishing Company, 2013) 28-29.
[3] Clive Edwards, "'Home is Where the Art is': Women, Handcrafts and Home Improvements 1750-1900," in *Journal of Design History* 19: 1 (2006) 18, 19.
[4] Preston's creative practice made me recall the room's surface, color and texture in the semi-autobiographical essay by Charlotte Perkins Gilman's *The Yellow Wallpaper* and more specifically how the primary room the young female character inhabits or is required to dutifully rest in would eventually facilitate her psychological unhinging. The narrator's intricate attention to surface detail in the room, the affect of light on the wallpaper pattern works towards her demise and disintegration.
[5] Lori A. Brown, "Introduction" and "Conclusion", *Feminist Practices Interdisciplinary Approaches to Women in Architecture* edited by Lori A. Brown (Surrey, England: Ashgate Publishing Company, 2011).
[6] McDowell, *Gender, Identity & Place,* 7-8.
[7] Sandra Harding, "Introduction Is There a Feminist Method?" in *Feminism & Methodology* edited by Sandra Harding (Bloomington: Indiana University Press, 1987), 7.
[8] Sandra Harding, "Conclusion Epistemological Questions" in *Feminism & Methodology* edited by Sandra Harding (Bloomington: Indiana University Press, 1987), 182.
[9] Harding, *Feminism & Methodology,* 183.
[10] Elizabeth Grosz, *Architecture from the Outside Essays on Virtual and Real Space* (Cambridge: The MIT Press, 2001) 59.
[11] Brown, *Social and Spatial Practices*, 36-37.
[12] Brown, *Feminist Practices*, 4.

Lori A. Brown has developed a creative practice focusing on the relationships between architecture and social justice issues with particular emphasis on gender and its impact upon spatial relationships in hopes to broaden the discourse and involvement of architecture in our world. She is the co-founder and co-leads ArchiteXX, www.architexx.org, a women and architecture group seeking to bridge the academy and practice in New York City. Her two books include *Feminist Practices: Interdisciplinary Approaches to Women in Architecture,* an edited collection of a group of international women designers and architects employing feminist methodologies in their creative practices (Ashgate 2011) and *Contested Spaces: Abortion Clinics, Women's Shelters and Hospitals* exploring highly securitized spaces and the impact of legislation and the First Amendment's affect upon such places (Ashgate 2013). She is an associate professor of Architecture at Syracuse University and is a registered architect in the state of New York.

Introduction – *Following the Material, or Materially Situated Learning*

Hélène Frichot

A woman with her thicket of white-grey hair, her head bent over in concentration, and the paradox of a calm expression worrying her face. She moves slowly, rests often, as though testing the proprioceptive relation of her material body to itself. Sometimes her arms sweep arcs through the air as she redistributes the diverse materials of her environment-world. She expresses bursts of material exuberance. Or else she remains quiet, curled up, exhausted. She inhabits a sealed room, viewed only through a restricted portal. What else? A bale of greasy wool, a blanket, a candle, some water, some gingernut biscuits for sustenance. *Room, wool, me, you.* And over three long days the woman redistributes the wool, as interior carpet landscape, or else she packs it tight so that it blocks the recess of what is the main door, which is, in any case, locked closed. The smell of greasy wool must be pronounced. A bale of greasy wool is as good as a coyote, she says to herself.[1] I love the greasy wool and the wool loves me, and between the two a relation is discovered that transforms each party. I love to you, she murmurs. It is an Irigarayan call: "*I love to you* means I maintain a relation of indirection to you. I do not subjugate you or consume you".[2] And Julieanna knows that the 'you' does not have to be a human actor, but pertains to anything one holds to intimately.

Julieanna Preston is a New Zealand academic and creative practitioner of architecture and interiors who asks persistently, what can an interior surface do? Who thereby insists through this probing that we will not get to the end of what an interior surface can do. This assumes that a lasting and prudent experimentation is required.

With this introduction to Julieanna's ongoing creative practice I do not presume that it is possible to commence from the beginning, as though a tame chronological account could be given. Instead I want to insist that the only viable entry point requires an acknowledgment of the persistence of utter matter, and that material immersion persists at ever turn. You are in the midst of things, and with these things you form confederations, corpuscular societies, molecular collectives. Privileged position is a kind of conceit you construct to get by. If you can claim a privileged position, it is only ever temporary, partial, and fragmentary. Given Julieanna's keen appreciation of her material relations, and the close or haptic vision this proximity demands, it would be inappropriate anyway to offer a sweeping overview of her creative labours. The work has neither beginning nor end, and in any case beginnings and ends are of little interest. The work instead draws urgent attention to material relations that are increasingly at risk of becoming exhausted, especially because what a material can do has not yet been given sufficient consideration. For too long mere matter and its special relationship with the interior has remained that which has been taken for granted, a situation that Julieanna has already done a great deal to remedy, in that she *follows the material*, rather than imposes pre-established ideas upon it.[3]

Julieanna uses an exacting, exhaustive material approach to speculate on political events, real and speculative, using fictional writing and imagery, as well as sculpted objects or props, installation and performance pieces. Her work has driven her incrementally toward a series of site-specific installations where she explicitly acknowledges that her performing body is one medium amidst many. She has frequently addressed the interior materials of her local institutional environments so as to allow them the opportunity to speak, but she has also ventured further out into less circumscribed environments to engage with the mud of toxic rivers. Her engagement with the vibrant matter of her local problematic field is a question of creative resistance. In recognising the immediate and inextricable condition of material relations and flows, resistance can provide the means by which a claim can be made sufficient to define a project. The challenge is how to act from amidst the flux of material relations and flows, so as to secure some material resilience for the time being. Creative resistance, as Julieanna demonstrates, can quite simply be related to material resilience, how a certain material is resistant to moisture, another to sound, and how resistance at times may also have something to do with yielding.[4] Julieanna reclaims the priority of resistance as a creative act. While at first seeming to respond to a pre-given oppressive force, through her creative works (including the poetic process that is her 'spatial writing practice') she turns resistance around so that it is no longer a question of *freedom from*, but a *freedom to* act amidst her encounters in an environment-world.[5] Resistance, rather than being a retroactive response to a given situation that is found to be oppressive, instead procures an inaugural act as an affirmative expression of the power of difference. Creative resistance is an acknowledgement of material relations and the potential, and responsibility, you hold to remake yourself and the present otherwise.

This persistent stress on the centrality of material relations is intended, as Julieanna's work, conceptual and material, makes a specific contribution to the burgeoning area that has come to be called 'new materialism.'[6] Julieanna reminds us that fundamental to this area of enquiry, including its redefinition of material not as something mute, but lively, vibrant and also politically entangled, is a debt that is owed to feminist thinkers. Luce Irigaray, Donna Haraway, Rosi Braidotti, Elizabeth Grosz, Moira Gatens, and more recently the architect and architectural theorist Katie Lloyd Thomas, the feminist theorist Karen Barad, and the political theorist Jane Bennett have all drawn crucial attention to revitalised engagements with matter. The contemporary resurgence of feminist practices is a crucial context for Julieanna's work, and many of her own tactics have been resituated into the domain of architecture and design from earlier feminist art performances that incorporated processes of materially oriented embodiment.[7] These precedent explorations, more familiar to artists than designers and architects, continue to open up a promising swathe of approaches, especially in light of the rise of creative works research and research by design.[8] It's also worthwhile issuing a pre-emptive retort to an occasional critique that is addressed to feminist practices generally, one that suggests that such practices are anachronistic. This critique is more disturbing even than the real risk that feminist practices might be perceived as threatening or exclusive (a risk easy enough to diffuse). There is a great deal at stake with respect to the generally undervalued and underrepresented material and immaterial labour of creative minorities, intersectionally applicable well beyond the gender assignation 'woman.' In taking creative resistance seriously as a form of feminist practice, Julieanna approaches a broader spectrum of material (human and non-human) things and their relations and offers a crucial reminder of the inheritance that new materialism receives from its feminist predecessors.

Feminist practices do not depend on identification per se, and you don't have to claim the political identity of 'feminist' to value the kind of practices you might discover should you remain open to the radical potential of material encounters. An emphasis can be placed here, in Julieanna's creative practice, on the priority of events and material relations: Something happens, and slowly, in fits and starts the subject (whoever she is) emerges as a process of subjectification amidst her seething material environs. Neither entirely 'constructed' nor entirely given, the erstwhile privileged point of view habitually ascribed to the self-same phenomenological subject is rather constructed by the world, or else emerges amidst an environment-world or milieu. But what then? The challenge becomes how you can develop an ecological sensibility that attends to the horizontal relations between material humans and material things. Donna Haraway celebrates such immersive relations in the following way: "I love the fact that human genomes can only be found in only about 10 percent of all the cells that occupy the mundane space I call my body; the other 90 percent are filled with the genomes of bacteria, fungi, protists, and such..."[9] To recall again this back-history of feminist practices, it's worthwhile looking more closely at what Haraway has famously called 'situated knowledges', which is about celebrating diverse feminist formations of knowledge where a necessarily partial and fragmentary situation is acknowledged, but one still adequate to make a rich account of a world, at least in a local way.[10] Between arguments concerning radical social constructivism, on the one hand, and sometimes arrogant expressions of positivist science, on the other, Haraway stresses that it is still crucial that adequate ways to make an account of the world are tested, even if those accounts can only address the very immediate world of your close-at-hand experience. Now, while it might be easy to mistake this for a license to produce auto-biographical meanderings that get stuck on personalogical habits, 'situated knowledges' do not forward a subject-centred approach, nor an opportunity to relate pre-packaged stories of your memories, your life, your travels, your dreams, your fantasies.[11] Instead your experience, situated for the time being only, constructs you and continues to do so as your respective field of action contracts and expands as a result of so many micro and macro-encounters, stirred up in material and immaterial forces. It is also important to remember that the things around you do not depend on you to achieve their own significance. Neither does this mean that the accounts you do hope to offer are merely or only 'constructed', instead it's a question of a "radical multiplicity of local knowledges."[12] In the encounters procured between the subject in formation and their seething environment-world the power of feminist situated knowledges emerges. Complementary to situated knowledges, 'situated learning', or rather 'situated material learning' offers yet another way of exploring feminist practices and what they have to offer amidst a multiplicity of ever-transforming local conditions.

There is a progression through Julieanna's project that I neither want to identify as linear nor chronological, yet I do want to suggest certain material lessons are learnt along the way exactly by *following the material*. To follow the material in order to ask what an interior surface can do is an ethical call that demands you pay head to future peoples and worlds: What environments do you propose to pass on to them? What is your eco-ethical approach? By complementing Haraway's discussion on situated knowledges with situated material learning, eco-ethical projects such as Julieanna's demonstrate the importance of remaining open to a process of learning. While I want to resist the idea of a chronological progression through Julieanna's works, yet there is the suggestion of a material learning that is incrementally produced: First there are the sculptural objects, seeming to stand alone, they are discrete and perhaps they are still overly 'representational'. Sometimes Julieanna even falsifies their environments through 'photoshopped' means of postproduction. There is something both necessary and yet unsatisfactory about these props, though exquisite they have too much of a story to tell. Then there is a testing of the limits of standard off-the-shelf materials, an experiment that is more processual, and where we begin to see the power of the female body labouring away in contact with her immediate and available materials.[13] Then there are the performative installations dedicated to a critique of the institution, and how the institution can at the same moment enable action and gag dissenting voices. By increments the projects arrive at a powerful performative moment, but that is not to say that they have to dispense with the usefulness of sculptural props. Here it is also interesting to draw attention to the precedent work of Mierle Laderman Ukeles, especially her Maintenance Art Manifesto of 1969, she is an important precursor, acknowledging the invisible labour of undervalued workers, the cleaners who make good our institutional environments, the garbage truck drivers who shovel our waste out of sight.[14] Again, I do not want to make it sound like there is a linear progression through Julieanna's materially engaged experiments, though there is the sense of a growing urgency. Ever more appears to be at stake.

Feminist practices, and what Haraway calls 'collective discourses' as exemplified in Julieanna's work, do not constitute a mere special interest group, but contribute to a "earthwide network of connections, including the ability partially to translate knowledges among very different – and power-differentiated- communities."[15] It is a question of deploying a feminist objectivity as partial vision, limited location, situated knowledge *and* material learning. The lesson to be learnt here is: A practice is never independent of its environment or milieu, and you do not know in advance what a practice can become, it's a matter of experiencing-experimenting.

[1] Julieanna's *BALE* (2011) can be situated as a feminist reinterpretation of Joseph Beuy's famous 1974 performance piece, *I Like America and America Likes Me*. Arriving in an ambulance and swathed in a felt blanket, Beuys shared a room in a gallery space in New York with a coyote for eight hours over three days, and during this time engaged in the spare materials available in this constrained environment, such as straw, the felt blanket in which he had arrived, his leather g oves, the cautious coyote itself, before leaving again without effectively setting foot in America. The video documentation of this performance was entitled, Room, Wool, Me, You.
[2] Luce Irigaray, *I Love to You: Sketch of a Possible Felicity in History,* trans. Alison Martin (London: Routledge, 1996), 109.
[3] See Julieanna Preston and Mark Taylor, eds. *Intimus: Interior Design Theory Reader* (London: Wiley Publishers, 2006); Julieanna Preston, ed., *Interior Economies, IDEA Journal* (Australia and New Zealand, 2011). http://idea-edu.com/journal/2011-idea-journal/
[4] See Julieanna Preston's works *SHEET GOODS*, 2008-2010, discussed in Chapter Two: *The Yield Principle*, an antigen to rigor mortis.
[5] See Elizabeth Grosz, "Feminism, Materialism, and Freedom", in Diana Coole and Samantha Frost, eds, *New Materialisms: Ontology, Agency, and Politics* (Durham and London: Duke University Press, 2010), 140.
[6] See the following collection all treating the rise of 'new materialism': Diana Coole and Samantha Frost, eds, *New Materialisms: Ontology, Agency and Politics*, Durham and London: Duke University Press, 2010; Katie Lloyd Thomas, ed., *Material Matters: Architecture and Material Practice* (London: Routledge, 2007); Rick Dolphijn and Iris van der Tuin, eds, *New Materialism: Interviews and Cartographies* (Ann Arbor: Open Humanities Press, 2012). See also Jane Bennett, *Vibrant Matter: A Political Ecology of Things* (Durham and London: Duke University Press, 2010).
[7] Lebovici offers an account of how women have taken up their own bodies in art practice as a means of manifesting female agency through practices of embodiment. See Elizabeth Lebovici, "This is not my Body" in Éric Alliez and Peter Osborne, eds. *Spheres of Action: Art and Politics* (London: Tate Publishing, 2013), 65-77.
[8] A selection of excellent publications would include: Jane Rendell, Barbara Penner, Iain Borden, eds. *Gender Space Architecture: An Interdisciplinary Introduction* (London: Routledge 2000); Doina Petrescu, ed., *Altering Practices: Feminist Politics and Poetics of Space* (London: Routledge 2007). Also books dedicated more directly to women architects in the profession, as distinct from more specifically operating in the difficult domain of practice based research, such as, Francesca Hughes, ed. *The Architect: Reconstructing Her Practice* (Cambridge, Massachusetts: MIT Press, 1998); Tanja Kullack, Architecture: A Woman's Profession, Berlin: Jovis, 2011; also Naomi Stead ed. (2012) "Special Issue: Women, Practice, Architecture" in *ATR* (Architectural Theory Review), (Issues 2-3, Vol. 3). The excellent website Parlour which collects research undertaken within and beyond an Australian Research Council funded research project entitled Equity and Diversity in the Australian Architecture Profession: Women, Work, and Leadership is also important to note here, Parlour: Women, Equity, Architecture. http://www.archiparlour.org.
[9] Donna Haraway, *When Species Meet* (Minnesota: University of Minneapolis, 2007), 3.
[10] Donna Haraway, "Situated Knowledges: The Science Question in Feminism and the Privilege of Partial Perspectives" in *Feminist Studies* (1988) 575–599.
[11] In his brief and beautiful essay, "Literature and Life", Gilles Deleuze insists: "To write is not to recount one's memories and travels, one's loves and griefs, one's dreams and fantasies", instead to write is about following the power of the impersonal, whereupon all these acquisitive, personal and possessive qualities take flight. Gilles Deleuze, "Literature and Life" in *Essays Critical and Clinical*, trans. Daniel W. Smith and Michael A. Greco (Verso, New York, 1998), 2.
[12] Haraway, "Situated Knowledges: The Science Question" in *Feminism and the Privilege of Partial Perspectives*, 580.
[13] See also Rendell's account of Preston's work with off-the-shelf sheet materials. Jane Rendell, "Critical Spatial Practices: Setting out a Feminist Approach to some Modes and What Matters in Architecture" in Lori Brown, ed. *Feminist Practices: Interdisciplinary Approaches to Women in Architecture* (Farnham, Surrey: Ashgate, 2011), 28.
[14] See Gunnar Sandin's forthcoming essay on institutional art. Gunnar Sandin, "Modes of Transgression in Institutional Critique" in *Transgression, AHRA Critiques: Critical Studies in Architectural Humanities* (Routledge, Abingdon Oxon and New York, forthcoming).
[15] Haraway, "Situated Knowledges: The Science Question" in *Feminism and the Privilege of Partial Perspectives* 580; 582.

Hélène Frichot is a researcher and teacher in Critical Studies in Architecture, School of Architecture and the Built Environment, KTH Stockholm. She has co-curated the Architecture+Philosophy public lecture series in Melbourne, Australia since 2005 (http://architecture.testpattern.com.au). Between 2004-2011 she held a continuing academic position in the School of Architecture and Design, RMIT University. Here she led the Architecture+Philosophy research stream with a focus on how to integrate critical theory into the emerging domain of research through design. While Hélène's first discipline is architecture, she holds a PhD in philosophy from the University of Sydney (2004), and her research examines the transdisciplinary field between architecture and philosophy.

Preamble

There is perhaps no other space or place so entangled with issues of surface and matter than that of the interior. Since its emergence in late nineteenth century Western European culture, interior design has been commonly understood as the selection, specification and organisation of material goods and products that support the inhabitation of environments inside buildings, most notably, domestic settings. A vast collection of paintings and drawings of interior environments complimented by a text that traces the social history of interiors as sites of human interaction and inhabitation in Mario Praz's *An Illustrated History of Interior Decoration from Pompeii to Art Nouveau* yields evidence of the industriousness of upholsters, then interior decorators, then interior designers to bring comfort, propriety and taste to the fore through the artful arrangement and application of material surfaces and furnishings.[1] Focus on the material wealth, even decadence, of interior environments has persisted through to modern history to extend architecture and design's contentious relationship with ornament and decoration.

Notable scholarship in this area tends to examine the objects and artefacts of domestic interiors as indices of class, gender and style whereby an interior signifies its owner, occupant and keeper (often not the same person). Methods of analysis common in anthropology and material culture studies are predominantly used in this research where by the material object is understood from a human and social-centric perspective. In this instance I am referring to the rich contributions to the field by historians such as Judy Attfield, Catherine Beecher and Harriet Beecher Stowe, Alice Friedman, Pat Kirkham, Grace Lees-Maffei and Rebecca Houze, Penny Sparke and Edith Wharton.[2] These scholars have drawn interior design across the cusp of the twentieth century from the Victorian era into modernity. One constant amongst all of the works by these pioneering historians is their attention to the pattern, colour, texture, scale, motif, organization and experience of material surfaces pervading interior environments. For example, in *Woman's Domestic Body: The Conceptual Conflation of Women and Interiors in the Industrial Age*, Gordon's analysis of an interior room draws relations between a female inhabitant's identity, the pattern of her garment, the wall paper lining the room and the general atmosphere of the space to signal an intermingling, even a blurring, of the physical boundaries between these interior elements.[3]

Fig 1 (p.15) J.Preston, *SWOON* (2009). A faux fur wrapping a live fleshy body is used to explore the liminal state of slumber to wakefulness.
Fig 2 (p.16) J.Preston, *LASH* (2009). A detail image of the juncture between the three-dimensional scaffolding.

Another constant amongst this body of literature is the presence of women in the domestic scene, the identification of woman with that of the home, and the association of women with home decoration and ornament. Judy Attfield's and Pat Kirkham edited book *A View from the Interior: Women and Design* is but one of the significant pieces of research on this topic that bears vestiges of interior design's emergence as an aesthetic realm and professional discipline in its own right.[4]

This compendium of literature prompted me to wonder if 'woman' and 'interior' were synonymous. Hers is a world filled with material things to arrange, drape, maintain and clean. Issues of surface appearance, surface application and superficiality skulked in the texts amongst notions of the proper place of woman, her alleged status as a weaker sex and her long-term association with all things tangible and sensible including emotions and earthly matter. As architectural practitioner and theorist Katie Lloyd Thomas points out, the roots of such conflations can be traced as far back as Aristotle's *Metaphysics* where form (associated with men) and matter (aligned with females) were split apart and form is privileged over any other attribute not withstanding the original idea. My cause advances from Lloyd Thomas' to examine the relationship between women, the built environment and material objects, to combat biologically-determined gender prejudice, to rescue language from its patriarchal pollution and to recast matter's vibrancy. There is no shortage of historical or theoretical literature and creative practice aligning design and architecture to feminism. Beatriz Colomina's book *Sexuality and Space*, Debra Coleman, Elizabeth Danze and Carol Henderson's book *Architecture and Feminism,* Doina Petrusca's book *Altering Practices: Feminist Politics and Poetics of* Space and Jane Rendell, Barbara Penner and Ian Borden's book *Gender Space Architecture: An Interdisciplinary Introduction* are, for me, some of the more significant sources.[5] While none of them focus explicitly on interiors, matters of interiors pervade their discussions which is not surprising given the way that discourse on the interior, interiority and spatiality cross disciplinary boundaries so readily.

The quantity of extant theoretical and historical material drastically reduces when the search is narrowed specifically to interior design and feminism. Though the emergence of interior design as a professional practice parallels the suffragette movement, the use of the word 'feminist' in interior design literature is used infrequently. Even Joan Rothchild's celebrated book *Design and Feminism: Re-visioning Spaces, Places and Everyday Things* omits interior design from the discussion.[6] Given the strong historical connotations between 'women','interiors' and 'matter' mentioned above, it is not surprising that the first professional interior designers were women and that women constitute a large majority of contemporary interior design professionals and educators.[7] Many scholars, many women and many interior designers would point to this fact as a sign of women's achievements and note the significant contributions made by feminist designers, writers, artists, architects and performers. Notable in this arena is the work of interior design educator Lucinda Kaukas Havenhand who speaks to gendered ways of learning and knowing with a focus on issues of gender and identity as well as design's role as an empathetic and transformative agent in today's society. Havenhand writes:

> Both Interior Design and women have responded in a similar fashion to their identification as inferior to their counterparts – men and architecture. In the first-wave of feminism women struggled to show that they were as capable as men and that with proper access to education and experience could do the same jobs they did. Interior Design similarly has fought hard to show that is as competent and professional as Architecture … feminism has now critiqued this strategy of comparison and has moved on to a new phase in its theoretical approach to identity politics.[8]

Performing Matter: interior surface and feminist actions presents a creative practice-led research project that considers the impact of constructing, inhabiting and thinking of interior environments in the manner outlined above and, in response, intervenes to reconceptualise interiors in relation to contemporary philosophy and transdisciplinary performative and material practices.[9] In this case, I borrow philosopher Rosi Braidotti's use of 'transdisciplinary' to mean "the crossing of boundaries without concern for the vertical distinctions around which they have been organized. Methodologically, this style comes close to the 'bricolage' defended by the structuralists, especially Levi-Strauss; it also constitutes a practice of 'theft', or extensive borrowing of concepts that, as Cixous puts it, are deliberately used of out context and de-routed from their original purpose. Delueze calls this technique 'deterritorialization' or the "becoming-nomad of ideas."[10] Mine is a speculative project that employs methods and values aligned with material feminism while exploring the capacity of an interior to be live, politically charged, affective and affirmative. It asks: *What can an interior surface do?* This open-ended question acknowledges a contingent agency to materials and objects, in particular interior furnishings and finishing products, intimately entwined with and yet surprisingly also distinct from human activity. The contingent aspect lies in the conviction that matter is not inert in which case, agency, the capacity of individuals to act independently and to make their own free choices typically reserved for human's is extended to non-humans, i.e. things, stuff, and materials.[11]

My motivation to engage this research has been two-fold. For twenty-five years my practice has, most curiously and uniquely, inhabited a space that bridged construction and philosophy and dwelt primarily in the art and craft of making objects: buildings, interiors, furnishings and sculptural objects. Throughout this research project I have gained appreciation for the beauty of these former works and their attentiveness to material detail as conceptually construed and aesthetically meaningful. And yet, I have also found the insight and courage to reflect on them critically: they now feel like closed, symbolically laden, rarefied, dead things to me.

This observation was formed while creating *vCase*, the first suite of creative works in this research project. Consisting of four sculptural objects (*LASH*, *HEDGE*, *HEAR* and *mute*), *vCase* attempted to bring to the fore metaphoric analogies between interior finishes and the linings of everyday objects such as vests, coats, satchels, hats, shoes and cases for storing and transporting precious objects.[12] (Fig 3-6) Having found four old and abandoned timber violin cases, each piece developed in response to a case's shape, structure, paper pattern, hardware or use and a condition of lining that was transferable to a human-scaled interior environment. Where *LASH* proposed that an interior space could be structured internally to support a luxurious external (and aggressive) skin, *HEDGE* veiled the remnants of a violin that had been trapped inside the case with perforated paper foliage to emphasise the power of pattern to produce spatial depth and camouflage. *HEAR* finds a violin case flooded with plaster and carved as a cavity for listening and handling. It was created to invoke the act of touching an interior surface, to feel your way across its topography with sensual pleasure. Lastly, *mute* stands as a yet un-activated performative sculpture commemorating a 1971 New Zealand feminist protest and a critique of that event's ineffectiveness forty-two years later. It will 'go-live' on 17 September 2014 when some of the original protestors and invited contemporary NZ feminist artists will open and close the barnacle or wreath-encrusted coffin-like lid and a plume of ash will fill the air. This work played between the seething underground forces of volcanoes and feminist agendas — both assumed to be dormant and harmless. I believe that these issues and concerns have found their way into the chapters and works that follow but with less overt reliance on symbolism and metaphor than *vCase* depended upon, greater subtlety in directing interpretation, and more respect for the body of matter I encounter.

As a necessary and enlightening phase of the project, *vCase* exposed the nexus of building construction and philosophy in my practice and the value that making with my body and materials at full scale has on my learning process. I find poetry in building. Building is my path towards embodied knowledge including knowledge as conceptual and abstract as philosophy. To inquire about what an interior surface could do required full-scale, direct and intimate engagement; representation would not suffice. Some people have called this construction-philosophy identity a duality and they imply that it is something to resolve which usually means that the two are too different to inhabit simultaneously, fruitfully. It was one thing for Jane Rendell to build a productive transfer between art and architecture because those two fields of practice share a common heritage under the auspices of 'the arts'.[13] Perhaps the space between the technical, matter-of-fact, pragmatic and concrete face of building and philosophy's concern for fundamental problems related to reality, existence, knowledge, reason, values, mind and language is too big to breach? To these comments I reply: This is how I make sense of the world. I am not bifurcated, I am one.

The second motivation for this project dates back to when life circumstances prompted me to shift from teaching architecture and building science to interior design. I was confronted by the discipline's penchant towards trends, forecasting and consumer products and its historically-driven identity related to domesticity and ornament. The dearth of critical theory underpinning its practice confounded me.[14] I became embroiled in the discipline's internal haggling over its own future and its contentious relationship to architecture.[15] I was intrigued by an interior's resistance to being generalised by virtue of its porous boundaries and spatial proclivities, and yet slightly horrified by the rate that interiors get redressed. Such ambiguity and changeability suggested that interiors are not stable or fixed entities but rather temporal, affective states. Though interiors are often

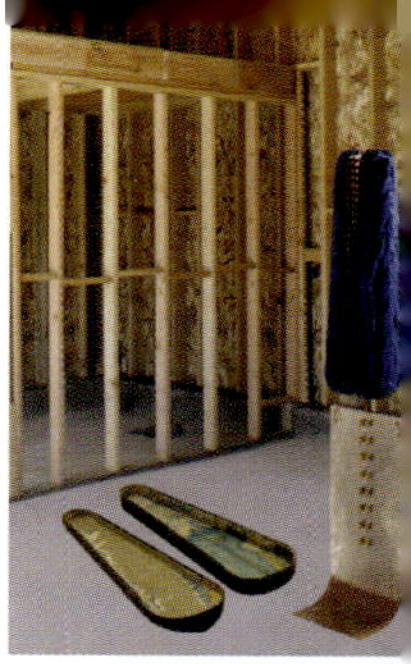

Fig 3. J. Preston, *LASH* (2009). A membrane of blue velvet supported on scaffolding encloses a hollowed out space as a means of contesting assumptions about surface as a superficial two-dimensional condition.
Fig 4. J. Preston, *HEDGE* (2009). A cloud of fragile paper mimicking the pattern of the violin case's lining shround the remnant of a violin's body as a means of addressing decoration as a hiding technique.
Fig 5. J. Preston, *HEAR* (2009). Plaster fills the interior of a violin case as an acoustic terrain operating between the ear and the posture of handling the instrument.
Fig 6. J. Preston, *mute* (2009). A wreath encrusts the lid of a violin case remade as a coffin ready to spew ashes as a commemoration of a significant New Zealand feminist protest in the 1970's.

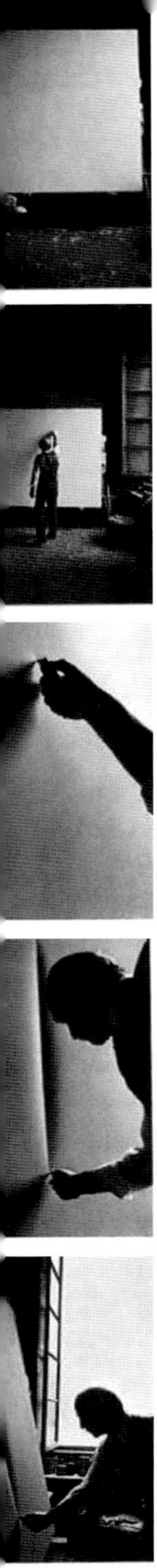

thought to be containers of consumptive goods and they are constructed with tangible materials, they themselves are elusively vibrant given the multitude and diversity of human emotions, activities and actions that occur in them. So why is it that so many interiors look the same, feel the same? Why do so many interiors hide expressionless in their own margins and with muted voices? What untapped potential resides in an interior if it is understood as the confluence of live spatial and material forces inclusive of the force of my own building body? How might a room constructed with seemingly lifeless matter be just as oppressed as a woman that watches after it? What happens when an interior performs as an active feminist agent? This collection of questions register how the research began as a project aimed at liberating interior surfaces from an inert quality attributed to them by (patriarchal) human-centred philosophic concepts. Feminism has been steadfast as a personal value and methodological provocateur throughout the project. It has assumed three distinctive voices, which offer a measure of how the project has matured and shifted over the course of four years. In the beginning, the feminist aspect of the project was one of resistance and criticism that saw a 'problem' (to fix) in the production of interiors generated by industrial construction processes and materials. 'I' was being held back by a homogenous, uniform and unyielding material domain erected by a patriarchal culture (of architecture) hopelessly bound to values of efficiency, progress and capital gain.

Not surprisingly, this problem drew associations with material attributes such as smooth, seamless, continuous, undifferentiated, flat and modular, and led to investigation of textile fabrication processes such as cutting-in, distressing and relaxing. In the initial stages of this research, I operated with feminist agency to liberate — not women, but the physical stuff of the realm attributed to them by default — the interior. These rebellious, repairing or re-doing acts were signified graphically by the double-lined score that cuts through the term 'inertia' to reflect an action of doing and undoing. This crossing out act teeters between violence and creativity in the same way that Lucio Fontana's sliced canvases exposed the material substrate of a painting as far more participatory than a representational plane or neutral substrate. (Fig 7) If inertia reflects a property in matter and material things

Fig. 7. Argentine-Italian artists Lucio Fontana (1899-1968) shown creating a "spatial painting" in 1958. http://www.corriere.it/cultura/10_febbraio_21/quello-sfregio-ai-tagli-di-fontana-quando-l-arte-suscita-rabbia-paolo-conti_dbc4545c-1ecd-11df-89bb-00144f02aabe.shtml Accessed 12 July 2012. In public domain.

to have no inherent power of action, motion or resistance whether in rest or moving in a uniform straight-line manner, ‘~~in~~ertia’ signals an unleashing of a state-altering force.

Performing Matter: interior surface and feminist actions consists of four distinct suites of creative projects. (Fig 8) Each suite includes works that played minor roles in advancing the topic and others that had resounding impact on the trajectory of the inquiry. Each chapter presents and expands upon one or two creative works and, in the process, significant creative exemplars and scholarly references are woven into the text as a means to probe the issues, support the argument or demarcate a field of

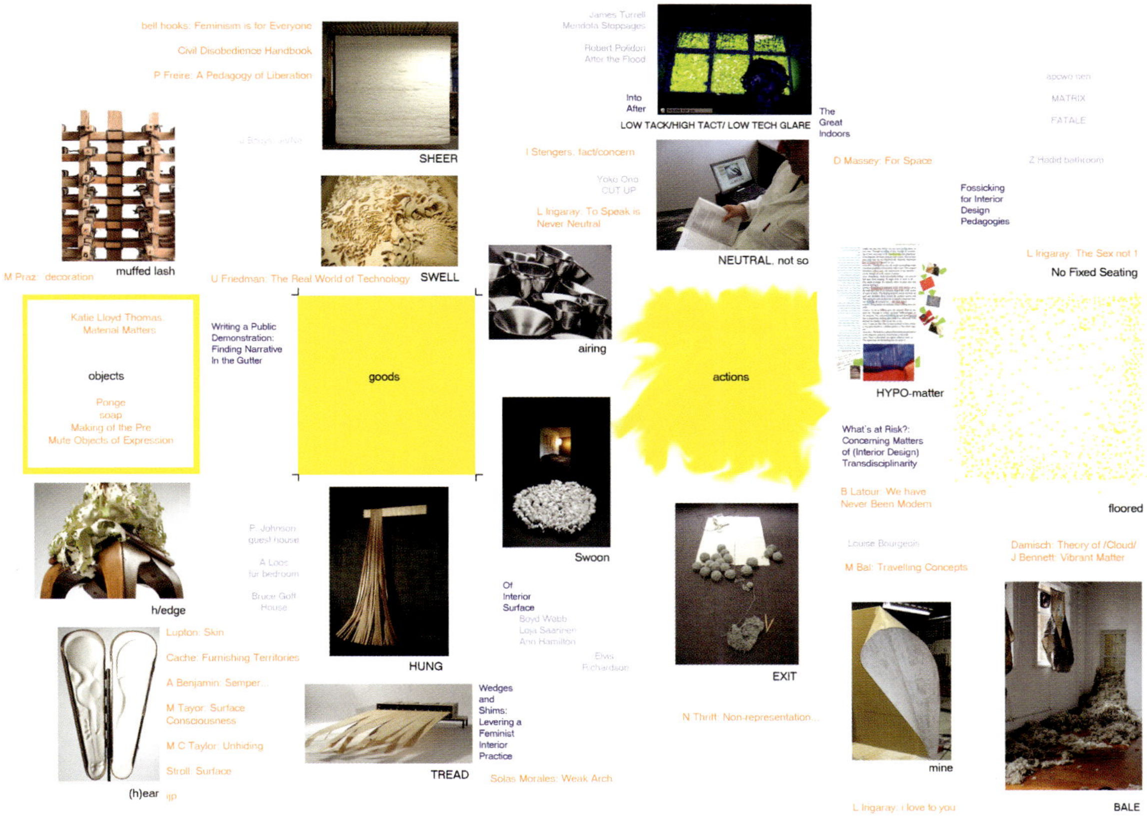

Fig 8. J. Preston (2012). A visual diagram mapping the four suites of major and minor creative works, scholarly publications and related readings and creative works by others significant to this research project.

concern. While these chapters follow the chronological development of the project and maintain some semblance of autonomy from each other with a distinct purpose, voice and tone with respect to the creative works that spurred them on. This effort

demonstrates my conviction that language, written and spoken, has a material constitution and therefore is complicit with the project's attention to the affective nature of material surfaces. In addition, this book offers a link to a collection of videos featuring videos, which revisit the creative work(s) discussed in each chapter. I am not claiming any expert status as a video artist; I regard these videos as visual, aural and spatial narratives that look into the work rather than define what it is or was.

The sculptural works *SHEAR* and *SWELL*, presented in Chapter 1: *The Yield Principle*, exemplify this approach best. (Fig. 9) Both works developed using processes that tamper and tinker with the structural integrity and aesthetic programme of standardised materials. It was here that I was operating with the idea of emancipating an industrial interior finishing material and hoping that the act might catalyse an interior to shed the burdens and stereotypes of interior design's history and its own modularity and smoothness.

NEUTRAL, not so, a creative work addressed in Chapter 2: *Voice Lessons,* operates in a similar way. It is a performative installation that found me repairing the walls of an office interior and reading selected texts aloud as a protest against neutrality's use as a cultural concept, a defence of prejudice and as a popular interior design colour palette. As such, *NEUTRAL, not so* registered the high-pitched emotions of a public rally that made me aware of an ensuing reciprocity between my actions and intentions and the materials and surfaces I was employing. Looking back on these works, I note the way that I was literally using material to wage a protest, and yet it was primarily my protest; interior materials were instruments not participants.

Fig. 9. J.Preston, (2009). *SHEAR* and *SWELL* exhibited in the mechanical space of their making.

Though I consider it a minor part of the overall project, *SWOON* was a work that attempted to correct the unbalanced power relationships I experienced in *NEUTRAL, not so*. (Fig 10-11) *SWOON*'s focus on the external surface of interior furnishings was a creative response to design historian Penny Sparke's pivotal essay "The Things Which Surround One: The Domestic Aesthetic" which documents the early modern notion of taste as something that is moulded by objects and consumer products selected and arranged by a housewife to propagate a sense of goodness and beauty.[16] *SWOON* attempted to de-objectify a Victorian villa interior as a site of consumption; thingness was replaced by the experience of sensate envelopment. Soft clay balls were pressed into the surface of my bedroom at critical horizontal datum created by the room's furnishings: skirting board, bed, dresser, desk, window sill, door header, window mullion, soffit moulding, foil wallpaper, synthetic fur duvet and so on.

This process registered an interface between my fingers and these objects; the clay balls lost their Euclidian form. Photographs taken at close range to these surfaces were assembled as a temporal sequence and the balls were strung as a beaded necklace and analogue mapping. Each of these actions was guided by a desire to capture the semi-conscious state of falling into or transitioning out of sleep, or more properly, a swoon. Though *SWOON* got closer to realising a practice that was less hierarchical in nature, it still maintained a highly symbolic and human-centric narrative, a characteristic I was seeking to dispense with or at least redirect via an expanded interpretation of what Sparke called a "sensibility of softening."[17]

Fig 10. J. Preston, *Neutral, not so* (2009). A "whites and neutrals" paint chip colour chart inspired this work's attention to interior renovation and political issues of whiteness. Courtesy Resene New Zealand.
Fig 11. J. Preston, *SWOON* (2009). A domestic bedroom interior in a turn of the century New Zealand house became the site of an exercise that attempted to measure the room's surface while enveloped by it. Balls of clay pressed between finger and wall surface formed a unique and lasting registration of the exchange. Strung in accordance with the datums, the beads continue to shape an interior space, in this instance one of adornment.

My performative installation *LOW TACK/LOW TECH/HIGH TACT GLARE*, expanded upon in Chapter 3: *IN wildness*, was an effort to step away from a practice that utilised, exploited or consumed materials to one that set the scene for something to happen. (Fig. 12) In this creative work my role was much more passive; I was a watcher, a recorder, an interpreter and a sentient. The sun, the window, the tape and the walls did all the work. This installation was a pivotal moment in the project where my poetic sensibilities were attuned to what an interior surface could do if I just let it. The anger of protest and the cause for emancipation transformed to a quieter, subtler and non-objectified form of creative practice, one that fused interiors as physical rooms and furnishings with the phenomena, experience, sensation and subjectivity associated with interiority.

The next phase of the research developed sites of demonstration in all senses of the word, i.e. "Be the change that you wish to see happen" or "Excel in the face of adversity." This shift is inspired by the affirmative tone in the work of feminist scholar Rosi Braidotti. She advocates "radical immanence" as a means to think through the body as "enfleshed" or "embodied materialism" in support of positive difference in contrast to distancing the body through "the fixity and lethal inertia of conceptual thinking" that has "frozen processes, fluid in-between flows of data, experience and information in spatial, metaphoric modes of representation which itemise them as 'problems'."[18] I was especially moved by social activist and feminist writer bell hooks' declaration, "Feminism is for everybody" which situates feminism less as a defence mechanism and more as a humanitarian call for freedom from oppression across a wide gamut of life situations, not all of them specific to being female. My performative installation *No Fixed Seating*, presented in Chapter 4: *making note(s) OF Surface*, offers visceral and temporal evidence of this way of thinking. It is here that I 'decorated and furnished a room' in a mode that sought to provide comfort and individuation to a public event. This work embraces (and advances) philosopher Luce Irigaray's persuasive calls for sexual equality and her argument that the privilege of one sex over the other limits the potential of both.[19] In making and installing *No Fixed Seating,* I took Irigaray's metaphor of fluids seriously: at every turn I perforated, permeated, filtrated and punctured material and space to support not just women, and not just women and men, but every different body, including the chairs. It was at this point that I ventured in Actor-Network Theory with caution over its social science leanings, enthusiasm for

Fig 12. J. Preston, *LOW TACK/LOW TECH/HIGH TACT GLARE* (2009). A selection of stills from the light infused event.

the way sociologist, anthropologist and theorist Bruno Latour seeks to form a parliament of democracy amongst all things and, admittedly, a suspicion that art and design practice was already assembling, circulating and associating forceful alliances. (I hesitated and still do to some degree, to fully yield to and embrace Actor-Network Theory because I have never found scientific models compatible or endearing to the conceptual and speculative nature of creative arts practices. At the same time, I am attracted to the bluntness of its ambitions and the overtones the theory makes towards discussions of systems, matter and forces that enable me to find synapse befitting transdisciplinarity.) *No Fixed Seating* clarified what an interior surface could do as a temporal encounter between material bodies. (Fig. 13) Two thin, fused films helped foster this exchange and convert a dialogue between two things into a symposium amongst many.

The third feminist voice in the project realigned the terms of respectful engagement between action and matter, an intellectual shift I credit to Luce Irigaray's demonstration of the consequences of yielding to hierarchical power structures pronounced in her essay, "i love to you." Irigaray's insertion of the word "to" is the "guarantor or indirection ... the sign of non-immediacy ...the site of non-reduction of the person to the object ... a barrier against alienating the other's freedom in my subjectivity, my world, my language ... guarantor of two intentionalities: mine and yours."[20] In the installation *BALE*, a performance where I lived with a bale of wool and a gallery space, I noted latent forces emerging in our mutual exchange beyond hierarchical human/non-human, organic/synthetic, affective/effective essential modalities.

Chapter 5: *utter matter* extends that understanding through an experimental site-writing text that revisits the event chronologically but rewrites it as a script for a play that is yet to be staged and where all things are actors; all things are matter and all things utterly matter. These forces are mute voices that circulate amongst vast complex tangles of associations shaping things physically, politically and spatially. In the process of performing this work, I experienced alternative modes of relating to material with respect to its own potential animation and, in doing so, I dwelled upon political theorist Jane Bennett's challenge to take seriously "the capacity of things — edibles, commodities, storms, metals — not only to impede or block the will and design of

Fig. 13. J. Preston, *No Fixed Seating* (2010). A still image taken at the moment between installation and human interaction.

humans but also to act as quasi agents or forces with trajectories, propensities, or tendencies of their own."[21] Such a horizontal realignment of authority is witnessed in the works of French poet and essayist Francis Ponge who does not speak for but speaks through things. His proems preserve a thing's individual identity as multiple and inseparable from a broader physical and cultural ecology, a trait with currency in much of contemporary continental feminist discourse and creative work. Ponge's literary voice and Bennett's theoretical proposition serve my feminist aims well. *BALE* and its expository text *utter matter* clearly evidence a transformation of my practice. I continue to speculate on what interior surfaces can do, what they utter, in a spatial and performative practice that includes language, text and image as equally pliable and politically active matter. (Fig. 14) This alternative form of democracy helps me to reconcile how the concreteness of my actions can be locally specific yet intertwine with complex forces outside my control and subject to generative modes of translation. For me, this is an ultimate form of liberation inextricably related to my feminist values, my female body and the ethical agency it bestows through creative action.

[1] Mario Praz. *An Illustrated History of Interior Decoration from Pompeii to Art Nouveau*. (London: Thames and Hudson, 1964).

[2] The literature addressing the topic of interiors, women and furnishings is substantial. Notable examples spanning late eighteenth century to late twentieth century include (in alphabetical order): Judy Attfield. *Wild Things: The Material Culture of Everyday Life.* Oxford: Berg, 2000. Beecher Catharine E. and Harriet Beecher Stowe. *The American Women's Home*. Edited and introduced by Nichole Tonkovich. New Jersey: Rutgers University Press, 2002. Alice T. Friedman. *Women and the Making of the Modern House: A Social and Architectural History.* New York: Abrams, 1998. Pat Kirkham. *The Gendered Object.* Manchester, UK and New York: Manchester University Press, 1996. Grace Lees-Maffei and Rebecca Houze, ed. *The Design History Reader.* New York: Berg, 2010. Penny Sparke. Modern Interior: A Space, a Place or a Matter of Taste? In *Interiors: Design, Architecture and Culture 1* (1-2) (2010): 7-17. Edith Wharton and Ogden Codman. *The Decoration of Houses.* B.T. Batsford: United States, 1898.

Fig. 14. J. Preston, *BALE* (2011). A single still image of a moment amongst many new materialist actions.

[3] Beverly Gordon. Woman's Domestic Body: The Conceptual Conflation of Women and Interiors in the Industrial Age. Winterthur Portfolio, 31 (4) (1996): 281-301.
[4] Judy Attfield and Pat Kirkham, eds. *A View from the Interior: Women and Design*. London: Women's Press, 1995.
[5] Though I am not a proponent of canons in general, my research on the subject of women, design/ architecture and feminism consistently underscores the importance of these texts to contemporary discourse: Cheryl Buckley. "Made in Patriarchy: Toward a Feminist Critique of Design." *Design Issues 3* (2)(1986): 3-14. Debra Coleman, Elizabeth Danze and Carol Henderson, eds. *Architecture and Feminism.* New York: Princeton Architectural Press, 1996. Beatriz Colomina, ed., *Sexuality and Space*. Princeton, NJ: Princeton Architectural Press, 1992. Pat Kirkham and Ella Howard, eds. "Women Designers in the USA, 1900-2000." *Studies in the Decorative Arts* 14 (2000-2001). Leslie Kanes Weisman. *Discrimination by Design: A Feminist Critique of the Man-Made Environment.* Urbana and Chicago: University of Illinois Press, 1992. Doina Petrusca, ed. *Altering Practices: Feminist Politics and Poetics of Space*. London and New York: Routledge, 2000. Jane Rendell, Barbara Penner and Iain Borden, eds. *Gender Space Architecture: An Interdisciplinary Introduction*. London and New York: Routledge, 2000.
[6] Joan Rothschild, ed. *Design and Feminism: Re-visioning Spaces, Places and Everyday Things.* New Brunswick, NJ: Rutgers University Press, 1999.
[7] Emma Ferry, "'Decorators May be Compared to Doctors': An Analysis of Rhoda and Agnes Garrett's Suggestion for House Decoration in Painting, Woodwork and Furniture (1876)," *Journal of Design History* (2003) 16(1): 15-33. Ferry's article identifies Agnes and Rhoda Garrett as the first professional interior designers. Locating world-wide data on this statistic is challenging to impossible.
[8] Lucinda Kaukas Havenhand. "Interior Design, Identity Politics, and Feminism: Problems, Parallels and Possibilities," (abstract and bibliography only), 2003 Interior Design Educators Council International Conference in San Diego, California. Accessed 12 August 2012. http://www.idec.org/pdf/03ConferenceProceedings.pdf#page=23. See also Lucinda Kaukas Havenhand, "A View from the Margin: Interior Design," *Design Issues* (Autumn 2004) 20(4): 32-42.
[9] This is a richly populated arena. I found my practice developing in association with the following individuals or group with regard to feminist material practice: FATALE "is a group of researchers and educators at the School of Architecture, KTH, pursuing research and education within, and through, feminist architecture theory – a critical practice where gender acts as a significant analytical category, often through the intersection with other power relations." Ella Finer, Emily Orley and P. A. Skantze performed Salt and Water at Whirlwinds, a symposium within the *Sexuate Subjects: Politics, Poetics, Ethics Conference*, Dec 2010, UCL, London. See http://www.ucl.ac.uk/sexuate-subjects/abstracts/abstractsPDF. Accessed 2 July 2012. "Three women, three artists, three theorists, three activists, a trio of roles and intentions, working in different media, gesture, object, movement and voice. This performance is an intervention, an infiltration, not in a covert sense of spying on the enemy camp but a fluid and windy intermixing. Using salt and water, materials, which can and cannot hold the traces of the physical marks made on them, and other fragile materials like words and dance. With a performance construction whose nature it is to disappear and endure, to be relentless in its repetition, we will attend to 'the third agency,' the real, saying until you respond we will be here." LIQUID INC: Amy Landesberg and Lisa Quatrale operated an architectural practice in the 1990s called LIQUID INC. Together they produced a series of spatial and material works that probed the feminine, ornamental and material such as "see angel touch" featured in Coleman, Danze and Henderson, *Architecture and Feminism,* New York, Princeton Architectural Press, 1996, 60-71. Accessed 1 June 2012. http://www.alarch.com. Matrix Feminist Design Co-operative "was set up in 1980 as an architectural practice and a book group that grew out of the Feminist Design Collective, itself an off-shoot of the New Architecture Movement's feminist group. They were one of the first architectural groups in Britain to take an overtly feminist stance in their way of working and designing, and in the projects they took on. The practice was run as a workers' co-operative with a non-hierarchical management structure and collaborative working. Accessed 12 July 2012. http://www.spatialagency.net/database/matrix.feminist.design. co-operative muf Architecture: "Since 1996 muf has established a reputation for pioneering and innovative projects that address the social, spatial and economic infrastructures of the public realm. The practice philosophy is driven by an ambition to realize the potential pleasures that exist at the intersection between the lived and the built. The creative process is underpinned by a capacity to establish effective client relationships that reveal and value the desires and experience of varied constituencies. Access is understood not as a concession but as the gorgeous norm; creating

spaces that have an equivalence of experience for all who navigate them both physically and conceptually, muf deliver quality and strategic durable projects that inspire a sense of ownership through occupation." Accessed 12 July 2012. http://www.muf.co.uk/ taking place "is a group of women artists and architects. Mierle Laderman Ukeles is an artist well-known for her work *Washing/ Tracks/ Maintenance,* 1973 performed at the Wadsworth Atheneum, Hartford, Connecticut where she washed the floor of the gallery to perform all her domestic duties in public. Lippard comments, "She sees women's roles ('unification ... the perpetuation and maintenance of the species, survival systems, equilibrium') as representing the life instinct in art. This opposes the death instinct, or the reigning principle of the avant-guard ('to follow one's own path to the death — do your own thing, dynamic change'). She thereby airs the real problem; what she calls 'the sour ball of every revolution: after the revolution, who's going to pick up the garbage on Monday morning?'" Lucy R. Lippard, *The Pink Glass Swan: Selected Essays on Feminist Art.* New York: The New Press, 1995, 65.

[10] Rosi Braidotti. *Nomadic Subjects: Embodiment and Sexual Difference in Contemporary Feminist Theory.* New York: Columbia University Press, 1994, 37.

[11] Susanna Kuechler. "Beyond Objects: Art and Agency and the Emerging Theorization of Materiality." The Centre for Research in the Arts, Social Sciences and Humanities: The Centre of the University of Idea: "Art and Agency Ten Years On". November 2008. Accessed 15 August 2012. http://www.crassh.cam.ac.uk/events/545/programme/

[12] vCase has been previously published in two locations: Preston, Julieanna. Lining Stories: Conversations with Inside Trades." In *Meanings of Designed Spaces,* edited by Tuii Vaikla-Poldma, 224–229. New York: Fairchild, 2013. Preston, Julieanna et.al. "an Antipodean imaginary for Architecture + Philosophy: Ficto-critical Approaches for Design Research Practice." In *Footprint: Delft School of Design Journal,* 2013, 69–96.

[13] Jane Rendell, *Art and Architecture: A Place Between.* London: I. B. Tauris, 2006.

[14] Mark Taylor and I addressed this gap in knowledge with our co-edited book Intimus: Interior Design reader (wiley, 2006). It is credited as, if not the first, then one of the first volumes of its kind.

[15] So much so that I wrote "Fossicks for Interior Design Pedagogies," in *After Taste: Expanded Practices in Interior Design,* edited by Kent Kleinman, Joanna Merwood-Salisbury and Lois Weinthal. New York: Princeton Architectural Press, 2011. That book chapter introduces the founding principles around interior design as a site of transdisciplinary practice that are informing the conclusions of this doctoral research project.

[16] Penny Sparke, "The Things Which Surround One: The Domestic Aesthetic," in *As Long as it is Pink: The Sexual Politics of Taste*. London: Pandora, 1995, 31.

[17] Sparke, "The Things Which Surround One," 40.

[18] Rosi Braidotti, *Metamorphoses: Towards a Materialist Theory of Becoming* (Malden, MA: Polity, 2002), 2-4.

[19] Luce Irigaray, *The Sex Which is Not One*. Ithaca. NY: Cornell University Press, 1985.

[20] Luce Irigaray, *i love to you: Sketch of a Possible Felicity in History*, trans. Alison Martin. New York and London: Routledge, 1996, 109-110.

[21] Jane Bennett, *Vibrant Matter: A Political Ecology of Things* (Durham and London: Duke University Press, 2010), 10.

Fig 12. (p.31) J.Preston, *HEDGE* (2009). A detail image of the paper "dress" rasterized by a laser cutter to reinterpret the lining of a floral patterned surface lining the interior of a abandoned violin case.
Fig 13. (p.32) J.Preston, *SWOON* (2009). A detail image of the individually shaped clay beads formed by pressing thumb to wall surface at various datums around the room.

Chapter 1

THE YIELD PRINCIPLE
an antigen to interior rigor mortis

As a radical standpoint, perspective, position, 'the politics of location' necessarily calls those of us who would participate in the form of counter-hegemonic cultural practice to identify the spaces where we begin in the process of revision ... I locate my answer concretely in the realm of oppositional political struggle. Such diverse pleasures can be experienced, enjoyed even, because one transgresses, moves 'out of one's place.' For many of us, that movement requires pushing against oppressive boundaries set by race, sex and class domination. Initially then, it is a defiant political gesture. Moving, we confront the realities of choice and realms of power relations - do we position ourselves on the side of colonising mentality? Or do we continue to stand in political resistance with the oppressed, ready to offer our ways of seeing and theorising, of making culture, towards that revolutionary effort which seeks to create space where there is unlimited access to the pleasure and power of knowing, where transformation is possible?[1]

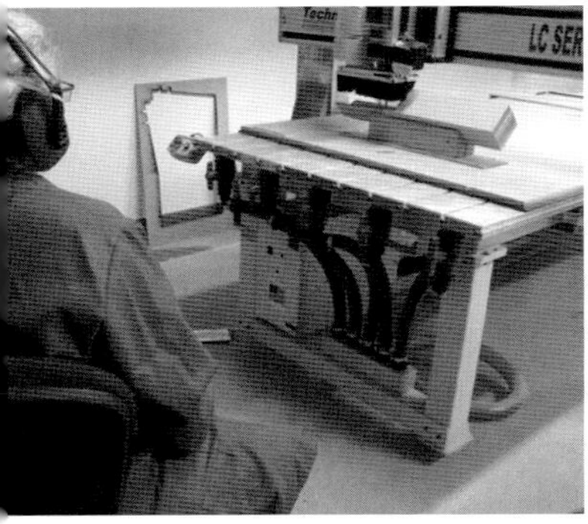

Fig 1. (p.33) J. Preston, *SHEAR* (2008). Close up detail.
Fig 2. (p.34) J. Preston, *SHEAR* (2008). A filleted sheet of gypsum wall board hangs in-situ amongst engineering tools for measuring material strength.
Fig 3. Ukraine topless feminist protesters arrested at Kiev Euro 2012 Stadium Opening Ceremony, Oct 10, 2012. Image courtesy of photographer John Webb.
Fig 4. Watching the CNC machine from the margin.
Fig 5. J. Preston and D. Scott, *() +)(* (1996). A handful of feminist tools made from pewter and timber poised ready to fill the gap.

My first reading of this text by bell hooks occurred while monitoring a full bed computer numerically controlled three-axis router. (Fig 3) The machine had been triggered by a relatively simple code to run a file that it calculated would take twenty-eight hours to complete. My research assistant and I took shifts 'babysitting' this monster, our perch located at the periphery of the room out of the way of flying debris generated by the process and within arm's reach of the (red) panic button that would shut it all down. Earmuffs softened the noise of the cutting tool as it encountered the resistance of the sheet material. The longer I listened the more attuned I became to the subtle shifts in sound when the tool changed direction or speed. Its drone repeated a hypnotic lullaby. I recall wondering if we were there to protect the life of the machine or issue an authority (marked by my official lab coat) over its possible anarchy. From the centre of the room, it exerted a power far greater than the 240 volts it drew from the electric wall outlet, the switchboard down the hall, the substation on the waterfront and the hydroelectric turbines stealing energy from a stifled river in the New Zealand wilderness.

Reading bell hooks' text to pass the time, I sat covered in dust, mesmerised by the machine, isolated by ear muffs and sound-insulated walls, in the bowels of the basement workshop. I realised how hooks' call to choose the margin as a space of radical openness made sense of my ambitions to operate from a feminist perspective on another kind of marginal space, interior environments. To occupy the margin is not to be deprived or in despair but quite the contrary; it is a "site of radical possibility, a space of resistance … not just found in words but in habits of being and the way one lives".[2] According to hooks, inhabiting the margin fuels one's capacity to resist oppression, exploitation and colonisation.[3] In the wake of this resistance, new worlds can be imagined. When silence is unhinged, as hooks suggests, space is "interrupted, appropriated and transformed through artistic and literary practice".[4] In this chapter, I narrate an emerging feminist interior practice situated at the confluence of gender, politics and technology. The wedge/shim is exercised as a multi-purpose low-tech building device that emphasises the instrumental nature of tools to 'make work'. The act of driving, shoving, sliding, slipping, tucking or jamming this cutting lever into place is metaphorically linked to civil disobedience and shown to be politically significant when applied to seemingly inert, banal interior finishing materials. Two creative works, *SHEAR* and *SWELL*, are explored in light of the wedge/shim's facility to employ feminist strategies that help to imagine what an interior surface can do.

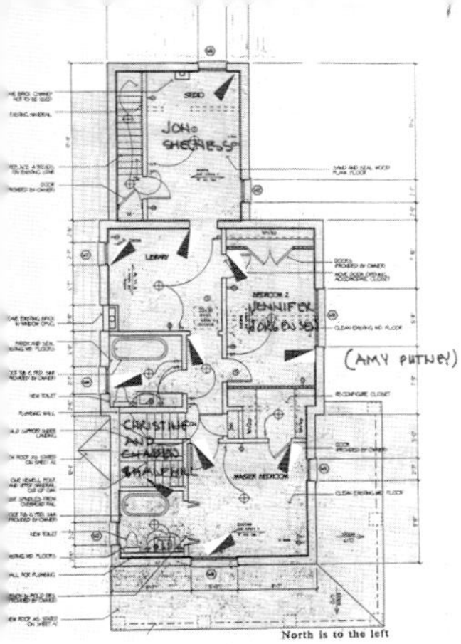

Fig 6. J. Preston and D. Scott, *() +)(* (1996). A second floor plan noting the most significant points of structural weakness.
Fig 7. J. Preston and D. Scott, *() +)(* (1996). Wedges/shims were strategically inserted into cracks and crevasses that required attention to bring the house back to a level of stability and inhabitability. Each tool was embossed with ')(' to mark a place of prying apart or '()' to signify a point to fill up.

Tool-ing

One body with two planar surfaces converging towards a common (sharp) edge or two planes veering away from one another as if taking flight towards different infinities, not a perspective, but a common ordinary unassuming sliver of material fashioned to cut/fill a gap, to shore/split something up, to prey/prop something open or to lever/level it away: this is the wedge/shim.[5] (Fig 5)

When you stop and look, you will find the wedge/shim everywhere. I do. I did. In 1996 Emily and Mike Donovan purchased a house on the fringes of an historic neighbourhood close to the centre of Des Moines, Iowa, USA. The house and its immediate surroundings were victims of the urban blight that to this day still plagues the city. The house was but a frame without full enclosure, heat, windows, doors, plumbing or internal linings, effectively a carcass of a past inhabitation. After braving the elements and the local drug scene, the Donovans were informed by council that, as a historic landmark building, any improvements to the house must comply with standards of preservation, the cost of which was more than ten times the purchase price and beyond the owners' means. As architects themselves, the Donovans invited fourteen artists to make installations within the house to wage a public and productive protest; subsequently, the policy minders decided it was better to have the house renovated and occupied than empty and derelict.

Furniture designer and sculptor Deb Scott and I were one of the groups of artists invited to contribute to this protest. Our collaboration adopted a grass-roots approach where many small acts (and voices) serve to overwhelm a dominant power structure. Figured as political irritants and conciliatory structural details, two hundred pewter-capped timber wedges and shims were inserted into the dilapidated house to literally pry open gaps and shore up walls, stairs and flooring. (Fig 6) This approach employed two notions of tolerance simultaneously: political tolerance and the tolerance factored into joining two or more materials together. While the house could have easily benefited from thousands of these tools, the reflection of silver caps on the exhibition opening night spoke to the distress of the situation.[6] Each individual cap signified a point of political contention and material weakness. Collectively, they signalled the extent of repairs needed to simply stabilise the frame by virtue of their cutting (critical) edge. (Fig 7)

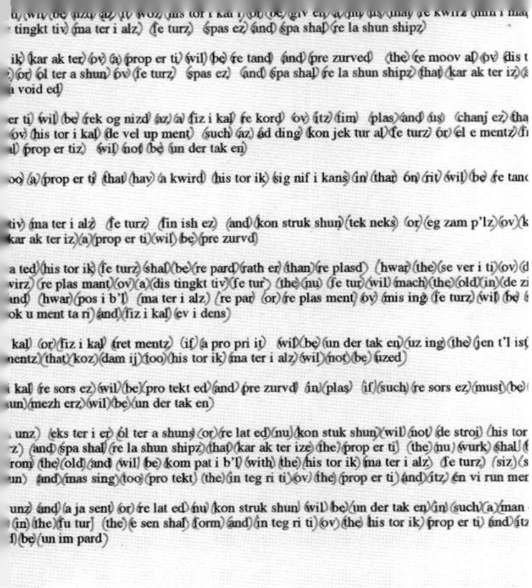

Fig 8. J. Preston and D. Scott, *() +)(* (1996). The Historic Places Trust Mission statement displays a plethora of inflections, insertions and modifications (possible weaknesses) when rewritten phonetically.
Fig 9. J. Preston, *My Feminist Survival Kit* (2012).

Our installation *() +)(* included a poster plastered to a piece of plywood temporarily serving as a front door, traditionally the site of public notices such as quarantine, eviction, condemned or, more familiarly, 'go around to the back', 'door bell not working, please knock' and 'please leave the package on the porch'. The poster was a copy of the historic landmark mission statement rewritten phonetically in order to emphasise spoken (immediately present) over written words (officially sanctioned), as well as to locate the wedge/shim as a tool shaping a protest language and a political and economic argument. (Fig 8) Each hyphen, accent, long and short vowel sign and parentheses marked a detail of similar weakness to the house.

This is my first recollection of feminism's presence in my practice as an architect, builder, interior designer and artist. This is the story of how the wedge/shim got added to my material and conceptual repertoire. The relation it has to language, especially punctuation, is something that still lingers in my practice. So is its sense of aurality, the spatiality of language.[7] The wedge/shim operates with positive friction. I keep one with me at all times in my feminist survival kit which holds a needle and thread, a wad of beeswax, a rubber band, an aspirin and a piece of chalk.[8] (Fig 9) The wedge/shim is the most useful tool in the kit, the best a girl could have to 'make work'. Its effect is directed by intent managed by the force of the hand that wields the mallet behind it. It makes up or it makes the difference.

Making the difference does not by any means occur in a singular way in feminist theory and activism. One of the strongest points of contention amongst feminists is whether or not one can work within an existing context, organisational system or regulatory process; whether the existing context is susceptible enough to be undermined, sabotaged or even simply used as the foundation for its own critique. This point appears to mark the difference between radical feminists poised to wage public protest and overturn political establishment for a cause (working in opposition to a system), and liberal feminists, who deal with matters within existing processes of dispute or grievance (working within a system). I explored the limits of these two feminist strategies in the context of a project called *SHEET GOODS*, which consisted of a series of sculptural objects linking actions of civil disobedience to standardised unit materials specific to interiors such as plywood, Medium Density Fibreboard (MDF), T&G flooring and gypsum board. With each material, I sought to operate with the parameters established by the material's physical character and with reference to its common use as an interior surface as a means of subverting it and possibly replacing it or even revitalising it. In this case, the wedge/shim tool served as a conceptual

Fig 10. An interior view at a local building supply store of future standardised interiors stacked flat and waiting for consumption and distribution across the region. J. Preston (2008).
Fig 11. A photograph of a contemporary apartment interior demonstrates the impact of standard industrial materials and details. J. Preston (2008).

mediator between complete destruction of a material's structural integrity and a posture of subservience to dominant cultural norms.

At the time of writing this book, I live in New Zealand; after seventeen years, it has become my homeland and the site of many of my creative works. Like most post-industrialised countries, New Zealand's building industry is still geared to standardised unit materials that, by virtue of their modularity, uniformity and pre-designed integration, reduce production costs (theoretically). And just like many other nations, the country's economy is driven by the construction industry, in particular the housing sector. As a small nation with a small manufacturing base, we rely almost exclusively on importation of these unit goods. (Fig 10) And in turn, as a result of New Zealand's idiosyncratic adherence to a second degree of thriftiness and expediency, our built environments, particularly interiors, tend to attain an aesthetic rendered as a consequence of material sheets goods joined by generic details. Speaking very generally, I observe that the interiors in my everyday life as a New Zealander harbour an overpowering trace of the 1200 x 2400mm sheet – a smooth, rigid and homogenous surface applied in uniform thickness to a structural frame.

This unit is a dominant ordering factor to the visual experience of interiors. The sheet material simply mimics the regulating lines of code, structural efficiency, thermal bridging and property boundary setbacks. In the zeal to maximise floor area, the difference between inside and outside is reduced to a functionally driven membrane. With such adherence to industrial tenets, interior space becomes anonymous and unresponsive to inhabitation of the particular. In this scenario, design of the interior is at risk of becoming the mere specification of surface appearance, a threat I observed in my former life as an architectural intern where I spent most of my time copying approved generic details from catalogues and writing construction specifications, most of which included the phrases 'as equal', 'equivalent to' or 'as required', legal short-hand for the status quo. (Fig 11) I don't believe this phenomenon is exclusive to New Zealand; it pervades most developed countries.

Smooth, rigid and homogenous are more than formal qualities of manufactured goods; they present an acculturated presumption about material as inert substance. *SHEET GOODS* inquires about interior finishing materials as affective sites of political resistance. It pries into the material in search of what might be suppressed in the surface and tamed by normalising processes. *SHEET GOODS* sought to expose a dimension to material surfaces typically assumed to be superficial, ornamental,

Fig 12. This image of a woman being beaten and dragged in a recent protest in Greece was reported in the BBC news. Her 'Go Limp' posture proved ineffectual to the violence of the state troops. Still image taken from video posted at http://www.bbc.co.uk/news/world-middle-east-16267436 Image in public domain. Photographer not identified.
Fig 13. Women lie prone in the street as a means of disrupting passage. From http://www.theatlantic.com/infocus/2011/08/student-protests-in-chile/100125/ Image in public domain. Photographer not identified.

without meaning and depth, and therefore without consequence. To find depth in an interior finishing material seems to confound what 'surface' is typically understood to be; surface depth is something that goes against each term's identity and yet, suggests that 'surface' and 'depth' might co-exist as an 'intra-action'. As feminist theory writers Stacy Alaima and Susan Heckman state, "We need ways of understanding the agency, significance, and ongoing transformative power of the world – ways that account for myriad 'intra-actions' ... between phenomena that are material, discursive, human, more-than-human, corporeal and technological."[9] Dwelling on the intra-action between surface and depth of standardised interior finish materials framed the work in a manner that recognised the dichotomies of mass-produced to crafted, structural to decorative, and profound to frivolous.[10]

In *SHEET GOODS*, I applied techniques of civil disobedience to common building construction materials in an effort to cast aside assumptions about their status as dead stuff. Handbooks on civil disobedience highlight several forms of non-compliance and protest. The most instructive piece of advice stated in the Civil Disobedience Manuals put out by ACTup is to 'Go limp', a posture which makes carrying a protester away more difficult and, in many political states, it is not interpreted as a crime.[11] (Fig 12, 13) This non-compliance gesture has been used throughout history by individuals and groups refusing to co-operate with injustice, yet "the fusion of organised mass struggle and nonviolence is relatively new".[12] Feminist movements have successfully employed this tactic in boycotts, non-cooperation, limited property destruction, civil disobedience, mass marches and demonstrations in an effort to fill the jails and disrupt public ceremonies to make their causes publically visible.[13] The transformation from a rigid and upright state to a limp, supple and yet heavier state (thus making it more difficult to arrest and transport a protester) is not a sign of giving in or being without power.[14] On the contrary, it is deemed as an effective force of resistance that allows the anger and emotions of injustice (another sign of life) to rise to the surface in healthy expression.

Curiously, in feminist literature, Canadian academic and feminist Ursula Franklin equates violence with resourcelessness and English Quaker feminist Jo Vellacott aligns nonviolent civil disobedience protest with the agency of resourcefulness. Seeking to extract the 'source' of power that knits women with peace, Vellacott rejects what the world prescribes as her power and opts for a power source kindled by personal belief and strengthened through collective effort. "Power does not come from focusing ... on our disabilities. Power is more likely to come by just going ahead and doing the thing in which we fear our inadequacy".[15] I wish to add that resourcefulness also carries connotations of thriftiness (economy) and cleverness (creativity), skills often credited to women in general and more often skills linked to survival.

The resistive yet yielding principle 'Go limp' resonates deeply with the iterative performances entitled *CUT PIECE* where Yoko Ono kneeled willingly, patiently, trustingly, vulnerably, subserviently and perhaps stoically on stage as audience members used a pair of large shears to cut her garments. This performance, produced iteratively between 1964 and 2011 as nuanced variations, inspired – maybe even incited – me to add 'Go limp' to my feminist tool box. What power it must have taken to sit there so serenely, unflinching, and unconcerned with what a pair of scissors is capable of doing! Furthermore, this performative work of art enabled me to situate my creative practice in relation to what Daniel Barber calls militant architecture, a phrase he borrows from Antonio Negri "who uses the term to describe the activity of being inside history, of 'doing, making, constituting history'. [16] 'Militancy, in this sense, is not based on duty and discipline, on fidelity to an ideal plan, but rather on the insistence that social conditions are constantly constructed with and by our everyday actions and formalised practices. Within architecture this concept has particular relevance: every project is based in specific social, political, and environmental conditions. The work of the militant architect is to identify and respond to these specific conditions rather than conform to a pre-existing model, to extract from these conditions the political goal most relevant to them. Militancy is the organisation of constituent power, power from below, 'capable of crossing all borders and reaching everywhere."[17]

No matter how persuasively these concepts on militant architecture are intellectualised or how they mirror my overall intent to bring interior environments into political discourse, the pacifist in me will never accept their overriding link to war and violence. I simply assert that acts of un-doing tender forms of emancipation. Power itself is not derived through violence, though history is not short of examples where violence is used as a tool of domination. According to ACTup, governmental power is often maintained through oppression and the tacit compliance of the majority of the governed. Any significant withdrawal of that compliance will restrict or dissolve governmental control. Apathy in the face of injustice is a subtle form of violence. Struggle and conflict are often necessary to correct injustice; struggle is not easy. The strength of nonviolence comes from a willingness to take personal risk without threatening other people. It is essential that one separate the individual from the role she/he plays. The 'enemy' is the system that casts people in oppressive roles. [18]

If the nonviolent civil disobedience motto 'Go limp' suggests an affirmative bodily protest action, then other acts of un-doing lend fruitful avenues for finding feminist agency in material processes and practices. This relational mode of thinking led me to employ processes such as draping, distressing, cutting out and relaxing to sheet good materials that I saw as unjustly suppressed and oppressed. Primarily used by fashion and textile designers, these material processes induce a greater degree of pliability, tactility and variable density to a given textile whereby structure, pattern and surface texture are indistinguishable. The process of increasing weight and vulnerability while exponentially increasing surface area, selectively slicing threads to tinker with the structure of the weave bring 'a perfectly good material' to the brink of failure with the intentional application of heat and chemicals; they offer modes of fertile protest. This process exemplifies the transfer from a protest carried out primarily through social action to a protest lodged specifically in materiality. It anticipates my own protest against material inertia, a pervasive notion that renders material substance as lifeless – rigor mortis.

Japanese textile manufacturer *NUNO* produces fabrics called *BORO BORO*, which demonstrate such material un-doing. They use techniques that, as they claim, translate emotional states into new textiles: ragged, tattered, worn-out, dilapidated, shredded, cut to ribbons, rumbly, brittle, fragile, falling (reduced to pieces), worn to a frazzle, frayed (at the edges). The textile processes challenge the fibres' structural integrity and at the same time elevate their expressive qualities exponentially. "It's not that our fabrics are bad as woven, but that stresses and hardships bring out character in even inanimate objects ... [they] tug at our hearts with a mysterious emotional warmth." [19] Though I am dubious about the link between emotional states and textile design, I am keen to expand their use of such processes to reveal the animate in supposed inanimate materials. Contrary to being described as 'cruel and unusual treatments' by the *NUNO* designers, I consider these un-doing processes as part of a nonviolent transformative course of action aimed at liberating inert substance as live and expressive. They are simply applications of the yielding principle which employ creative tempering acts not to anneal or align molecules for ultimate strength and virility, but relax, drape and wear in affirmation of the weak and fragile.

Such subtle shift in thinking and intent registers with Katie Lloyd Thomas' discussion

Fig 14. J. Preston, *TREAD* (2008). This work finds a 1200mm x 2400mm panel of tongue and groove pine flooring sections cantilevered off a wall. Its tapered ends confuse normative expectations that it functions as a floor or step.

of Aristotle's differentiation between the 'hylomorphic' material as inert and undifferentiated, the servant of form which gives material presence, and a prime matter called 'hypokomenon,' which is located in the substrate, literally lying beneath the surface – "it has the sense of something behind, something perhaps which can be deduced rather than touched".[20] Aristotle is partially responsible for establishing form's tyranny over matter's chaotic nature and geometry's privilege over material's plurality despite its plastic nature, a prejudice that Lloyd Thomas states is deeply and persistently embedded in architectural practice.[21] In Aristotle's terms, material is fixed, supplementary, interchangeable and superficial, all attributes that signify it as inert and, in the case of my project, relegated as mere interior surface decoration.

TREAD, the first in the series *SHEET GOODS*, represents my first effort using the yield principle to expose the tactile voice of a material surface such that the surface is not divorced from the material as a finish or appearance. (Fig 14) I tapered the ends of a section of tongue and groove pine flooring using a spoke-shave tool. Removing material in this way translated a structural engineer's equation called the modulus of elasticity into a physical reality – the tampered end started to droop. These thin and fragile tips behaved as if they were heavy. Because *TREAD* was situated as a plateau positioned just above the floor, this yielding surface obfuscated any effort towards ascension or, in feminist terms, 'immanence', a hierarchical goal associated with patriarchy. It asks anyone who seeks to 'step up' to surrender to the material. At the local level of interiors, *TREAD* highlights the artificiality of interior floor surfaces and the inappropriateness of considering floors as stable and level or even synonymous with ground.

Of the five sculptural objects created in the suite of *SHEET GOODS* projects, *SHEER* and *SWELL* offer the most critical and visceral response to what an interior surface can do given a feminist interior practice and a standardised interior sheet good material. They were conceptualised independently from one another but made in tandem, which revealed a curious relationship bound up with assumptions of material standardisation and homogeneity.

Fig 15. J. Preston, *SHEAR* (2008). Filleting the sheet of gypsum board the long way meant negotiating its 10mm internal plaster flesh with an oscillating saw. This gesture found me bifurcating what appeared to be an endless horizon of matter.
Fig 16. J. Preston, *SHEAR* (2008). As I cut, the sheet peeled away from itself (with the aid of a pulley system), confronting me as a new wall surface.
Fig 17. J. Preston, *SHEAR* (2008). Double its standard surface area yet thin, fragile and littered with rents, the sheet of gypsum wall board bore all the supposed flaws of an imprecise cutting process that found the Achilles' heel of the material.

Shear-ing

A uniform 10mm thickness of gypsum plaster is sandwiched between two paper sheets, which counter the plaster's brittleness and contribute to its global mobility. The edges are tapered ever so slightly in anticipation of joining it with another like edge. If you run your fingers to the back edge of the sheet you will feel where the two paper faces overlap. They are different surfaces. One surface will entrap the dark dusty space between studs with its slightly furry surface and the other will, over the years, flaunt a multitude of slick coloured coats. I have an intimate relationship with gypsum wall board, one that is kindled by a fascination of its plastic, rigid, fragile and forgiving personality and a gut-wrenching repulsion over the way it sucks moisture out of everything living thing around it, demands constant attention (maintenance) and always mirrors my flaws (as a builder) in its blemishes. This mixture of matters of fact and matters of concern introduce my creative sculptural work *SHEAR*.

Filleting a sheet of gypsum board is counter-intuitive, even counterproductive, to the practical properties the product offers contemporary interiors. (Fig 15) It negates its fire-resistant property. It propagates a dust-filled atmosphere. The energy to make it smooth is over-ridden by coarseness reminiscent of (unrefined) exterior rubble walls. However, the gypsum wallboard's acoustic value increases and the surface area coverage is doubled. At the start, all of these were good reasons to cut the sheet in half, 'the wrong way', to render it unusable (I was told), to go inside the sheet and turn its insides out. Such misuse of a perfectly good sheet of material afforded a contemporary twist of philosopher Elizabeth Grosz's now well-worn postmodern catchphrase 'there is no outside (of discourse, patriarchy, history, power)'; inside is everything.[22]

I could never figure out if it was the way the filleting raised a cloud of dust that settled on every surface and clogged the air filters, or the persistent whine of the oscillating saw probing the (dry) fatty tissue that caused a fuss in the workshop. Day after day, five to be precise, I worked tediously to unfold, unfurl, this dead sheet of calcified velvet. (Fig 16) I admit that there were moments it felt less like shearing a sheep and more like an autopsy than I preconceived. (Fig 17) This being the third of five works in the series *SHEET GOODS*, I could already see a trend; undoing was my form of resistance and the economy was one of gift and sacrifice; all I had to give was my body, my labouring body.[23] Artist Ann Hamilton's guardian sitting in the gallery amongst the work oblivious to any other human presence, tediously reading a

Fig 18. Ann Hamilton, *tropos* (1993). Serving as a combination of docent, guardian, sentient and spatial facilitator, a reader sits undeterred by gallery visitors amongst a sea of swirling horsehair. Image with permission of the artist.
Fig 19. Ann Hamilton, *tropos* (1993). A reader is occupied solely with the task of crossing out the text of the book with a soldering iron line by line, eradicating its legibility and scoring its presence. Image with permission of the artist.

book line by line, burning each line in the process, consuming the book literally and conceptually - this image stood fast with me as I persevered.[24] (Fig 18) That was my gift to the cause: to undo, cross out, cross over inertia, to work and write over lines demarcating fortified boundaries between women, men, material, property and space. (Fig. 18) Over and over again, line after line, working left to right, the saw dug into a horizon line that slowly bore a (radical) openness to the sheet such that, in the end, it hung as architecture, amongst a room of calibrated calculating instruments and an argument against the perils of industrial manufacturing processes. (Fig 19) In addition, these actions bore out an advocacy for weak architecture, a term coined by Ignasi de Solà-Morales, which in its rejection of classical mimesis and monumentality, looks to the gesture of 'the diagonal cut' to render the world (and architecture) not as a totalised, closed and complete universe but instead, as non-linear, plural, multiform and complex experiences.[25] Though Solà-Morales speaks to the act of detection and excavation from an archaeological perspective linked to recollection, a trajectory not aligned with my research project, his notion of weak architecture promotes processes of decomposition and decoration away from the sense of ugly, vulgar, trivial or mere embellishment towards the secondary function linked to the aesthetic of the accident rather than industrial ambitions overpowers assumptions about material as inert and dead substance.[26] Architectural theorist Jonathan Hill argues:

> This notion of a deeper or 'embodied' form of knowledge, arising out of the body's interaction with physical 'things', is something to which an expressive and articulated architecture can help provide access. The key is to re-establish the link between the eye of the perceiver and the hand of the maker, by inscribing in the surface of the material the 'story' of the making process – restoring the dialectical relation between the 'construction of knowledge' and the 'knowledge of construction', implied in the word technology's coupling of techne and logos. Paradoxically, it is the surface of a material that reveals its true importance for the issue of a narrative dimension in technology. Just as poetry makes use of a kind of 'thickening' at the surface of language in order to heighten the awareness of its own materiality, a poetically articulated technology can help renew our sensibility towards the particularities and pleasures of bodily experience. It is here that the possibility of a symbolic technology begins to emerge, as the full implications of the 'lost' language of tectonic expression become apparent. [27]

Fig 20. Maison Martin Margiela défilé Spring – Summer 2008. An example of Margiela's deconstructed fashion design. Image courtesy of the designer.

The surface thickens. My concerns for liberating an interior finishing material with the actual and metaphoric aid of a wedge/shim had not yet taken responsibility for the aesthetic language it was bound to produce. This became ever so apparent when I considered the deconstructed fashion designs by Martin Margiela leading an international fashion trend often referred to as 'unfinished', 'coming apart', 'recycled', 'transparent' or 'grunge'. Margiela creates new garments from linings extracted from vintage dresses leaving their interior structural details of seams, darts, zippers and interfacings exposed. (Fig 20) In much the same way that sheet materials such as gypsum board plaster are used to line or 'fit out' an interior space, Margiela's fashion aesthetic showcases an investment of labour hidden behind the surface, a visibility Alison Gill names the 'structur-ing ontology' of the garment "... given to the simultaneous bidirectionality of the labour that the garment-maker and clothes perform – i.e., the garment-maker is simultaneously forming and deforming, constructing and destroying, making and undoing clothes."[29] Curiously, Gill reminds us that the etymology of 'garment' includes 'garnir': French for furnish, equip or fit out. Clearly in *SHEAR* I am bearing vestiges of a postmodern penchant for deconstructionism that has been used countless times to align various acts of assembly: writing, making and theorising.

This is something I struggled with throughout the research – this reliance on language, obsession with the written text, word play and how language inculcates patriarchal dominance. At every turn I tried to channel that way of thinking back to a material language or process, hoping that text would translate as a texture, something one could feel rather than read. For example, another *SHEET GOODS* project *HUNG* plunges towards the floor as a bundle of fragile wafer-thin strips compressed by a horizontal beam. It recalls the decorative figure of curtain, drapery, pelmet and valance.[30] This work reconstitutes a sheet of cabinet-grade birch veneer plywood, 25mm thick x 2500mm long x 1200mm wide, successively ripped into 1.5mm strips, the finest slice before the alternating layers of ply start to disintegrate. The sheet's structural value, married with its natural wood grain surface, lends to its prudent and judicial application as an interior finish. And yet it also serves as a mask behind the thickness of its face such as in a built-in storage cabinet or partition wall. Such economy is not specific to New Zealand. The fact that more than 65% of the sheet was lost to the dust extract system and it took two people more than eight hours to slice the sheet upset the New Zealand building ethics associated with its extravagant $400 price tag. (Fig 21) This project reinforced my (human) inability to replicate what machines

Fig 21. J. Preston, *HUNG* (2008). This work tampers with the structural integrity of laminated layers and industrial ambitions to exploit the material's supossed inertia.

are supposedly so apt at doing perfectly and repetitively – laborious tasks – only to underscore Irigaray's call for a shift of economy, as architectural theorist Jane Rendell eloquently writes:

> An economy of the capitalist market is based on pricing mechanisms – specialisation, efficiency, scarcity, maximisation of profit and utility, and on principles of homogeneity, rationalism and calculation. This masculine economy requires strict delineation of property from the ownership of one's body to the ownership of the fruits of own labour, it is an economy of appropriation and of the self-same. This exchange economy of masculine subjects involves the pleasure of appropriation, ownership and exchange of women's bodies in space. Within the masculine economy of patriarchal capitalism women are feminine products of exchange.
>
> Irigaray rejects the masculine libidinal economy and gestures towards a female libidinous economy – a gift economy based on generosity and not lack – endless and without closure. From woman's ability to have a child within her body and yet allow its existence, comes an image of positive giving, an ability to embrace difference and the other, not to dominate and to incorporate. The ability to sustain this diversity contradicts the phallic desire for unity and appropriation and stems from a woman's closer links to the imaginary, where the difference between mother and child has not yet been established. The économie feminine could be described as a theoretical construct or poetic utopia which can inform practice – showing that profit maximisation is not universal and inevitable in all spheres of exchange.[31]

Swell-ing

A 1200 x 2400mm sheet of Medium Density Fibreboard (MDF) lay prone on the router bed. Back and forth, back and forth, up and back, the router's gantry surveyed the sheet's surface; the logic of its path was far from legible or predictable. (Fig 22) The cutting bit spun indifferently to the sheet's matrix of homogenous fibres bound in agreement to be planar by resin, heat and compression. MDF is a standard material used prolifically in interior building construction. Its relative low cost (because the

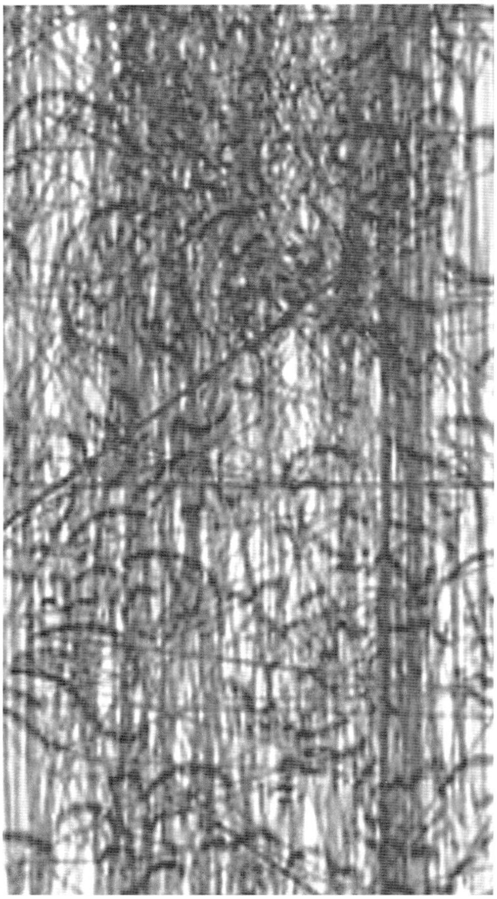

Fig 22. J. Preston, *SWELL* (2008). This image registers the path of the CNC cutting tool across the MDF sheet surface, a drawing that appears anything but logical.
Fig 23. An example of a period style Victorian dining room panelled in timber and lined with one of William Morris' wallpaper patterns. Image in public domain on wiki commons.

fibres are ground wood waste), workability (because it has no grain) and its versatility lend to its application for cabinetry, furniture and wall linings throughout the industrialised world. Its suitability is linked to its internal make-up, which serves a now well-recognised lingering modernist desire for smooth surfaces. This same structural characteristic belies its Achilles' heel: MDF cannot withstand strain at the site of fixings (hardware) or, most importantly, moisture.

Having been milled by the CNC machine, the sheet assumed a supine position on the workshop table. A portion of its body had been ground to dust and sucked up into the extract system. What remained was a firmly disciplined material body in the formalised image of a Victorian dining room panel complete with a textured wallpaper pattern borrowed from the William Morris collection. (Fig 23) Those who know how such wall panels are crafted would not be impressed with the pristine homogenous surface of this faux wall section, a simulacrum indeed! For they would see the rounded corners and the ridges left by the ball-tipped router bit, a geometrical trace of the technology, less superior to the hand that would have selected every piece with concern for its colour and grain, mitred the pieces to meet precisely at 90 degree angles and lovingly tapped the mouldings into place with fine brads. And yet, it was a technological feat to get the computer file, the tool bit and the machine's passes and speed working in unison to carve a mundane sheet of MDF into something other than a smooth rigid and practical shape.

The reference to domestic scenes of the late 19th and early 20th centuries, at least those dominating interior design history and theory, was critically purposeful towards building a network of associations between interior design's emergence as a professional discipline, its historical identity linked to decoration and domestic environments, its changing relationship to technology, industry and feminism for social change. The panelled wall would have witnessed most of this flux. A wall panel would have certainly graced the interiors that Walter Benjamin dubbed as phantasmagoria, the English bourgeoisie interiors full of social proprieties and boredom, heavily gilded and draped by linings that protected a private retreat from the external urban realm of soot, crime and finance.[32] Panels such as these featured in Catherine Beecher and Harriet Beecher Stowe's redesign of the typical American house with concern for health, industry and economy from a Christian woman's point of view.[33] These women would have flourished amidst the antics and totalising creativity of the Bloomsbury group.[34] Panels such as these would have been at the scene when the Garrett cousins became the first professional interior decorators rather

Fig 24. Robert Polidori, 52520 Deslondes Avenue, New Orleans, Louisiana, March 2006. Image courtesy of the artist.
Fig 25 – 26. Robert Polidori, 6539 Canal Street, New Orleans, Louisiana, March 2006. Image courtesy of the artist.

than homemakers.[35] Edith Wharton employed, amongst other elements, timber-lined wall panels to bring social, moral and economic order to the home.[36] It is out of these same interiors that Elizabeth Wilson coaxed women to inhabit the city for its liberating potential.[37] And the same kind of interior that Jane Rendell's critical texts opened the door: London's panel-lined men's clubs, dark, leather-bound and panelled as they were (are).[38]

The sculptural object *SWELL* brings that history of the interior in contact with contemporary manufacturing technology to critique its craft and revel in the transformative potential it realised. At the same time, *SWELL* raises environmental concerns where the interior is no longer a private retreat but complicit with global well-being. *SWELL* is a wake-up call to the huge contribution MDF interior furnishings, cabinetry and wall linings make to landfill each year. Its use in interior construction persists despite having been proven as carcinogenic and in spite of the short life any product made of it has.

Over the course of a week, a wallpaper steamer infused the MDF sheet with moisture. Sections of the surface blossomed as particles freed themselves from the hold of resinous glue. They extolled the non-homogenous quality of the sheet's interior at a macroscopic scale. A hideous beauty emerged akin to Robert Polidori's photographs of New Orleans *After Katrina*. Both works register the entanglement of forces both human and not. Polidori's images speak to the conscious of everyone associated with the building of the levees, the re-enforcement of poverty for the sake of capital gain, the development of disaster preparedness schemes and the convenient ignorance which kept these interiors out of sight until Katrina struck and Polidori ventured inside.[39] (Fig 24-26) *SWELL* is purposefully beguiling and contentious. I watch people encounter it; their first impulse is to poke at it, ruffle the surface, rub the gritty particles between their fingers, marvel at the artificial growth as if the material had gone wild. And then they shudder at the risk they might be putting themselves in upon remembering that airborne MDF particles have been linked to cancer; the particles are so small that when inhaled, they lodge themselves into the smallest pockets of the lung and cause obstructions to oxygen exchange. The dryness of MDF's material body equals its political candour. (Fig 27–28) The sense of beauty conjured by *SWELL* turns to an emotionally charged sense of horror. I recall the proclivity of using MDF in contemporary interiors. I note that while women have expanded their horizons beyond the household to the academy, the office, the factory, the boardroom and parliament, the environments they inhabit consume them, do them (and the planet) harm.

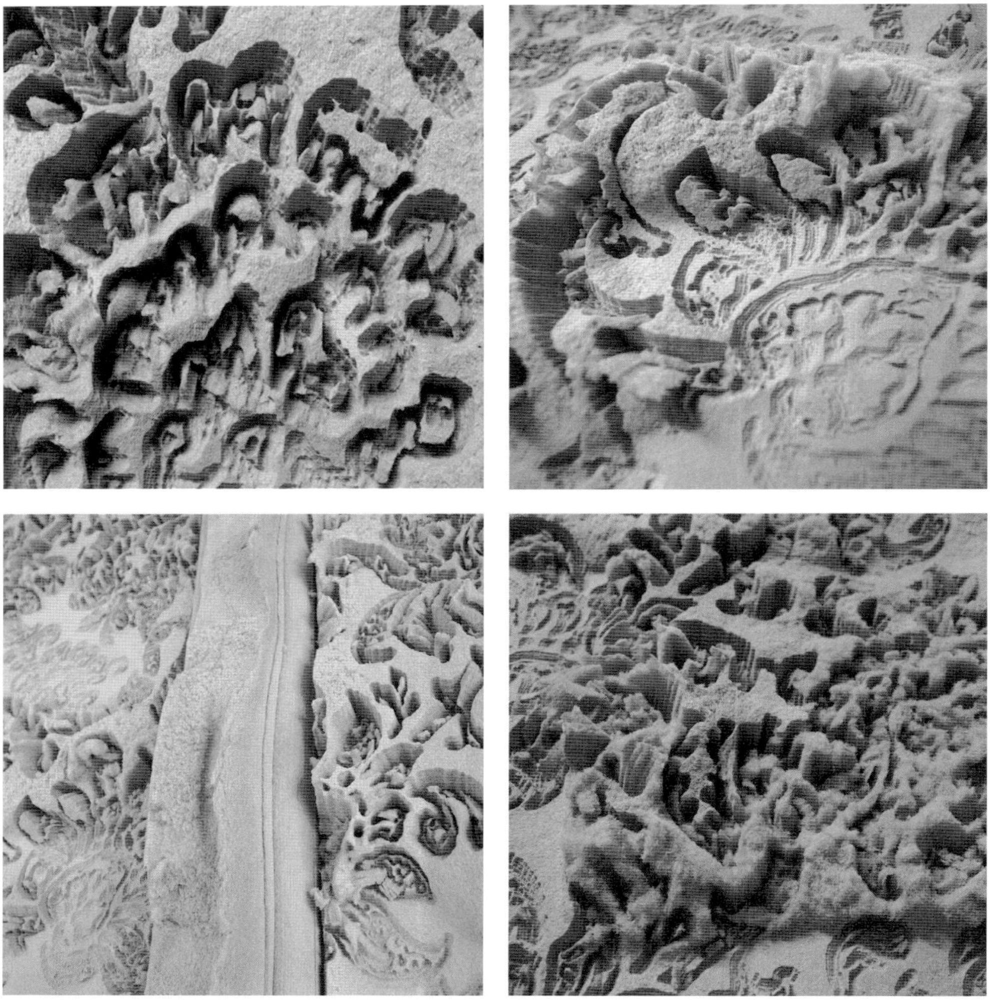

Fig 27. J. Preston, *SWELL* (2008). Close up details of MDF's response to moisture and its not so homogeneous or complacent material matrix.

Yield-ing

My feminist interior practice did more than emerge in the duration of creating these works: it advanced, raised doubts, circled back, reinforced, shed and produced. What grew out of naiveté has stuck hard and fast. (Or should I say soft and yielding?) First, directing my energy to interiors and the materials commonly used to line them, finish them, to initiate that first decorative gesture, was initially intuitive. I quickly identified the quagmire of trying to qualitatively or quantitatively measure the impact interior environments have on those who sleep, eat, clean, work, bath, entertain, procreate and yes, die within them. That I could formulate some kind of thesis that equates the liberation of women to interior surfaces seemed foolhardy many points along the way. Such aim was a hangover from my education in the 1980's where behaviourism induced a cause and effect relationship between that which was social and that which was material, people and environment. I have now cast that way of thinking aside along with any pretension of answering questions about the gender of space. When asked if a space could be feminine or whether the architect was a man or a woman, Elizabeth Grosz calls for the focus to shift to "ways of occupying space and producing places that somehow contest, challenge, and problematise the dominant modalities of organisation, of space and place".[40]

Second, I am keenly aware that *SHEET GOODS* started as a quest to figure out what kind of feminist I was and identify how to liberate women from some evil oppressor, as if something or someone was holding me, us, them, back from some kind of utopian dream of democracy and free will. I came to realise in my own terms that feminism is not a singular identity or political marker. Throughout this project I have witnessed feminism as a label that has the power to unite but, more usually, it shuts down conversation; people stop listening as if 'the fight' is already over, it is too difficult to discuss or it was never worth fighting for to begin with. I now understand the criticism levelled at how it has been pigeon-holed into three waves, a convenient and simplistic framework that denies its messy internal tensions and nuanced practices from surfacing and multiplying. My own intellectual and making practices were equally as messy, non-uniform, and showing no allegiance to a single platform of feminism but certainly veering towards an emerging model Alaimo and Heckman call 'material feminism' which explores "the interaction of culture, history, discourse, technology, biology, and the 'environment,' without privileging any one of these elements".[41]

Fig 28. J. Preston, *SWELL* (2008). In its final state, the MDF decorative panel stood dry, spongy, and once again vertical.

Rather than represent the body, material feminism considers bodies as multiple and corporeal and having lived experiences and biological substance as part and parcel of the concrete world in which they inhabit with other bodies, human or not. This approach is significantly different from postmodern feminist theory dominating the scene for the past two or more decades, effectively a shift away from the textual, linguistic and discursive concerns focused on over-turning gendered dichotomies and a move towards bringing material concerns to the fore. In the instance of my creative practice, the body is not a concept, it is a body -- a material, sensing, fleshy, live bundle of physical, chemical and psychological forces. *SHEAR* and *SWELL* mediated between and meditated on these distinct paradigms. I see this as a tension in the work. Language still plays a significant role in shaping my practice, as does the cultural and critical analysis that makes up the majority of theory on the interior. I would struggle to abandon these familiar forms of social construction yet I feel the pull of the new material ontology insisting on co-constitution of mind and matter, in many cases, matter-minding. My hesitancy to leap towards material feminism rests in the way it is situated primarily in the social sciences, territory not often traversed by artists, poets and designers. With my carpetbag of postmodern feminist theory in tow, and the wedge/shim tucked into my feminist survival kit, *SHEAR* and *SWELL* lent me the courage to venture into this new discourse.

Such a shift of focus enabled me to stop worrying if feminism was politically savvy to my doctoral project, my academic career or my creative practice. It spurred me to consider how practicing as a feminist I might not be defending the cause of women specifically, i.e. where women are the subject, but instead how I might use feminism as the agent of liberation in general. bell hooks' bold statement "Feminism is for everybody!" has refreshed meaning. This enabled me to reconcile my fears of embracing feminist philosophy such as those espoused by Luce Irigaray where the dominance of patriarchy is denounced in the same breath that women as equal (or better) is pronounced.[42] Though persuasive on many counts, this seems to me to only reinforce dualities. Surely the notion of two is not ample enough to represent the diversity of the world. (Fig 29) What I learned in the project *SHEET GOODS*, in particular *SHEAR* and *SWELL*, is that my feminist interior practice was to extend ethical care to materials that we live amongst and to attend liberally to the surfaces that negotiate the threshold between intimate and immense. This is what this project has affected and where my practice then journeyed.

[1] bell hooks, "Choosing the Margin as a Space of Radical Openness," in *Yearning: Race, Gender, and Cultural Politics* (Boston, MA: South End Press, 1990), 145.
[2] hooks, *Yearning*, 149.
[3] hooks, *Yearning*, 150-1.
[4] hooks, *Yearning*, 152.
[5] This conceptual trope was first developed in a keynote lecture I presented at Interior Tools, Interior Tactics Conference (2008, Edinburgh) which was further developed as a book chapter "Wedges and Shims: Levering a Feminist Interior Practice," in *Interior Tools, Interior Tactics: Debates in Interior Theory and Practice,* edited by Fleming, Hay, Hollis, Milligan, Plunkett, 264-274. Oxfordshire: Libra Press, 2011.
[6] The exhibition opening of *Re: BIRTH* occurred at 905 Eighteenth Street Des Moines, Iowa, USA, November 16, 1996. It was curated by Peter Goche.
[7] See Chapter 3: *Voice Lessons* for a discussion on my project *Neutral, not so* which tests this concept.
[8] *This is my feminist survival kit* (J. Preston, 2010) was shown at the exhibition 13.3%, WUHO Gallery, Pasadena, California 2010. This exhibition considered the contributions women have made to the practice of architecture since Lucy Lippard's 1973 landmark exhibition that contested a statement that there were no women making art at the time and also structured by the use of manila folders.
[9] Stacy Alaimo and Susan Heckman ed., "Introduction: Emerging Models of Materiality in Feminist Theory," in *Material Feminisms* (Bloomington and Indianapolis: Indiana University Press, 2008), 1-22.
[10] These dichotomies have long been present in my research and creative works. For further reading, see Taylor, Mark, Julieanna Preston and Andrew Charleson. *Moments of Resistance*. Sydney: Archadia Press 2003. Julieanna Preston, "Soft Stuff," in *The Sensuous Intellect,* edited by Ross McLeod, Patricia Pringle, and Christopher Kaltenbach, 142-155. Melbourne: RMIT Press, 2006. Julieanna Preston, "Sewing Architectural Fragments," *Architectural Design Research* 1 (2005): 53-61. Julieanna Preston, "Shifting between Economy and Cladding." *IDEA Journal: Between Excess and Austerity*, (2003): 117-129. Julieanna Preston, "Structure and Ornament: The Veritable and The Spurious", Presented at the *Second Annual Symposium of Architecture History Architecture and Authenticity,* Savannah College of Art and Design, Savannah, Georgia, 2001.
[11] *Actup*, 2 accessed 22 April 2008, 12:38 p.m. http://www.actupny.org/documents/CDdocuments/ACTUP CivilDisobedience.pdf
[12] For example: "In 1980 women who were concerned with the destruction of the Earth and who were interested in exploring the connections between feminism and nonviolence were coming together. In November of 1980 and 1981 the Women's Pentagon Actions, where hundreds of women came together to challenge patriarchy and militarism, took place. A movement grew that found ways to use direct action to put pressure on the military establishment and to show positive examples of life-affirming ways to live together. This movement spawned women's peace camps at military bases around the world from Greenham Common, England to Puget Sound Peace Camp in Washington State, with camps in Japan and Italy among others." See *Actup*, 3.
[13] James Tracy ed., *The Civil Disobedience Handbook: A Brief History and Practical Advice for the Politically Disenchanted* (San Francisco: Manic D Press, 2002), 77.
[14] *Actup*, 6.
[15] Jo Vellacott, "Women, Peace and Power", in ed. Pam McAllister, *Reweaving the Web of Life: Feminism and Nonviolence* (Philadelphia: New Society Publishers, 1982), 30-35.
[16] Daniel Barber, "Militant architecture: Destabilising Architecture's Disciplinarity," in *The Journal of Architecture* 10 (3) (2005): 246.
[17] Daniel Barber, "Militant," 246.
[18] *Actup*, 5.
[19] Richard Hodges, "Cruel and Unusual Treatment to Fabrics," in *BORO BORO* (Tokyo: NUNO Corporation, 1997), 4.
[20] Katie Lloyd Thomas, "Architecture and Material Practice," in ed. Katie Lloyd Thomas, *Material Matters: Architecture and Material Practice* (London and New York: Routledge, 2007), 4.
[21] Lloyd Thomas, *Material*, 4.
[22] Elizabeth Grosz, *Architecture from the Outside: Essays on Virtual and Real Space* (Cambridge, MA: MIT Press, 1995),

131.

[23] Though I came to this concept through my own making, credit is due to Jane Rendell's essay "The Undoing of Architecture" for enriching my practice and offering a conduit to her world where architectural construction and feminist philosophy meet. Rendell's essay takes on at least three different iterations between 1998 and 2010. This excerpt is specific to the iteration published in ed. Jonathan Hill, *Occupying Architecture: Between the Architect and the User* (London and New York: Routledge, 1998), 229-246.

[24] Ann Hamilton, *tropos*, Dia Center for the Arts, New York, 1993.

[25] Ignasi Solà-Morales, *Differences: Topographies of Contemporary Architecture*, trans. Graham Thompson, ed. Sarah Whiting (Cambridge, MA: MIT Press, 1997), 58-59.

[26] Solà-Morales, *Differences*, 69-71.

[27] Jonathan Hale, "Signs of Resistance: Remembering Technology," *The Journal of Architecture* 5 (2000): 94-5.

[28] Solà-Morales, *Differences*, 71.

[29] Alison Gill, "Deconstruction Fashion: The Making of Unfinished, Decomposing and Re-assembled Clothing," in *Fashion Theory* 2(1) (1998): 28.

[30] *HUNG* was curated by Volker Albus to feature in the international group exhibition *somewhat different: Contemporary Design and the Power of Convention* held in 2010 at The Museum Building, Wellington, New Zealand.

[31] Jane Rendell, "Undoing Architecture," 229-246. Rendell draws from Luce Irigaray, *Elemental Passions*, (London: The Athlone Press, 1992), 73.

[32] Walter Benjamin, *The Arcades Project*, ed. Rolf Tiedemann, trans. Howard Eiland and Kevin McLaughlin (Cambridge, MA: Belknap Press of Harvard University Press, 2002).

[33] Catharine Beecher and Harriet Beecher Stowe, *The American Woman's Home,* ed. Nicole Tonkovich (Hartford, Conn., Harriet Beecher Stowe Center; New Brunswick, N.J.: Rutgers University Press, 2002).

[34] See for example Christopher Reed, *Bloomsbury Rooms: Modernism, Subculture, and Domesticity* (New York: Bard Centre, 2004).

[35] See for example Emma Ferry, "'Decorators May be Compared to Doctors': An Analysis of Rhoda and Agnes Garrett's Suggestion for House Decoration in Painting Woodwork and Furniture (1876)," *Journal of Design History* 16 (1) (2003): 15-33.

[36] Edith Wharton and Ogden Codman Jr., *The Decoration of Houses* (London: Charles Scribner's Sons, 1897).

[37] Elizabeth Wilson, *The Sphinx in the City: Urban Life, the Control of Disorder, and Women* (Virago: London, 1991).

[38] Jane Rendell, *Pursuit of Pleasure: Gender, Space and Architecture in Regency London* (London: The Althone Press, 2001).

[39] For a fuller account of this analysis see Julieanna Preston, "Into After," in *Proceedings of Interior Space and Other Places*, IDEA 2010 Symposium, Brisbane, AUS. http://www.idea-edu.com/Symposiums/2010-Interior-Spacein-Other-Places

[40] Joan Rothschild and Victoria Rosner "Feminisms and Design: Review Essay," in *Design and Feminism: Revisioning Spaces, Places and Everyday Things*, ed. Alethea Cheng (New Brunswick, NJ: Rutgers University Press, 1999), 36.

[41] Alaimo and Hekman, *Material Feminisms*, 7.

[42] For example, see Luce Irigaray, *The Sex That is Not One* (Ithaca, NY: Cornell University Press, 1985).

Fig 29–30 (p.69, 70). J. Preston, *SWELL* (2008). The representation of a dining room timber panelled wall is appropriately displayed in the industrial site of its making.

Chapter 2

Voice Lessons

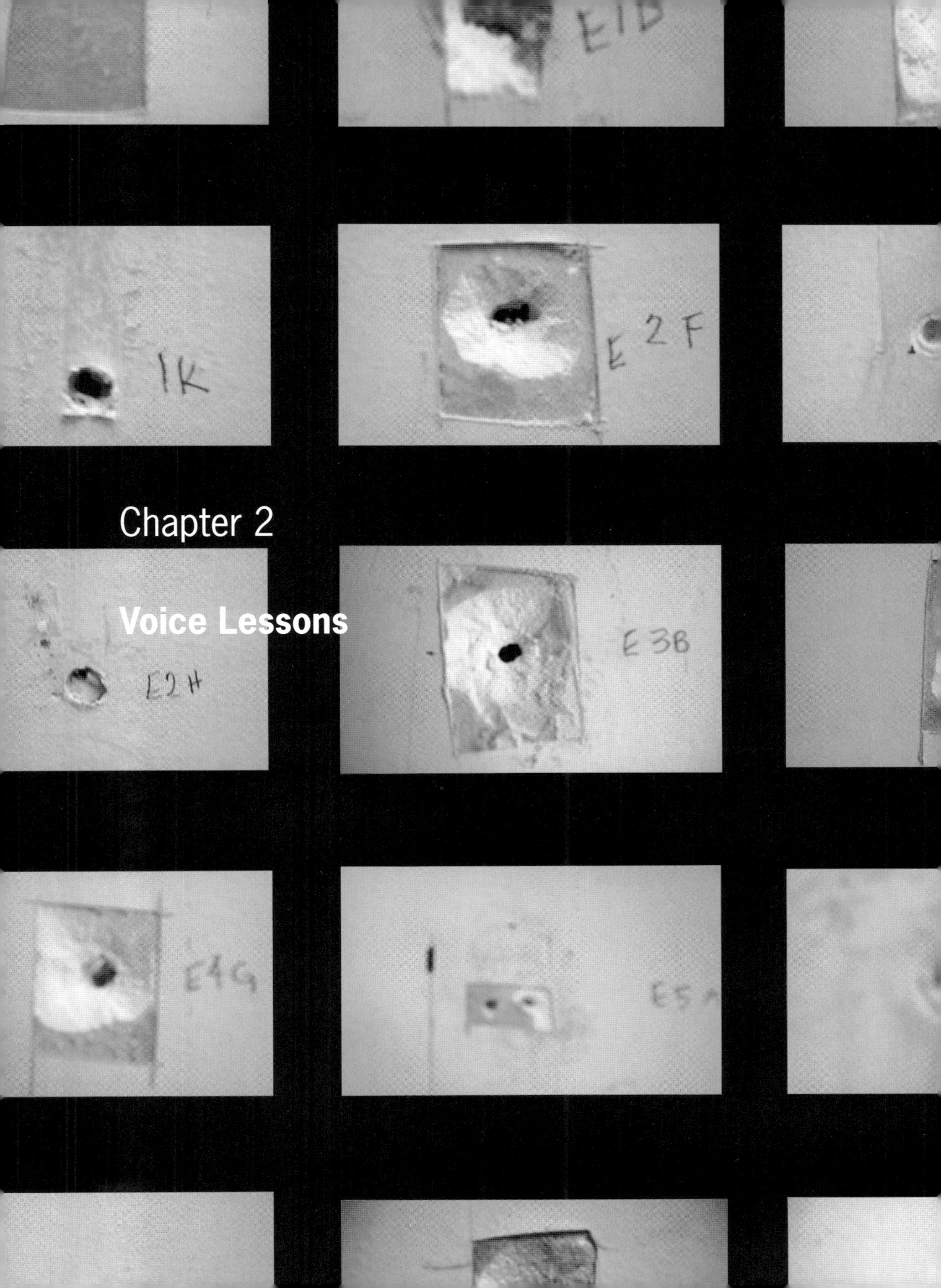

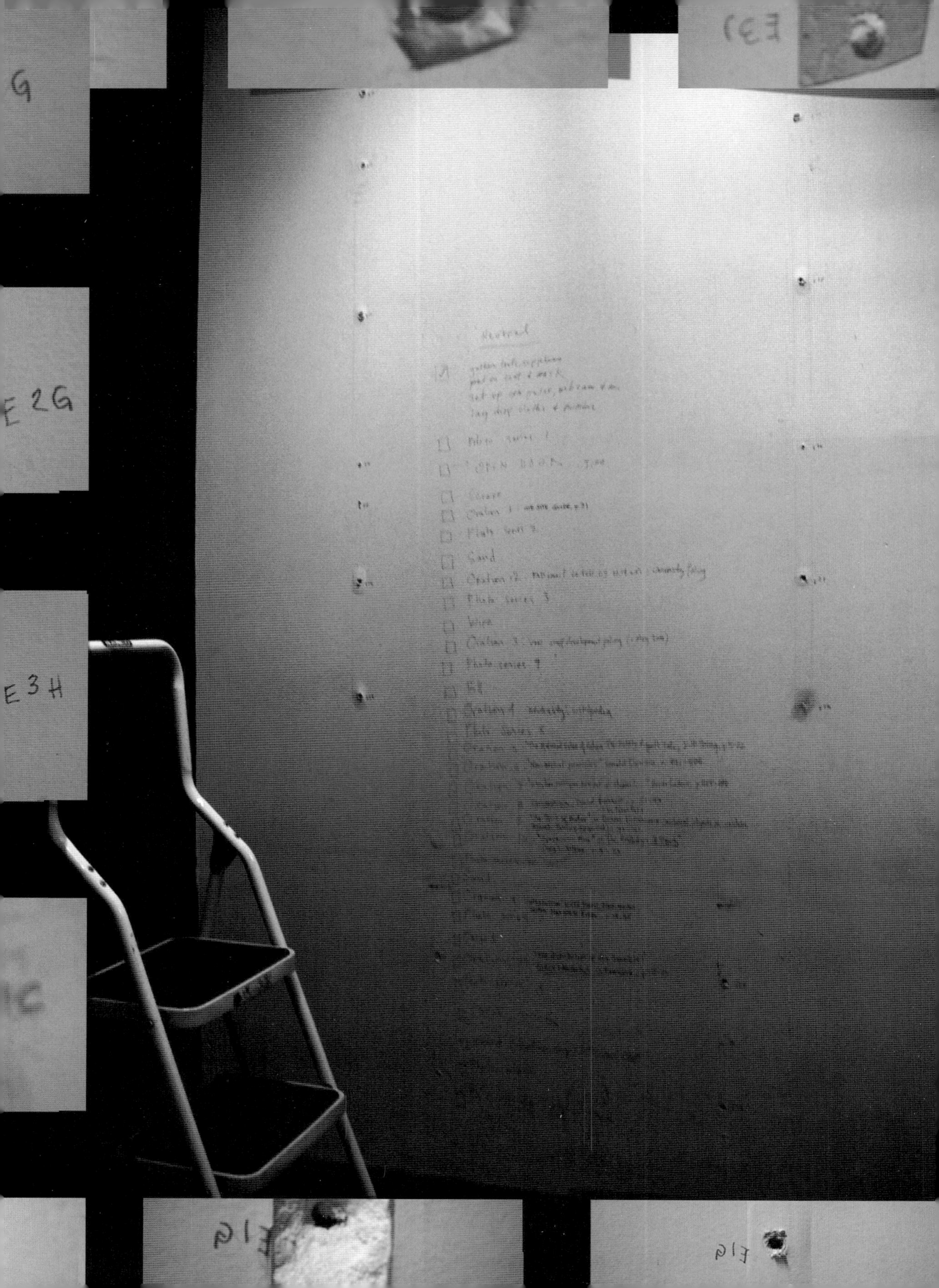
G
E 2G
E 3 H

How does an interior surface participate in the politics of neutrality?

In 2009 I repaired the wall surfaces of a small institutional office space as a creative form of protest against the pervasive use of neutrality to uphold a political position and a material quality without bias. This performative installation, entitled *Neutral, not so,* tested the political agency of a generic interior surface. A script, scribbled on the wall, structured a typical nine-to-five workday as a one-act play with eight scenes comprised of a repetitive sequence of work tasks.[1] The performance cycled through acts of repair (cutting, filling, sanding, wiping and painting seventy-nine holes left in the walls by the removal of shelving), oration (reading aloud from texts on topics associated with neutrality) and documentation (archiving each scene through still and video images). Through these acts I was exploring the capacity of these walls, these interior surfaces, 'to speak'.

This chapter is directed by several senses of what it means to demonstrate. As instruction, to demonstrate means to impart practical knowledge, in this case, to disseminate information about several industrial construction products, specifically, a standard partition wall, gypsum wall board and white latex interior paint. (Fig 1) Here, demonstration offers instruction on how to carry out a procedure or activity. Such instruction is typically offered to provide basic understanding and optimise end results, the foundation of 'do-it-yourself' pamphlets and videos. Demonstration also refers to the exhibition of rhetorical expression, such as communication calling for resistance as protest often taking the physical form of flyers printed and distributed en mass 'to the people' in good proletariat style. The graphic quality of these flyers plays a strong role in their message – short punchy bullet points, clear legible fonts, slogans and logos. And finally, demonstration is found in a persuasive argument relative to a political issue, specific to my cause, the capacity of neutrality to be oppressive. One finds persuasive arguments most notably in the context of editorials and most formally in a speech such as in a political campaign or a legal summation to the jury or, as I demonstrate here, in the written form of an essay expanding and reflecting on a creative work. Eloquence mixed with logic and relevant case studies, perhaps even a touch of Socratic Method, render the essay as a far more narrative form of demonstration than the others. The essay builds the case, tells the story, lures the reader in and levies a position with convincing effect.

Fig 1 (p.71, 96). J. Preston, *Neutral, not so* (2009). The spectrum of wall surface and holes under repair.
Fig 2 (p.72). J. Preston, *Neutral, not so* (2009). The scene of a script on a hole-ridden wall.

Neutral, not so, itself a demonstration in several ways, cast aspersions on two dominate notions central to interior design and contemporary culture. First, that the smoothness, seamlessness and uniformity of industrial processes and products are motivated solely by economies that link industrial nations. Consider how design history has situated the advent of streamlining as a style aligned to evolution: "... sleek shape and its attendant qualities of maximised efficiency and hygiene ... streamline designers embrace the goal of producing 'ideal' product types ... that would, at least in rhetoric, contribute substantially towards the realization of an imminent utopia."[2] The smooth surfaces and organic forms found in nature offer inspiration for design's functionalist drive to minimise air resistance and energy expenditure—or, at the very least, appear to. Such economy is not just mimetic; it practices streamlining as design's alignment with evolutions' "paring away of 'parasite drag' caused by 'the unfit' ..." to serve "a modern aesthetic suitable for a 'civilized nation.'"[3] Given that building construction industries in general operate on the premise that producing quantities of the same item (goods/products) are designed to respond to the needs and use of most of the population (market), another kind of smoothness is articulated: the homogenising effect that the pervasive use of such products has on the constitution of interior space. Every smooth plaster wall surface registers a desire for complete control over a material, a desire that leaves no room for blemishes or idiosyncratic traces of the maker. While labour intensive, the mass-produced products and construction systems offer no space for the labourer's creative investment.

The second notion that this chapter will address is an assumption that to be neutral is to be without colour and bias, i.e. to be white. As estate agents confirm, neutral coloured interiors are more attractive to buyers.[4] This assumption emphasises the degree to which prevailing tenets of modernism serve to discipline interior environments and their occupation. Ostensibly, this performative installation work is about the office's two opposing white walls, which are framed by timber studs, sheathed in gypsum wallboard and finished with several coats of paint. Do not be fooled by this matter-of-fact description; as neither a knowhow/can-do manual nor homage to material science, this essay uses such data as a rhetorical platform to link conventional interior materials, finishes and installation processes to the seemingly un-contentious position of neutrality. Though I am utterly convinced by Bruno Latour's case to become the poet that follows the bird beyond the transparent window glass: to question, put aside to even abandon the idea of "letting reality return to our speech" in the search for exactness, truth, proof or other forms of quantifiable knowledge a dominant mode of inquiry, I remain committed to the interplay of facts and concerns as mutually entwined currents of recording and reflecting.[5]

Instructing

The scene of the performative installation was nothing more than a room measuring approximately 3 x 7 metres with an east-facing window. A cellular space amongst many in an urban environment, it is what one might call normal for a university workspace — nothing flashy, just standard issue. The performance began several days before the actual event as I shifted all my personal belongings out of the office. The need to vacate the office was the result of a dispute surrounding equity in the workplace, a situation that at the time was volatile and personal to me, but for the sake of this story, is only peripherally significant; it merely incited the opportunity to protest. Removal of all the metal bookshelves left ruptures in the walls that drew attention to the fact that they had not been safely secured to the internal structure, a frightening realisation considering the weight in books I had just removed from them. With nothing else in the space to distract me, I mused on what made these holes offensive so as to require that they be filled up and the surface continuum resurrected. Other than re-instating the shelves in exactly the same configuration, did the holes not offer any further possibilities? Could it be that the holes revealed breaches to the wall's interior where fumes, debris, and dead space had been banished? Did the holes insinuate a form of social neglect, abandonment or state of impoverishment? Or did the holes impart traces of occupancy too viscerally laden, like the odour of used footwear or the stains on mattresses found at the op shop? Inherently I knew the answer had something to do with cultural codes of propriety, a sense reinforced by the fact that every time I shifted house as a child (thirteen times in the space of eighteen years), my parent's insisted that we leave the house in a better state than that in which we acquired it. This was about duty and obligation, respect for the next occupant and the fine print of tenancy agreements. In academic terms, this impulse to repair the wall served to uphold what I have come to learn as lingering traces of a modernist ethic linked to simple forms, clean lines and smooth surfaces. To repair and repaint was to (hygienically and aesthetically) cleanse the space and dress it in the uniform of standardised interior building products.

Interior design construction manuals provide a glimpse of what that standard uniform is. (Fig 3) A typical interior partition wall consists of timber studs or light-gauge steel units assembled as a flat, even and rigid plane.[6] Structural members are located 16" or 24" on centre depending on the thickness of the drywall in order to maximise the efficiency of a standard sheet nominally measuring 4' x 8' (1200 x 2400mm). According to New Zealand Building Standards, gypsum wallboard, a.k.a. dry wall or plasterboard, "is a sheet lining material renowned for its properties of stability, fire resistance, acoustic control and bracing. It consists of a plaster core of gypsum encased in a durable face and backing paper."[7] Sheets are fixed in a horizontal orientation directly to the skeletal frame. Screw or nail heads are sunk below the board surface to enable smooth rendering with a plaster joint compound.

The wall is then 'primed' with a paint designed to saturate and unify the pores of the paper coating with the spackled plaster, a process followed by several coats of finish treatment, usually acrylic white paint with a flat, satin or low-sheen texture. A flawless wall surface is dependent on the coincidence of an industrial fabricated material, an installation process prefigured on modularity, power tools and the attention of a 'semi-skilled' labourer to maintain a low degree of tolerance throughout installation.[8]

In building construction, tolerance has become quantifiable — a part of science's role "to render everything measurable, to attach a number to it, and to make sure each thing keeps to its assigned class."[9] In this case, tolerance is the accuracy of fit between two or more components in a material join. Good fit takes into consideration how materials respond to heat and moisture, how they will be assembled together, and anticipate manufacturer's deviations in size.[10] I tend to think of it as the sociability factor between detail elements and the processes that bring them into a working relationship. More components equate to more meeting points and hence greater tolerance. Less tolerance yields a better detail, i.e. a detail cheaper to build. This is why buildings with fewer components, details and surfaces are less expensive and it follows, why generic details dominate building construction drawings as 'tried and true' examples with less risk of failure due to variation or deviation, in other words, points of difference. In exterior building details, more components mean more places that water is likely to get in. Interior details, however, are those that tend to keep the dirty outside - outside, as Shonfield calls it, "architecture's project against matter out of place".[11] (Fig 4) Note that the word tolerance means "1. The capacity to endure pain or hardship; 2. Sympathy or indulgence for beliefs or practices differing from or conflicting with one's own; 3.The allowable deviation from a standard," curiously, a word reaching well beyond the mastic caulking and joining edges, faces and margins of structural elements measured in millimetres.[12]

> In construction, common sense prevents one asking 'why'; the practical leaves one endlessly trying to find out 'how'. Books on construction are often presented in the form of a handbook, as something that is practically useful, like a guide to motor mechanics...[Their] bland, matter-of-fact style is singularly effective in eradicating controversy and loss of faith the presentation in the...manual makes the search for belief systems absurd. The details are drawn mechanically, with a constant line and a straight edge. Handwriting is eliminated, and with it any notion that circumstances might call for changes, adaptation or amendment. There is no reference to when or where they will be built; they are ahistorical, incontrovertibly valid for all time.[13]

The closer regulating standard practices are adhered to, the nearer a wall comes to a minimum level of tolerance. As Shonfield points out, ideology promoting an economically driven notion of what it is to be natural, rational and sensible takes the guise of product literature from the building-supply industry to reveal that "Common Sense, the Practical and the Classifiable, are alive and kicking."[14] The instructional practices put forward by 'do-it-yourself' literature support uniformity, i.e. to assume an air of perfection in terms of standard contemporary construction. Such instruction is promoted by the state that regulates health and safety measures and the manufacturer who distributes the product and communication on the means by which to install and maintain the product. Such instructions are written into the building code as performance indicators, pre-approved and sanctioned installation methods and construction documentation and specifications, and legislated in the guise of product warrantees.

As manufacturer advertisements attest, this is a good product! (Fig 5) Gypsum wallboard is relatively inexpensive, lightweight, easy to install, readily available, thermally and acoustically sound and if that is not enough, it helps keep you safe in the event of fire! What appears as a reasonable and innocuous promotion of material 'goodness' translates as a rhetorical construction of the 'conception of the good', a notion usually associated with social politics and the debate on if, how and to what

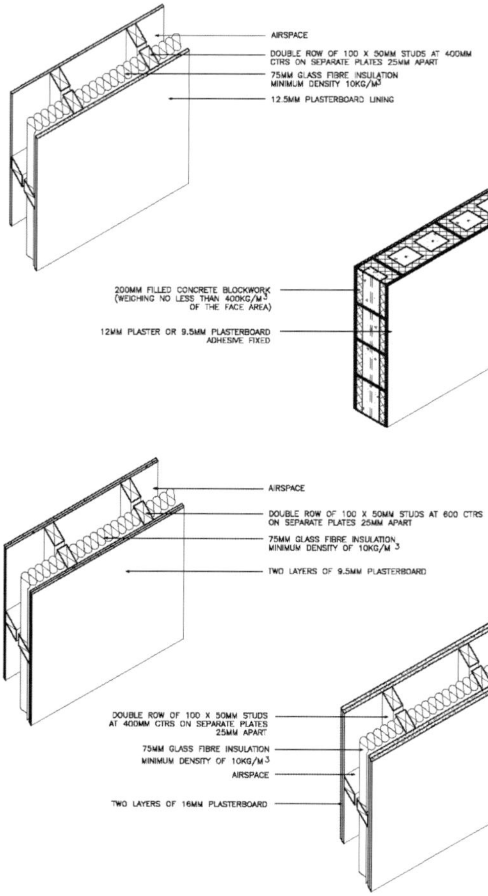

Fig 3. Non-load bearing wall partition construction details. Mark Burry and Julieanna Preston, *Construction Primer* (Wellington, NZ: VUW Press, 2000), 153. Primer © 2000

Fig 4. Katherine Shonfield and Frank O'Sullivan, *Dirt is Matter Out of Place* (1993), a subterranean public lavatory in Commercial Street London covered in white goose feathers. Katherine Shonfield, Purity and Tolerance: How Building Construction Enacts Pollution Taboos, AA Files, 1994. Courtesy of Thomas Weaver, Chief Editor of AA Files.

Fig 5. 1960's Industry advertisement singing the praises of plasterboard (aka gypsum wall board) to the American public. Sourced from http://www.ebay.com/itm/1907-Ad-Sackett Plaster-Board-Fire-Resisting-Housing-ORIGINA ADVERTISING-/300701319567. Image in public domain.

degree a government should regulate independent choice and action.

In recent years, many who call themselves liberals have maintained that the state should not favour, promote, or act on any particular conception of the good. Instead, it should simply provide a neutral and just framework within which each citizen can pursue the good as he understands it. To provide this framework, a government must sometimes interfere with liberty. It must restrict its citizens' options in order to insure security and stability, promote prosperity and efficiency, and make available various public goods. Also if justice requires more equality than unconstrained markets can provide, the state must intervene to equalize opportunity or resources.[15]

Gypsum board's abundant presence in the marketplace extends to most home and workplace environments. Such is the reciprocal nature of supply and demand in a free-market capitalist economy. But what does it mean to construct an interior partition that is as generic as the drafted detail that represents it? What level of choice, expression or situated specificity does the industrial system afford? How does such a managed system discipline the labouring body that builds it, or in this case, the labouring body inhabiting the office interior? The above quote suggests that there may be some liberty at stake. If the construction of a simple and common gypsum board interior wall partition is bound up in the political economy that Sher describes, how is the wall and the act of building the wall anything more than compliance to those forces and confirmation of gypsum's branding as a neutral product?

Acting within these insidious constraints, I felt obliged to repair the holes in order to bring this office space back into line with conditions illustrated by prominent examples of proper surface decorum. Such obligation gained prominence when weighed against the responsibilities between a person or state taking a neutral stance and that of an aggressor in the case of war:

> One of the fundamental doctrines of the modern law of neutrality is that a belligerent must refrain from committing hostile acts within the jurisdiction of a neutral power. Correlatively, the neutral is under duty to prevent the commission of such acts. A belligerent's failure to respect the neutral's right makes it liable to respond in damages to the neutral. A neutral's failure to carry out its duty makes it in turn liable to respond in damages to the injured party.[16]

Surprisingly, my sense of duty was slightly unwarranted. While the Residential Tenancy Agreement outlines a legal obligation to "not damage or permit damage to the premises" and to "leave a property clean and tidy, clear of rubbish and possessions at the end of tenancy", I found no mention in policy or contractual agreements towards the physical maintenance by staff of their university office spaces.[17] Motivated by custom and conscience, I referred to a local building supplier's installation pamphlet for guidance on repairing these holes.

For holes between 50 and 150mm in diameter a plaster board patch will be required.
1. Cut away the damaged area to a neat rectangular hole.
2. Sand the area around the repair to ensure the best adhesion between the compound and the painted surface.
3. Cut a piece of plasterboard that is slightly longer (approximately 20 mm) than the hole, but small enough to fit through the hole.
4. Place a 60mm flat head nail through the centre of the plasterboard and coat the ends with GIB Tradeset 20.
5. Insert the patch into the hole and pull forward using the nail.
6. Once hard (approximately 1 hr) gently push the nail back through the patch.
7. Using a broad knife, fill the hole flush to the surrounding area.
8. Leave to dry for approximately 48-72 hours. This longer time is required because the plaster is very thick.
9. Apply a thin coat of GIB Plus 4 over the patched area.
10. Leave to dry and sand or wet sand the area smooth.
11. Decorate the area as required.[18]

These helpful instructions facilitated a straightforward do-it-yourself task. However, these instructions also signified an allegiance to standard industrial building material products and systems, which, according to editor, typographer, writer and critic Robin Kinross, stem from the dream of "an ideology-free or ideologically neutral world made possible by advances in technology, by an abundance of material goods, by the spread of representative democracy and the eclipse of rival political systems, and by mass education."[19] Like Kinross, I am highlighting a binding relationship between material attributes and social politics such that building a simple wall is understood in a wider social context and regarded as a critical act no matter how banal the situation. What appeared to be a simple mending task, proved to be vestiges of "... the faith of modernism: the belief in simple forms, in reduction of elements, apparently not for reasons of style but for the most compelling reason of need - the need to save labor, time, and money, and to improve communication."[20] Such uniformity tends to infiltrate social norms through three modes of diffusion: information disseminated via mass media, sharing best practice in an innovative environment, and imitation in an effort to blend in or gain status. The level of uniformity is factored by the number of people who have access to the information, the relevance the standard has to potential users, the degree of interpretation embedded in the standard, and the effectiveness of their implementation.[21]

In their raw state, the holes spoke of the ways that this material had been manipulated to achieve its pristine and uniform state. After having been quarried, crushed, dried and ground to a fine powder, crystalline hydrous calcium sulphate is heated to 175° C where it loses most of its water content and gains its ability to fend off threatening flames.[22] A slurry of calcined gypsum, starch, water and sizing admixtures such as rosin and alum is poured between special paper faces and passed between sets of rollers that reduce it to the desired thickness.[23] The passage from a wet formless substance to a semi-dry stiff plane culminates as the continuous ribbon is sheared into desired lengths and sent to cure in a high temperature kiln. Stacked and bundled on palettes according to grades of moisture susceptibility, these uniform plates prefigure a future interior.

In contrast, my semi-unskilled labour highlighted plaster's propensity to elude regulation: the fine plaster dust permeated my pores, caked my nasal passages and infiltrated every nook and cranny of the room. There was no escaping it, no containing it; it was feral. Shallow reliefs of plaster (also known as 'holidays') made visible in the low angle of the morning sun exposed my inexperience at wielding the trowel. Trying to comply with but subvert science's glee to classify, to establish taxonomy of everything, I gave each hole a hand-lettered name according to its unique location on the wall, a process that formed the basis of organising my photographic archive.

Such up-close and personal scrutiny of each hole made me appreciate each hole's point of difference from the rest. And yet, as the performance progressed, each hole was absorbed back into the matrix of the wall in allegiance with the normative values inculcated by the dominant forces of an industrialised economy and the social mores of the workplace: a proper office should have smooth white walls, no holes. In this way, the performative installation's gesture to restore the wall's smooth, flat and seamless surface was an act that erased difference as it upheld the status quo, an act I saw as a critical rehearsal of everyday events with the material, in the office and in the world, in general. The critical commentary extended across scales of space and concern.

Neutral, not so was guided conceptually by Hans Haacke's site-specific artwork *Shapolsky etal, Manhattan Real Estate Holdings, a Real-Time Social System,* as of May 1, 1971, an exhibition displaying factual data taken from public records on a prominent New York family-based corporation The Shapolsky Group's real estate operations related to the sale and acquisition of large numbers of impoverished housing buildings in The Lower East Side and Harlem. (Fig 6-8) Citing the risk of subsequent legal action for "revealing the identity of private individuals and the clear intention to call their actions into question", the Guggenheim Museum director Thomas Messer (at the decision of the Museum's Board of Trustees) cancelled the show only to have the issues made public in the media shortly thereafter and the exhibition content find its way into a subsequent exhibition in 1985 at the New Museum of Contemporary Art, NY.[24] At the time, Haacke was one of a group of artists intervening in public institutions and discourse while testing public reception of works of art. Haacke was prepared to let the public draw their own conclusions as to the relations between slum lords, urban development, real-estate practices, the right to information and the role of the museum in mediating, supporting, defending or standing at arm's length from the reality of a heated political situation.[25] Rosalyn Deutsche highlights it as a sign of art's severance from economics and of art's retreat into the private autonomous and harmonious domain of the bourgeois interior (of the museum) sequestered from the conflicts and collision of interests of capitalist society, in her words, a shelter and citadel.[26] Deutsche claims that the specificity in Haacke's art work "militates against neutrality," the kind of neutrality that "interrogated modernist assumptions about the museum's status as a neutral arena cleansed of social and political concerns" signified in the white walls of the institution and the kind of neutrality that deflects engagement in deference to the consequences or the implications of aesthetic impropriety.[27] Haacke assembled maps, created charts, photographed buildings and plans and displayed them in the museum, effectively letting them speak for themselves. Ultimately this artwork was a demonstration on and of the museum as a politically charged but repressed public, but seemingly privatised interior. I learned a lesson from Haacke's work and Deutsche's essay: Raw data is telling. Facts have the capacity to be more than archival records; when assembled in systematic ways, they have the power to be hard-edged political instruments, just like the raw surfaces of the office interior of *Neutral, not so*. Advancing Haacke's tactic, I acted directly on and with those white walls.

212 E 3 St.
Block 385 Lot 11
5 story walk-up old law tenement

Owned by Harpmel Realty Inc., 608 E 11 St., NYC
Contracts signed by Harry J. Shapolsky, President('63)
Martin Shapolsky, President('64)
Principal Harry J. Shapolsky(according to Real Estate Directory of Manhattan)

Acquired 8-21-1963 from John the Baptist Foundation, c/o The Bank of New York, 48 Wall St., NYC, for $237 600.- (also 7 other bldgs.)

$150 000.- mortgage at 6% interest, 8-19-1963, due 8-19-1968, held by The Ministers and Missionaries Benefit Board of the American Baptist Convention, 475 Riverside Drive, NYC(also on 7 other bldgs.)

Assessed land value $25 000.- , total $75 000.- (including 214-16 E 3 St.)(1971)

214 E 3 St.
Block 385 Lot 11
5 story walk-up old law tenement

Owned by Harpmel Realty Inc., 608 E 11 St., NYC
Contracts signed by Harry J. Shapolsky, President('63)
Martin Shapolsky, President('64)
Principal Harry J. Shapolsky(according to Real Estate Directory of Manhattan)

Acquired 8-21-1963 from John the Baptist Foundation, c/o The Bank of New York, 48 Wall St., NYC, for $237 600.- (also 7 other bldgs.)

$150 000.- mortgage at 6% interest, 8-19-1963, due 8-19-1968, held by The Ministers and Missionaries Benefit Board of the American Baptist Convention, 475 Riverside Drive, NYC (also on 7 other bldgs.)

Assessed land value $25 000.- , total $75 000.- (including 212 and 216 E 3 St.) (1971)

Fig 6–8. Hans Haacke, *Shapolsky et al. Manhattan Real Estate Holdings, a Real-Time Social System*, as of May 1, 1971. Two maps (photo-enlargements) black & white photographs; 142 typewritten sheets; 6 charts; one explanatory panel maps: 24 x 20" (61 x 50.8 cm); photographs: 10 x 8" (25.4 x 20.3 cm); typed sheets: 10 x 8" (25.4 x 20.3 cm); charts: 24 x 20" (61 x 50.8); panel: 24 x 20" (61 x 50.8 cm).

Expressing

"Speak. Say everything that comes to you. Just as it comes to you, right here, now. Don't omit or exclude anything. Don't worry about contradictions or conventions. Don't organize what you say. Etc."[28]

During the performative installation, I read aloud excerpts from various texts on the subject of neutrality and allied topics of whiteness, standardisation, uniformity, generic, normal, equity, universality and so on. Donning a white dustcoat, I stood at the far end of the room, back to the camera and window, face to the door and anyone that might (dare) enter. The video audibly recorded these readings and visually recorded the surface of the white coat animated by my breathing and speaking. (Fig 9) At first my reading voice was edged by angry protest. Despite publicity generated by posters, email invitations and word of mouth, I was very much aware that I was shouting to an un-gathered audience. As the day wore on, I grew increasingly weary and indifferent to whether anyone was listening at all. I took note of the words I was expressing — how my mouth shaped them, how my breath regulated their flow, how enunciation changed their meaning and how my hand movements embellished their articulation. The surface and volume of the room echoed, absorbed and rattled in syncopation with my voice which was now lighter, more coy, more varied in intonation. Like a variant of the circular breathing technique developed by jazz musicians to inhale and exhale while simultaneously playing a saxophone, I gradually became more aware of the interplay between my body, its breath, its transmission of the text through speech and the role the room and its surfaces had in that exposition. Visitors entered, lingered, even leaned against the walls to listen. I would like to think that these orations practiced Irigaray's call to use speech as enunciation machinery against a form of gendered neutrality hidden in language.[29] Using the room and its surfaces as a site to pitch a verbal protest privileged 'the mother tongue' where the voice of speech is an "instrument of (re) production, as vehicle, or as object..." that crosses from the inside to the outside of discourse.[30] The room and I were neither container and occupant nor human and environment, but instead a network of coupled and entwined interiors sharing resonant wave lengths across surfaces that vary by corpuscles, coarseness, vibrato and reverberation indexes. In like manner, the readings were no longer texts written for academic consumption in the detached, disinterested and disengaged voice of proper social science research. They transcended their typographic bodies as

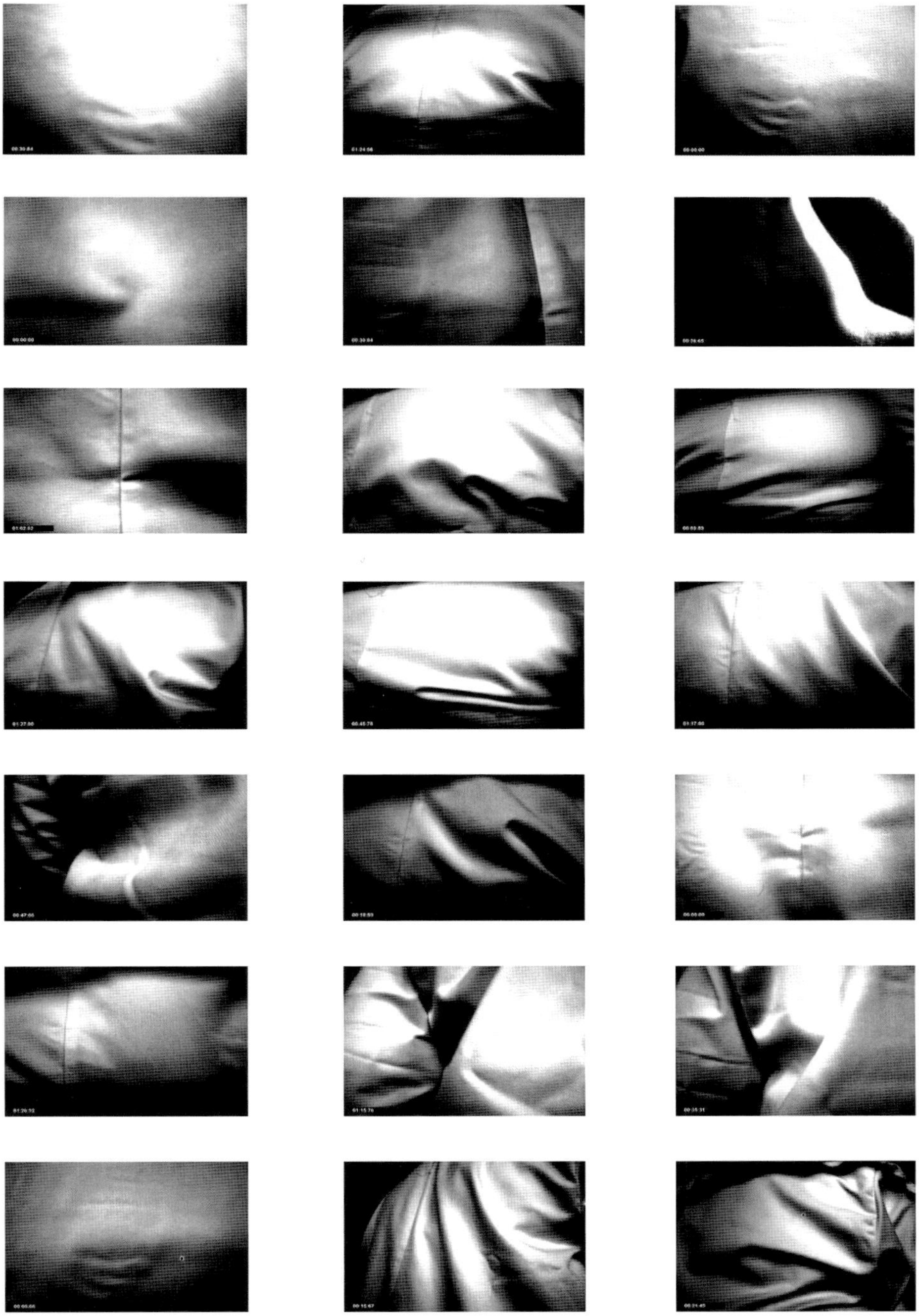

Fig 9. J. Preston (2009). *Neutral, not so*. A selection of still images extracted from the performative installation web cam videos. The expressive surface of a white dustcoat 'speaks' in synch with a body orating texts on neutrality.

black text, usually Times Roman or Arial font, on white paper. They were no longer harnessed by objectivity's aspiration "to knowledge that bears no traces of the knower - knowledge unmarked by prejudice or skill, fantasy or judgement, wishing or striving. Objectivity is blind sight, seeing without inference, interpretation or intelligence."[31] I subverted the neutered language of these texts through the accent, amplitude, range, inflection, intensity, timbre and volume of speech projected from my body into the room, onto the room, its surfaces acting reciprocally to absorb or reflect it. Such is the plain and simple stuff of acoustics.

At times this enunciation machinery (Irigaray's term) extended out into the corridor and the studio space beyond the office; the room became a megaphone. This transition of voice demonstrated Gui Bonsiepe's statement, gendered as it is, "As soon as he begins to give it concrete shape, to bring it within the range of experience, the process of rhetorical infiltration begins."[32] If rhetoric is the art of using language so as to persuade or influence others as well as the body of rules observed by a speaker or writer in order that she may express herself with eloquence, it must necessarily extend to communication via aesthetic visual and material objects. Though Kinross speaks specifically to information design, he reinforces my reasoning:

> [This is] a simple reminder that nothing is free of rhetoric, that visual manifestations emerge from particular historical circumstances, that ideological vacuums do not exist. In the context of the present rather intensely charged and volatile political atmospheres of even the "stable" Western nations, it may not be necessary to labor such truths. The rhetorical interlarding that these cultures effect in their material and visual production hardly needs decoding. That is certainly so if one thinks of the more blatant products of the Western cultures of consumption ... we need to keep awake, applying our critical intelligences outside, as well as inside, ... questioning and resisting.[33]

Therefore, it follows then that even a wall surface is capable of rousing a political rally, a useful realisation when the neutrality of commonly accepted design aesthetics is in question. So- how might an interior surface speak? Does it do it at the bidding of a human hand, the maker, who, in the making, invests meaning into mute or dead materials? Or does this action summon expression latently residing in a product's material interior substance?

Jacque Rancière assists in arguing the point:

> A 'surface' is not simply a geometric composition of lines. It is a distribution of the sensible. For Plato, writing and painting were equivalent surfaces of mute signs, deprived of the breath that animates and transports living speech. Flat surfaces, in this logic, are not opposed to depth in the sense of three-dimensional surfaces. They are opposed to the "living." The mute surface of depicted signs stands in opposition to the act of 'living' speech, which is guided by the speaker towards an appropriate addressee ... In opposition to the Platonic degradation of mimesis, the classical poets of representation wanted to endow the 'flat surface' with speech or with a 'scene' of life, with a specific depth such as the manifestation of an action, the expression of interiority, or the transmission of meaning.[34]

Engendering eloquent surfaces, manifesting a 'scene' of life, I profess, is one of the mainstays of an interior design practice. The selection and specification of fabrics, paints, textures and materials occupies the normative activities of the discipline. Orchestrating the spatial arrangement of these surfaces is a craft that draws on professional expertise. These attributes of interior design target more than competent provision of services; these are interior design's oratory tools. For example, what could be more rhetorical than the use of colour? As Robin Kinross exclaims, "Color is perhaps like music: It can play on our senses. How, we do not quite know. But suddenly we are seduced. And is not this a rhetorical manoeuvre, in the sense of a set of rules for making information eloquent and more easily understandable, and then - more than this - for sweetening it and slipping it down our throats?"[35] Though Kinross' statement emphasises the power of colour to invoke pleasure, it also has equal capacity to influence and punctuate social values including prejudice as a persuasive political tool.

The seemingly benign use of neutral colours in interiors then is cause for concern. Citing a tactic to increase spaciousness, sales and 'create a blank canvas', Diana Young's article "The Material Value of Colour: The Estate Agent's Tale" reveals the depths to which neutrality as a preferred aesthetic language permeates popular culture. It is here that the neutrality insinuated by shades of grey in Western science has been overturned for a fashionable hue of impersonal whiteness in Western interior environments.[36] As Young's interviews with estate agents attest, those hues signify a state of cleanliness associated with good morals and a high level of maintenance. Young writes:

> The 'blank canvas' nature of walls of beige, white, magnolia or cream minimizes their material presence ... In the critical discourses of modern architecture, white surface first becomes 'natural' and then gradually becomes just surfaces, all references to colors ceasing. Whiteness has become a 'given' of modernist history ... At the point of sale or rent, colour is too personal, too emotive, and too problematic and can only mar the product, making it appear unnatural and irrational compared with the socially acceptable, genderless, given currency of neutrality as well as producing the unfortunate effect of binding the property to its vendor.[37]

This practice of using colour as a rhetorical tool to erase the particularity of human presence incites a collection of critical descriptors: efficient, sobering, serious, frugal, fearful, oppressive, subduing, passive, tranquil, undemanding, "hovering on the brink of disappearance" and most germane to my protest, "embodying a socially constructed rationality."[38] To say the least, it makes me wonder about what was actually in play while cleaning all those houses I live in as a child. More importantly, how might the colour one chooses (innocently or not) to paint a room invoke gender, ethnic, cultural or racial bias to future inhabitants (however temporary their stay might be)?

Many passionate arguments have been made around race as a dominant form of whiteness, a convenient construct of deep-seated discriminating economic and material practices that are "designed to ensure long-term survival of the culture's worldview."[39] While the use of neutral colours may prove liberating within a housing market, the perception of skin colour has quite a contrary effect. Speaking to the subject of architecture and equity with a specific focus on whiteness, Craig Wilkins identifies "whiteness as a historical and socially produced concept that works to grant or deny different life opportunities. He argues that whiteness is a form of cultural capital, similar to economic capital, and he concludes that becoming aware of the advantage that whiteness provides is a necessary requirement to challenging it ... As such, whiteness is often discursively hidden within concepts like neutrality or universality."[40] Whether the pigment of paint or skin, it appears that colour is far from just neutral. As the preeminent tone of assumed neutrality, white and whiteness are shown to mask dirt, prejudice, imperfection and political values operating behind and on the surface.

A trip to my local paint shop confirmed what is obvious to every interior designer faced with specifying colours: white is more of an idea than a reality. Every white or neutral paint sample I looked at had a hint of another colour in it. Each sample I tested on the room's existing walls incited a phenomenal riot as it reacted with the colours in the carpet, my jersey, the façade of the building across the street and so on.

Persuading

What was contentious in this performative installation? The installation was a protest against neutrality as a common and unquestioned brand in contemporary culture. At a personal level, I was protesting a mandate made by my employer, which used workplace equity policies to withdraw support for my individual development as an academic researcher. This form of neutrality endorsed equal treatment for all at the expense of the pursuit of excellence for one; it supported mediocrity in the disguise of fairness. At a professional level, this performative installation sought to expose the degree to which interiors are governed by the standard industrial materials with which they are constructed. Thirty-one years of experience as art and design practitioner and educator reinforces my position that the specifying of construction materials, installation processes, fixtures and finishes does not typically include consideration of their political inclinations nor question the ethics or the values on which they are grounded. These processes and products are so readily available and frequently upheld as exemplars of 'good design' in popular and professional journals that the will power to resist employing them is weak. This protest was about bringing this issue to bear, making it apparent and obvious, making it a political issue specific to interior design but symbolically relevant to a larger audience entrained by assumptions over the neutrality of neutrality.

Neutral, not so was an experiment using my labouring body and the surface of the interior to mount a public and spatial demonstration. To do this necessitated re-enacting the forms of neutrality at play in the use of simple and banal building products, repairing them in line with the manufacturer's instructions and matching the colour through trial and error. In one sense, my performance was not unique in that all around the world on any given day the same task is repeated by many other labourers yet without the spectacle of academic discourse orated as if it were poetry. (Fig. 10)

As I reflect on *Neutral, not so,* I recognise the value architectural theorist Mark Wigley's book *White Walls Designer Dresses* had on theorising the event. Recharting canonical histories of modern architecture in relation to whiteness, surface and fashion, he uncovers the spatial politics of suppression and oppression in the guise of cultural codes to what is ordinary, standard and apparently acceptable. His cause, in part, was for architecture to recognize that it is clothing and that the default "fragile coat of white" was a dissimulation of "architectural discourse's institutionalised opposition to dissimulation."[41] He writes: "It is not a question of the idiosyncratic and suspect desires of particular architects and historians. Rather, it is a question of the institutionalized logic that they simply reinforce and exploit. Indeed, it is the very ordinariness of such statements that marks their force. It is the taken for granted status of these structural biases that is aligned with the white wall. They are its props. The wall can only be taken for granted when these biases are operational."[42]

I am reminded of my own fragile white coat visually sounding its own chorus of voices, those heaving, gesticulating and twitching voices spewing discourse, delivering a lesson. Despite enduring efforts to render neutrality as fair, equitable, and unbiased, the evidence suggests neutrality may at best signal non-commitment, refusal or inability to make a choice or it may offer a place of safe hiding. This is not the essay that will rectify that situation by introducing a new definition or big idea, nor is the installation meant to offer a solution in terms of an aesthetic design practice. What it does do, however, is augment existing literature, and more importantly, design practice, with more doubt and disbelief in neutrality's dominant character — to be distant, uninvolved, dispassionate, without opinion, non-positioned. It underscores the fact that interiors are political environments and their material construction and historical interrogation are anything but neutral. Though written with specific regard to the context of race and whiteness, I wish to invoke Lesley Naa Norle Lokko's question as a closing: "What are the implications — and alternatives — for both the maker and the product, if the vision [of neutrality] is no longer shared and the language no longer tolerable?"[43] It is unlikely that this essay will change the face of prejudice that concepts of neutrality promote. That is long term work much more demanding than filling holes in a wall. If it were to persuade interior designers to reconsider how and what materials are specified, how built environments reflect but also promulgate paradigms that reinforce nominal, generic, standard, homogenous space and therefore extend those qualities to the occupation of those spaces and places, this demonstration would have been heard.

Fig 10. J. Preston, *Neutral, not so* (2009). Orations occurred while seated at the window in a white lab coat between scenes of patching, sanding and painting.

Neutral, not so: **A Performance Script**

- Gather tools/ supplies, put on coat/ mask, set up computer/ web cam, lay drop cloths Photo series 1. Open door, 9:00 am.
- Scrape.
- Oration 1: "Repairing Small Holes", *GIB Site Guide: For Residential & Commercial Installations*, CBI 5133, Winstone Wallboards Ltd (May 2006), 90-91.
- Photo series 2.
- Sand.
- Oration 2: [FAD-Architecture] (email) Message from David Bibby, Thursday, 26 February 2009 10:14 a.m. sent by Diane Brand.
- Photo series 3.
- Wipe.
- Oration 3: Victoria University of Wellington Staff Development Policy, Human Resources Policy Group, Section 4.4 [internal document], (1 May 2008), 4.
- Photo series 4.
- Fill.
- Oration 4: "Neutrality" (philosophy), Wikipedia http://en.wilipedia.org/wiki Neutrality_(philosophy) accessed 16/09/2009.
- Photo series 5
- Oration 5: David Batchelor, *Chromophobia* (London: Reaktion Books, 2000), 9-11, 21-22.
- Oration 6: Luce Irigaray, *To Speak is Never Neutral*, trans. Gail Swab (London and New York: Continuum, 2002), 137.
- Oration 7: DJB Young, "The Material Value of Colour: The Estate Agent's Tale," *Home Cultures* 1/1 (2004): 5-22.
- Oration 8: Gerald Dworkin, "Non-Neutral Principles," *The Journal of Philosophy: Some Problems in Ethics* 17/17 (1974): 491-506.
- Oration 9: Gottfried Semper, "Preliminary Remarks on Polychrome Architecture," in *The Four Elements of Architecture and Other Writings*, trans. H. F. Mallgrave and W. Herrmann (New York, New Rochelle, Melbourne, Sydney: Cambridge University Press, 1989), 45-73.
- Oration 10: Craig L. Wilkins, *The Aesthetics of Equity: Notes on Race, Space, Architecture and Music,* Minneapolis and London: University of Minnesota Press, 3-23.
- Sand/ wipe
- Oration 11: Lesley Naa Norle Lokke, "Introduction," In *White Papers, Black Marks* (London: The Alone Press, 2000), 14-35.
- Paint
- Oration 12: Jacques Rancière, *The Politics of Aesthetics: The Distribution of the Sensible,* trans. Gabriel Rockhill (New York: Continuum, 2004), 12-19.
- Photo series 6
- Close door.
- Remove tools, supplies, step ladder and drop cloth
- Photograph room.
- Exit office 5:00 pm

[1] The script including the references to the orated texts is included at the end of this essay.
[2] Christina Cogdell, "Product or Bodies: Streamline Design and Eugenics as Applied Biology," *Design Issues* 19/ 1 (2003): 44.
[3] Cogdell, "Product or Bodies," 45. 4 DJB Young, "The Material Value of Colour: The Estate Agent's Tale," *Home Cultures* 1/1 (2004): 8.
[4] A 1960's Industry advertisement singing the praises of plasterboard (aka gypsum wall board) to the American public.
[5] Bruno Latour, "What is the Style of Matters of Concern?" (University of Amsterdam: Van Gorcum: 2008), 9-11.
[6] Francis D. K. Ching and Catherine Adams, *Building Construction Illustrated Third Edition* (New York: John Wiley & Sons, Inc. 2001), 10.10.
[7] Mark Burry and Julieanna Preston, *Construction Primer* (Wellington, NZ: VUW Press, 2000), 154.
[8] Edward Allen and Joseph Iano, *Fundamentals of Building Construction Materials and Methods Fourth Edition* (Chichester: John Wiley and Sons, 2004), 775.
[9] Katherine Shonfield, "Purity and Tolerance: How Building Construction Enacts Pollution Taboos," *AA Files, Annals of the Architectural Association School of Architecture*, 28 (Autumn 1994): 37.
[10] *Build* (BRANZ, October 1991): 22-23.
[11] Shonfield, "Purity and Tolerance," 37.
[12] *Miriam Webster Dictionary*, http://www.merriam webster.com/dictionary/tolerance accessed 9 April 2012.
[13] Shonfield, "Purity and Tolerance," 37.
[14] Shonfield, "Purity and Tolerance," 39.
[15] George Scher, *Beyond Neutrality: Perfection and Politics* (Cambridge: Cambridge University Press, 1997), 1.
[16] Philip C. Jessup and Francis Deák, *Neutrality: Its History, Economics and Law, Volume 1: The Origins* (New York: Octagon Books, 1976), 249.
[17] Department of Building and Housing/ Te Tari Kaupapa Whare, *Residential Tenancy Agreement* (Wellington: New Zealand Government, 2005), 4. wwwdhb.govt.nz accessed 23 June 2010
[18] *GIB SITE CODE For Residential and Commercial Installations:* CBI 5113, May 2006, New Zealand: Winstone Wallboards LTD, May 2006), 92. http:/ www.gib.co.nz/assets/Uploads/Gib-Site-Guide-2003.pdf accessed 24 June 2010.
[19] Robin Kinross, "The Rhetoric of Neutrality," *Design Issues,* 2/2 (1985): 27.
[20] Kinross, "The Rhetoric of Neutrality," 25.
[21] Nils Brunsson and Bengt Jacobson, *A World of Standards* (New York: Oxford University Press Inc., 2000), 138-150.
[22] Allen and Iano, *Fundamentals of Building Construction,* 761.
[23] David Bieri, et al., *Gypsum wallboard and Method for Producing Same,* Patent 3,389,042. United States Patent Office, 1968. Access 1 February 2010. http://news.google.com/patents/ about?id=VbdsAAAAEBAJ
[24] Deutsche cites a guest editorial written by Thomas M. Messer in Arts 45, no. 8 (Summer 1971). See Rosalyn Deutsche, *Evictions: Art and Spatial Politics* (Cambridge, Massachusetts and London: MIT Press, 1996), 179.
[25] Deutsche, *Evictions*, 162.
[26] Deutsche, *Evictions*, 165 and 192.
[27] Deutsche, *Evictions*, 161.
[28] Luce Irigaray, *To Speak is Never Neutral,* trans. Gail Swab (London and New York: Continuum, 2002), 137.
[29] Irigaray, *To Speak is Never Neutral,* 138.
[30] Irigaray, *To Speak is Never Neutral,* 140.
[31] Lorraine Daston and Peter Galison, *Objectivity* (New York: Zone Books, 2007), 17.
[32] Gui Bonsieppe, "Visual/Verbal Rhetoric," *Ulm* 14/15/16 (1965): 30.
[33] Kinross, "The Rhetoric of Neutrality," 29-30.
[34] Jacque Rancière, *The Politics of Aesthetics: The Distribution of the Sensible,* trans. Gabriel Rockhill (London and New York: Continuum, 2004), 16.
[35] Kinross, "The Rhetoric of Neutrality," 20-21.
[36] Young, "The Material Value of Colour," 9.
[37] Young, "The Material Value of Colour," 13.

[38] Young, "The Material Value of Colour," 15.
[39] Lesley Naa Norle Lokko, *White Papers, Black Marks: Architecture, Race, Culture* (London: The Athlone Press, 2000).
[40] Craig L. Wilkins, *The Aesthetics of Equity: Notes on Race, Space, Architecture and Music* (Minneapolis and London: University of Minnesota Press, 2007), 10.
[41] Mark Wigley, *White Walls Designer Dresses* (London and Cambridge, MA: MIT Press, 1995), 362.
[42] Wigley, *White Walls Designer Dresses*, 361.
[43] Naa Norle Lokko, *White Papers, Black Marks*, 27.

Fig 11 (p.95). Anything but white, a page from 2009 The Resene Whites & Neutrals Colour Chart. Image with permission from Resene.

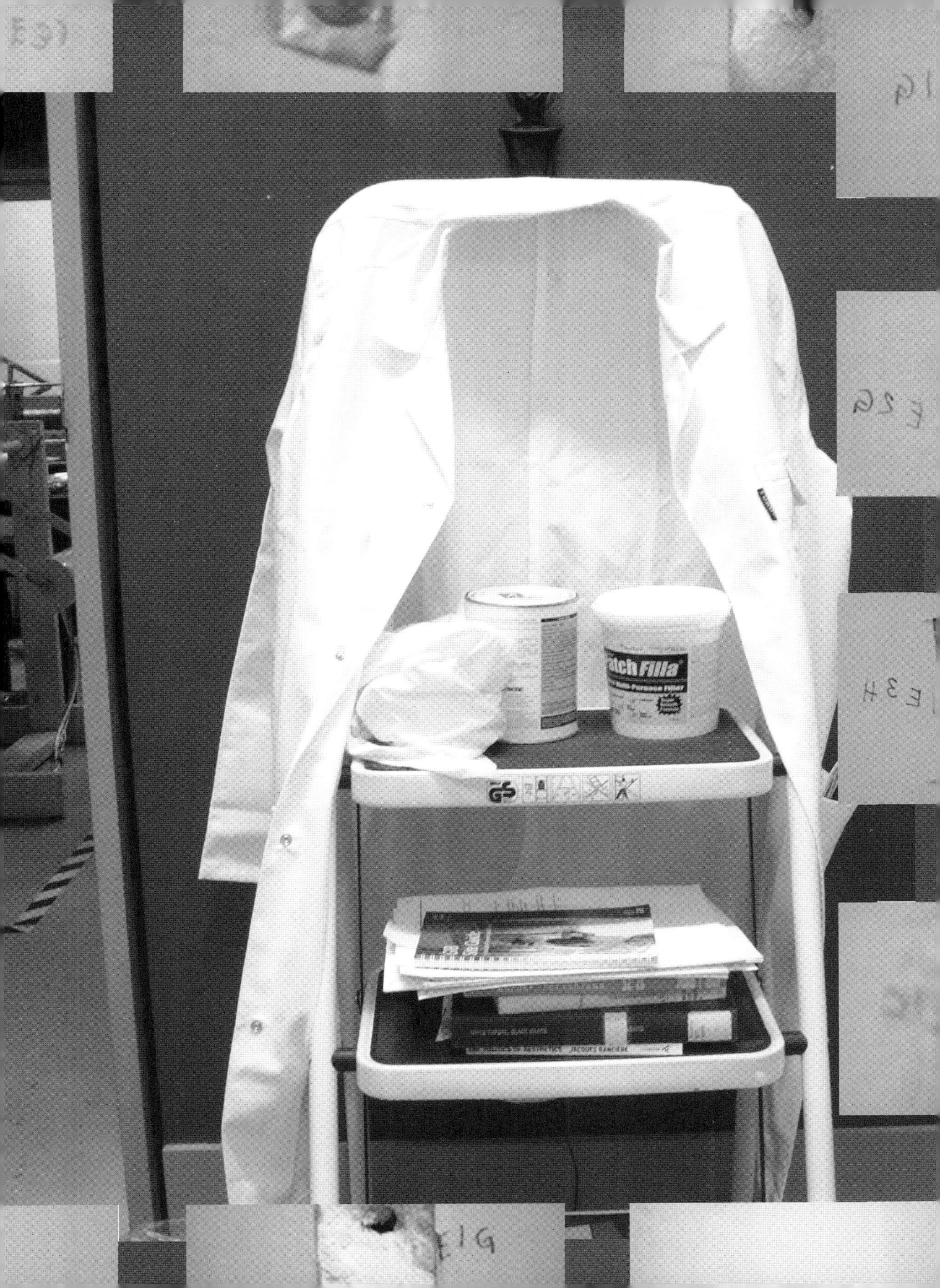
JACQUES RANCIÈRE
E1G

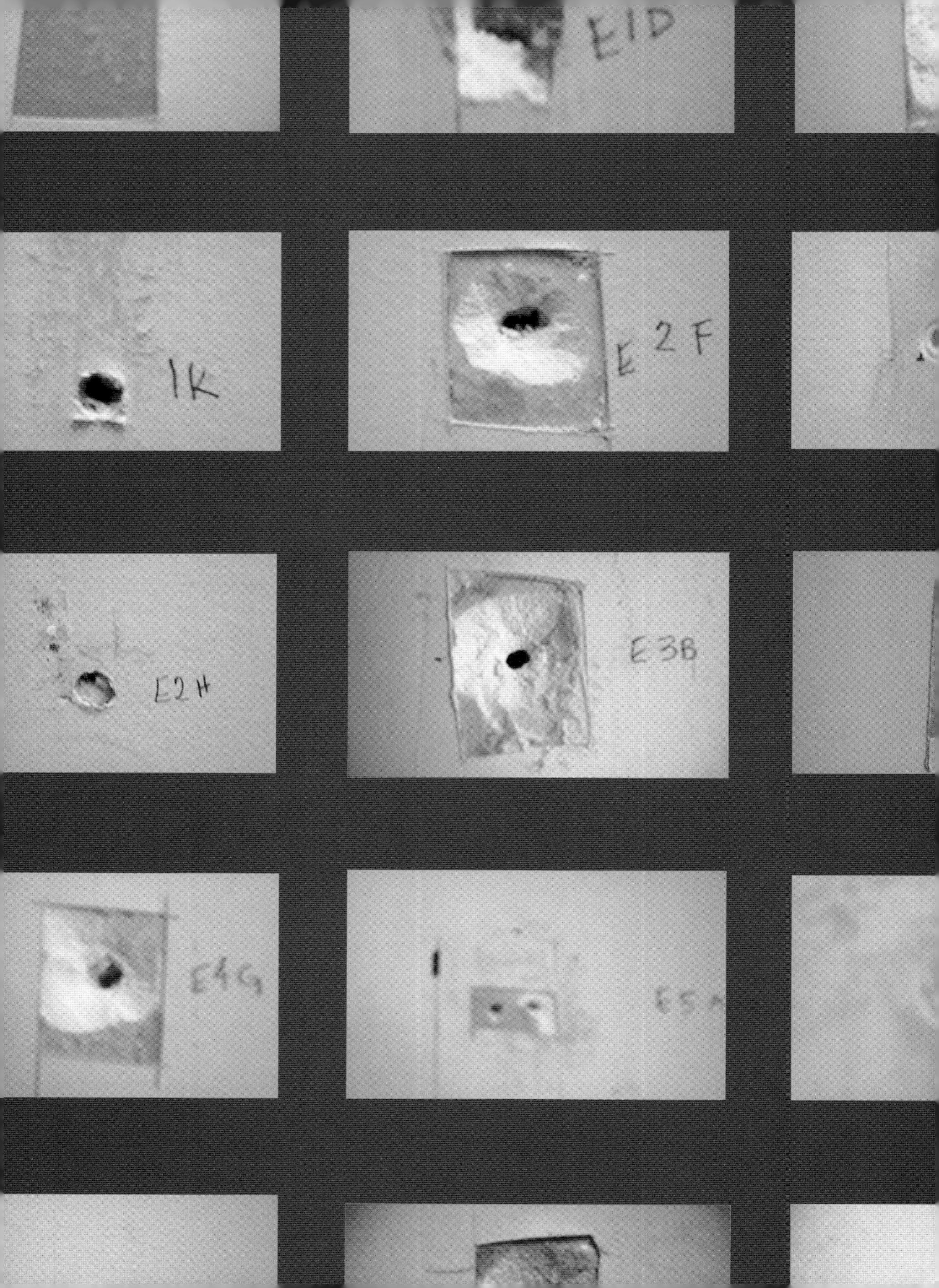
E1D
1K
E2F
E2H
E3B
E4G

Chapter 3

IN wildness

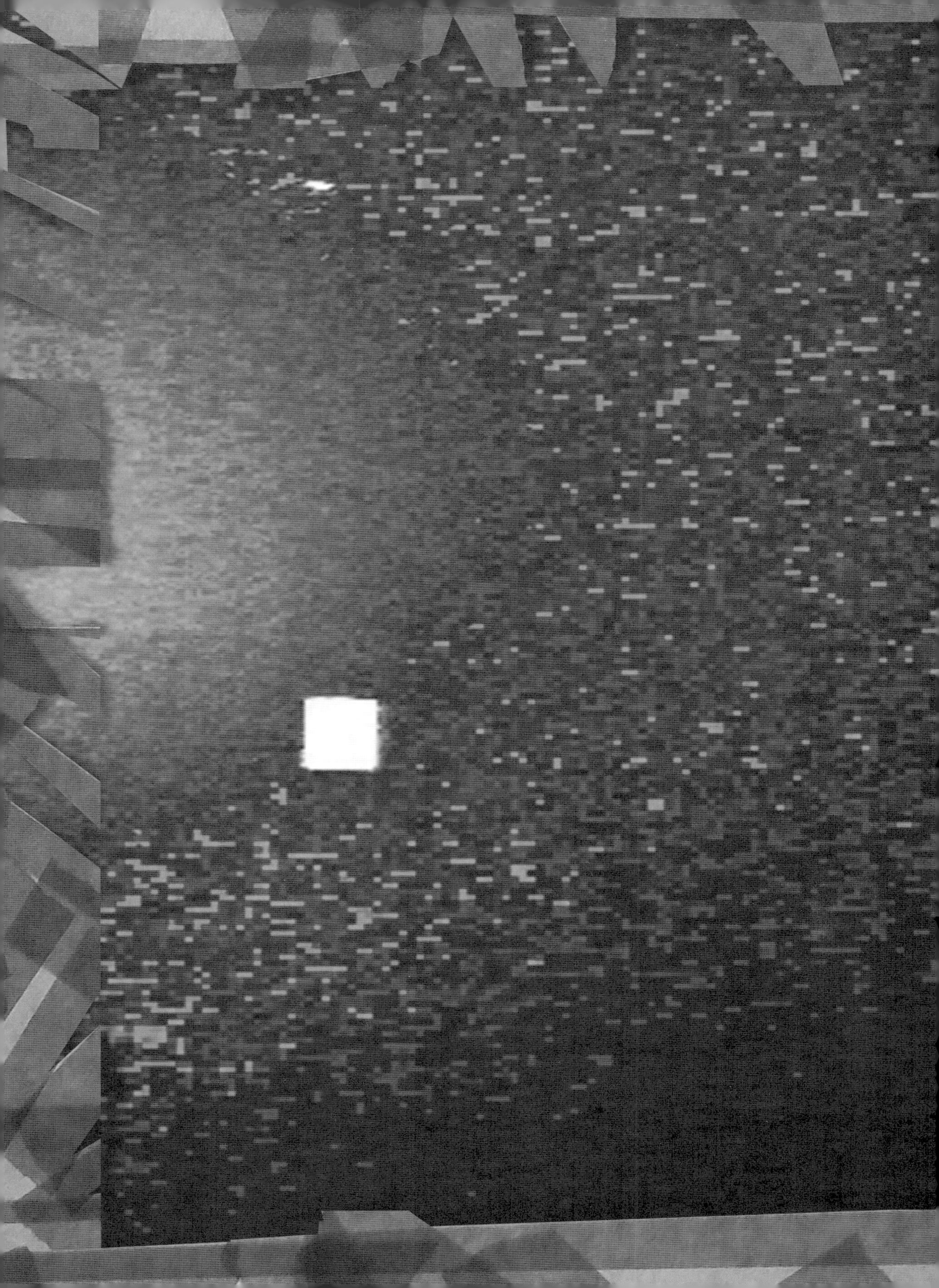

IN wildness tracks the transformation of an institutional office from a volume of functionalist interior surfaces to a vibrant network of spatial phenomena in the context of a performative and site-specific installation entitled *LOW TACK/LOW TECH/HIGH TACT GLARE.* A liberal application of masking tape to the room's large glass window wreaks havoc with its literal transparency and an association with modernist tenets and ideals of democracy. Noting the room's resemblance to a weather station and hunting blind, an eight-hour vigil was held during which I observed the emergence of wildness, an interior climatic weather pattern, conjured by feral forces transgressing the windowsill. A visual and textual record was made to qualitatively measure what an interior surface like industrial sheet glass can do when its transparency, and hence, the primacy of vision allied to the 'picture window' view is forsaken.

This chapter invites those who did not witness this installation into a exegetical space that expands the back story of the creative work; it avoids trying to represent the installation but instead, attempts to bring a reader/visitor to a similar slow experience through thick description, metaphoric association and frequent migrations across the boundary that holds wilderness at bay and a domesticated interior safe. This story is punctuated by a collection of found bits relative to wilderness, wildness, weather, New Zealand, interiors and glass that collectively position the creative work, and in the process, expose my transdisciplinary tendencies and penchant to assemble conduits between material, theory, factual data, emotions and poetry, thus coalescing a feminist approach to discursive text known as a spatial writing practice. Here one will find the authority of the argument 'coming and going,' and 'waxing and waning,' in the same tidal tempo as the performative installation. Such a ploy is punctuated by excerpts from *The Waves*, a book by Virginia Woolf, described as "a submarine book, every atom saturated"; "as if it were the product of secluded, disembodied sensibility … [yet] in an exploratory and sensuous narrative"; testing the demarcations between individual and collective experience; following a rhythm, not a plot; inhabiting the body; and, as Virginia Woolf declares, the book holds an insistence on substantiality that "goes along side a sense of how objects warp, bend, deliquesce and how the senses seize a world always irretrievably altered, endlessly contingent."[1] As in Woolf 's text, there is no outside space for the observer in the scene of *LOW TACK/LOW TECH/HIGH TACT GLARE.*[2]

Fig 1 (p.97, 132). J.Preston, *LOW TACK/LOW TECH/HIGH TACT GLARE* (2009). A common low tack adhesive decorator's masking tape forms a matted textile to circumnavigate assumptions about its limited expression.
Fig 2 (p.98, 131). J. Preston, *LOW TACK/LOW TECH/HIGH TACT GLARE* (2009). The textile made of tape and adhered to the window casts an unusual spectrum of colours onto the surfaces of the room as seen thru the technological eye of a webcam.

The sun laid broader blades upon the house.

The light touched something green in the window corner

and made it a lump of emerald,

a cave of pure green like stoneless fruit.

It sharpened the edges of chairs and tables and stitched white table-cloths with fine gold wires ...

Everything becomes softly amorphous,

as if the china of the plate flowed

and the steel of the knife were liquid.[3]

It was prime real estate for a university academic office: approximately nine square metres, adjacent to an open studio, private (not shared), and most of all, fitted with a large operable window. Though the radiator and blinds did not work, there was no direct sunlight (the office was located on the south side of the building), the walls were not sound-insulated, and a persistent draught transgressed the unsealed window frame, this was, on all accounts, a significant improvement from my previous office.

The height and the strength of the early spring sun asserted its power into the office by virtue of the heavily glazed apartment building façade a mere twenty metres away. Such proximity accelerated my anxiety over being watched by many of my students living behind its glass face as much as it promoted blinding glare on the smooth white surfaces of the office interior. During the day the glare was so strong it negated my ability to work in the office, a counter-productive factor to office life in general. At night, I was consistently startled by my own (distorted) reflection looming in the night glass. Glee with a new office quickly turned into a spatial design problem: How to mitigate the glare, retain the natural light and provide choice as to when and to what extent I chose to view or be viewed? The obvious solution would have been to have the blinds repaired or to install some other curtain condition. The anticipated number of calls, emails, requests and quotes for the expense and labour was impetus enough for a more inventive solution, one that I could do on my own and at little to no cost.

A roll of low tack adhesive tape lingering on my desk willingly offered itself to the cause. (Fig 3) Left over from the previous installation *NEUTRAL, not so*, its coiled lime green 25-millimetre-wide and 25-metres-long body expressed practical application. Relatively inexpensive and able to be purchased in bulk locally, it offers a high holding strength, clean removal, easy application, ready conformity to curves, contours and angles and an ability to mask a very sharp edge. It seemed to me that the pragmatic virtues of this common ordinary masking tape suggested more than a solution to the problem; it offered a green and slightly sticky spatial and political potential to exploit the glass pane's surface as a threshold between interior and exterior environments.

Over the course of several days, I applied the masking tape to the windowpane successively targeting those areas that appeared to generate the most glare and those areas overexposing my work activities to the prying eyes of neighbours. At one point I had to stop to clean the oily grime off the window surface, evidence that the urban atmosphere had already infiltrated my work cell. At first the application method was self-conscious of assuming any discernible pattern; this registered an efficiency quota about using as little tape as possible to cover the area and to do so in response to the tape's and the window's rectangular shape. The effect of glare however evades Euclidian geometric regulation and I found myself patching, scribbling and colouring in the transparency using sharp ripping gestures to produce short and medium-length strips to build up the surface as a textile fabric. This fabric was not the same warp and weft as in weaving looms; it was a tangle of matted fibres, much like seaweed coating the shoreline after a southerly storm or the comingling of debris in a landfill. The logic of overlapping segments of tape proved not only to produce a certain visual aesthetic; it provided a solution to the condensation that accumulated on the glass surface as the inside and outside temperatures gradually differed: on the inside my breath becoming warm and laboured. Tape to tape bridged over these moist spots where the glass was sweating. So while there was an overarching rhyme and reason that addressed the problem of glare, something else happened. As Woolf alludes to, as if liquid, everything became softly amorphous. I thought I recognised it as wilderness.

But what is that exactly?

Fig 3. 3M Scotch®Performance Masking Tape 233+

Now, too,

the rising sun came in at the window,

touching the red-edged curtain,

and began to bring out circles and lines.

Now   in the glowing light its whiteness settled in the plate;

the blade
condensed its glean.[4]

Fig 4. J. Preston (1979). A watercolour sketch of Thoreau's cabin in Massachusetts, USA.

Wilderness, the great outdoors

In 1845 Henry David Thoreau sauntered into the Massachusetts forest where he reportedly built a small dwelling with his own hands.[5] The makeshift structure has become emblematic for its frugal construction as provisional resistance to the pervasive climate and the tempering demands of civilisation. (Fig 4) As the story goes, the remotely sited, single-room cabin fostered an interior space in which Thoreau could think and write, a space so unencumbered by the ills and noise of everyday life that a work of prosaic philosophy could emerge. Thoreau explains: "I went to the woods because I wished to live deliberately, to front only the essential facts of life, and see if I could not learn what it had to teach, and not, when I came to die, discover that I had not lived."[6] Thoreau's *Walden, or life in the woods* is an address upon socio-political consciousness specific to mid-nineteenth century American life. As an introspective diary saturated by romanticism, material economy and social commentary, it is a text that rekindles poetic reflection, self-sufficiency and resilience towards political and cultural conformity. As such, Thoreau's poignant examination of life and thought in 'The New World' pinpoints a transitional moment in western culture's notion of wilderness.

In the Middle Ages, wilderness prevailed as a form of nature that instilled fear rather than wonder or pleasure. As landscape architect Linda Pollack states, it was a limitless and lawless state, a physical territory as well as a mental attitude strongly aligned with the rhetoric of the sublime.[7] Landscape historian J. B. Jackson claims that this notion of wilderness was replaced in the early eighteenth century by a view central to American history's relation to Nature Romanticism, whereby "the belief that any one exposed to the forest for a certain length of time underwent a spiritual awakening, became aware of the Seamless Web of Being, and thereafter renounced the world."[8] (Fig 5) As the means to possess and cultivate land in the early nineteenth century increased, the concept of wilderness acquired a pastoral and picturesque definition that saw it as an aesthetic and domesticated view hemmed in by wildness; i.e. wildness with reference to un-owned, as opposed to unknown. As early as 1888, American hunting groups with a goal "to promote manly sport with the rifle" formed the tenets of contemporary wilderness experience and land policy.[9]

This form of wilderness acquired two distinct identities: one, where 'wilderness' implied a state of mind, 'terra incognita' (a concept created and held by individuals and groups), and two, a political construct (a specific protected area defined and designated by government decree).[10] A prominent group of US forest ecologists draw the distinction even more decisively: "Land can be described in a space defined by two fundamental qualities: naturalness and freedom … Wilderness is that portion of land that is most wild, and wildness is a function of both naturalness and freedom from human control."[11]

On the other hand, wilderness, as a discrete physical entity, is central to a current legal battle between ecologists wanting to protect the last stands of wilderness from human intervention, and lobbyists sponsored by tourism, recreation and resource developers such as mining and logging, who support freedom of access and enterprise. A spatial and political inversion has occurred; wild lands are now contained and surrounded by domestic lands as *inter alia* i.e. land to be kept and maintained in a state of nature.[12] Wilderness as raw, unruly Nature has been recast as an interior. (Fig 5)

In a far more condensed period of time, New Zealand has adopted and adapted to all of these shifts in the notion of wilderness simultaneously. Boasting a stauncher bio-centric policy than the USA, New Zealand's management of wilderness seeks to eliminate "developments such as huts, tracks (trails), bridges, signs and mechanised access."[13] At the same time New Zealand has committed over thirty percent of its total land mass to conservation, touts itself as a protector of land, birds and water, and advertises itself as 'Paradise Lost' and 'God's Own', wrestling to balance a sustainable consciousness with a freedom associated with land rights and a desire to capture a flourishing tourist economy. As weather watcher and poet Hugh Barr writes:

> New Zealanders have always considered it their birthright to go to the beach, climb or ski mountains, tramp (a New Zealand term for backpacking or biking) the forests and wildlands, hunt for introduced deer, goats and pigs, and fish the rivers for introduced salmon and trout … [It] is a fundamental component to what New Zealanders see as quality of life and part of our identity as a fit and free outdoors people.[14]

This brief outline of wilderness' notional transformation establishes wilderness as a complex idea grafted with social values and political agendas not singularly defined or uniformly understood. And with a relatively short history of settlement, it reveals an allegiance to Western European landscape attitudes and its alliance with American land policy legislation, New Zealand sports an intensified and hybridised wilderness.

Fig 5. A photograph of Thoreau's cabin interior after its restoration. Image courtesy of K. M. Lynch.

The sun fell in sharp wedges inside the room.

Whatever the light touched became devoured with fanatical existence.

A plate was like a white lake.

A knife looked like a dagger of ice.

Suddenly

tumblers revealed themselves upheld by streaks of light.

Tables and chairs rose to the surface

as if they had been sunk under water

and rose,

filmed with red,
orange,
purple
like the bloom on the skin of ripe fruit.[15]

Island weather

From inside his cabin, Thoreau espouses a romantic notion of wilderness as he describes a seasonal shift:

> The change from storm and winter to serene and mild weather, from dark and sluggish hours to bright and elastic ones, is a memorable crisis which all things proclaim. It is seemingly instantaneous at last. Suddenly an influx of light filled my house, though the evening was at hand, and the clouds of winter still overhung it, and the eaves were dripping with sleety rain. I looked out the window, and lo! where yesterday was cold gray ice there lay the transparent pond already calm and full of hope as in a summer evening, reflecting a summer evening sky in its bosom, though none was visible overhead, as if it had intelligence with some remote horizon.[16]

In contrast to this gentle pageantry, New Zealand suggests a hybrid notion of wilderness: wild spirits and mythic creatures lurk in the flora, fauna and waters, yet one soon feels an eerie absence of mammals while tramping in the forest. It is not poisonous snakes, wolves or malaria-ridden mosquitoes that will 'get you' but a quick shift in temperature, wind direction or rugged terrain that claims the lives of more than eight people each year and necessitates many rescue operations.[17] Such differential is due to the islands' small land area and significant variable topography. Ensuing weather does not linger or gather – it rushes in and out. In a matter of an hour, winds can shift from south to north without hiatus, temperatures can plummet or soar from 8 to 38 degrees Celsius, a fog can brew in the harbour thick enough to close airports, plants can sprout a measurable length right before your eyes, and a year's supply of rain can storm the drains. Sometimes all of these events happen on the same day. According to regional weather map analysis, New Zealand is merely a minor blip of frictional resistance to large atmospheric forces operating at a global scale.

The magnitude of spatial forces enveloping New Zealand defies even the best forecasting methods. Weather is posited as the most variable and consistent characteristic of everyday life. As contemporary cultural theorists and landscape geographers argue as to the authenticity of New Zealand's modern landscape, and government continues to sanction large tracts of land and ocean as reserve, weather appears to be the last bastion of wilderness (and a rogue one at that) to elude the grasp of regulation and management. Always present, New Zealand weather lingers, hovers, thrashes and deluges every scene of every day as a high-pitched, dramatic performance.

The assertion that weather is New Zealand's most wild thing shifts wilderness from a quality or condition attributed only to land – solid ground, earthen matter – to a temporal and relational ecosystem. No less sublime than the wilderness of places such as the Congo Jungle, Antarctica or the Grand Canyon, this wilderness is not an objectified or contained place but a dynamic set of contingent forces. *LOW TACK/ LOW TECH/HIGH TACT GLARE* took that idea one step further; it observed those forces not from within an interior (via a picture window), but in an interior (by virtue of a resurfaced picture window). As the action or state of being wild, the interior witnessed a transformative live and active state – not wilderness, but wildness.

Wildness is a quality frequently attributed to things untamed and out of (human) control. And yet Thoreau saw great redemptive value in the natural world and animal kingdom:

> We need the tonic of wildness – to wade sometimes in marshes where the bittern and the meadow-hen lurk, and hear the booming of the snipe; to smell the whispering sedge where only some wilder and more solitary fowl builds her nest, and the mink crawls with its belly close to the ground. At the same time that we are earnest to explore and learn all things, we require that all things be mysterious and unexplorable, that land and sea be infinitely wild, unsurveyed and unfathomed by us because unfathomable. We can never have enough of nature. We must be refreshed by the sight of inexhaustible vigor, vast and titanic features, the sea-coast with its wrecks, the wilderness with its living and its decaying trees, the thunder-cloud, and the rain which lasts three weeks and produces freshets. We need to witness our own limits transgressed, and some life pasturing freely where we never wander.[18]

The sun struck upon the house, making the white walls glare between the dark windows. Their panes, woven thickly with green branches, held circles of impenetrable darkness. Sharp-edged wedges of light lay upon the window-sill and showed inside the room plates with blue rings, cups with curved handles, the bulge of a great bowl, the criss-cross pattern in the rig, and the formidable corners and lines of cabinets and

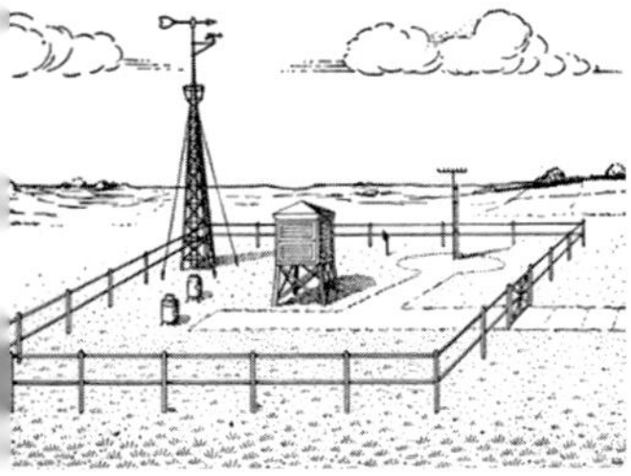

bookcases. Behind their conglomeration hung a zone of shadow in which might be a further shape to be disencumbered of shadow or still denser depths of darkness.

Calculated observation

The architectural response to the act of watching weather is remarkably similar to Thoreau's cabin: small and often for solitary occupation, simple and often temporary, and always sited in order to maximise monitoring of the surrounds. As data collection stations, weather observatories are designed to obtain a true and accurate measure of the vicinity's atmosphere based on universally standard procedures. (Fig 6)

> The site chosen for exposing the outside instruments should be the most unrestricted area possible. An open space 300 or 400 feet square without buildings or trees and without large areas of concrete bordering the site … would afford the ideal location. To prevent rays of the sun from falling on thermometers used for air temperature measurements, a screen, or instrument shelter, is required. It should be placed near the center of a plot covered by short, level grass, with a minimum area of about 20 feet by 20 feet … The rain gage (sic) should be about 10 feet from the shelter. The plot should be in an area of level ground.[20]

In this case, collecting quantitative data ranks more importantly than inhabitation and comfort: the inside of weather stations is typically small and unadorned. Technologically precise instruments external to the interior space detect cloud direction, cloud height, temperature, humidity, wind direction, wind speed, pressure and precipitation. As the instruments collect numerical and statistical information through highly sophisticated devices, phenomena such as cloud types, states of visibility and definitions of hydrometeors such as dry haze, damp haze, light fog, ice fog, smoke, dew, dust, frost and drifting snow are qualitatively described and annotated by a human observer.[21] Early twentieth century weather forecaster W. N. Shaw interpreted clouds as "heavy and swelling", "like waves of the sea", "in the form of upward hooks ending in a little claw" and "sprouting" whereby the sky is figured as a stage:

Fig 6. A sketch of an ideal weather station from Benarthur Castle Haynes, *Techniques of Observing the Weather* (New York: John Wiley & Sons, 1947). In public domain.

> There are occasions on which the sky is serene and the stage is empty, but generally there are clouds to be seen; they move, they change – all on business, with a purpose in their direction and behaviour ... The whole stage is full of action, the action which carries on the life of the world, for clouds are the precursors or survivors of the rainfall upon which the world thrives.[22]

Perhaps divulging meteorology's latent prosaic tendency, Shaw's metaphor is not a casual one: his weather watching occurred from within a weather station behind a relatively large picture window. (Let's not overlook the fact that the word 'window' results from the combination of 'wind' and 'eye', as Teysott suggests, an insulated interior eye separated from the windy exterior.[23] This large pane of glass served as the only hard-edged observational instrument to supplement qualitative interpretation. But sheet glass is not actually that hard-edged, except for perhaps when it breaks. (Fig 7) At a macroscopic level, glass is unlike the three ordinary kinds of matter: "A gas is an anarchy of molecules going every which way; a liquid is a tighter but still disorderly society in which molecules constantly dissolve and re-establish weak bonds; a solid is a molecular army in rigid formation. But glass is ... none of the above. It is rigid like a solid, but its molecules are not arranged in repeating crystals. It is amorphous like a liquid."[24] (Fig 8)

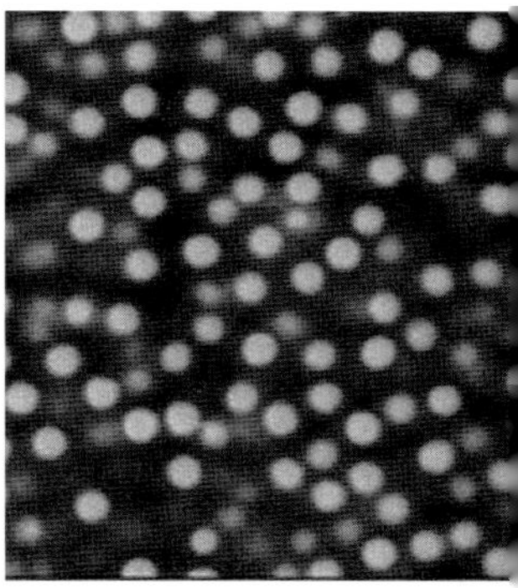

Myths perpetuating glass' un-crystallised viscous state claim that over time it slumps into a molten puddle at the bottom of the windowsill as its molten body constantly searches for equilibrium. A thin surface tension membrane is all that keeps the guts of the glass from escaping its own skin.But glass is ... none of the above. It is rigid like a solid, but its molecules are not arranged in repeating crystals. It is amorphous like a liquid."[25] (Fig 8) Myths perpetuating glass' un-crystallised viscous state claim that over time it slumps into a molten puddle at the bottom of the windowsill as its molten body constantly searches for equilibrium. A thin surface tension membrane is all that keeps the guts of the glass from escaping its own skin.The fact that some sheet glass becomes distorted

Fig 7. A microscopically enhanced view of glass crystalline molecules. http://prlo.aps.org/story/v20/st4. In public domain.
Fig 8. A close view of the bonds between glass molecules. http://www.dreamstime.com/stock photo-stock-photo-3d-glass-molecules image6022840. In public domain.

over long periods of time, centuries, is explained empirically only by flaws in the forming process or impurities in the originating silica mix. Though the myth has not been definitively disproven, scientists insist that the transparency of float sheet glass is not at risk of flowing away or distorting a clear view.[26]

What else might Shaw have observed in the sky through the large glass window as wind squalls invaded London, and much of the developed world at the time grappled with huge changes in labour, industry, and environment? Having published his book Forecasting Weather in 1911 on scientific matters of weather prediction, might Shaw have been one of the meteorologists in the audience at the London Institution where John Ruskin, an English art critic, patron of the arts, draughtsman, water colourist, prominent social thinker and philanthropist of the Victorian era, delivered his famous lectures *Storm-Cloud of the Nineteenth Century*?[27]

Cleverly wooing his audience of meteorologists, Ruskin's lectures draw parallels between the familiar experience of mist as an aqueous vapour that blurs distinction between cloud types – and social and political orders. In this lecture, Ruskin seems to play out a metaphor that launches criticism of 'unfathomable truth' attributed to the physical sciences and his sense that a fragmented harmony was emerging between phenomena and learning through observation. Ruskin's storm clouds are not merely gaseous volumes traversing the sky in a manner of everyday atmosphere-forming weather; they are signs of a world that is changing (for the worse).

Even Ruskin scholars cannot agree as to whether or not these lectures were forecasts of environmental doom or socio-political criticism craftily disguised as weather reports. Some critics and historians claim the lectures dwell on England's encroaching coal-induced pollution, a phenomenon Ruskin noted while watching the colourful effects of an inverted cloud layer on the sunrises and sunsets. "The black Devil cloud", "the blanched Sun, – blighted grass", in Ruskin's terms, presented an alarming prophecy.[28] This reading bolstered arguments of environmentalism as a precursor to contemporary concern for sustainability. Yet Ruskin's lectures are also read as a call to clean up, not the outside environment, i.e. the natural environment set apart from humans, but the environ within, the inside, and according to English literature academic Brian J. Day, the site of moral intuition. Day writes, "Ruskin's distinction between natural human perception and supernatural revelation not only foregrounds human moral agency but also emphasises perception as a moral act that with discipline can become a moral practice … Seeing, knowing, and feeling the world intuitively and morally, human beings come to understand its complex ecological order without recourse to instrumental science."[29] Day makes note that while Ruskin's plea is anthropocentric, it foregrounds a sensate and liberating agency common to human and non-human beings. This is important to our tracking of wildness. For while Day refers to a form of interiority to do with faith (or the lack thereof) in either the supernatural or in the scientific method (both understood to be ultimate, external and all-seeing forces), he leaves the window open just enough to let the atmospheric phenomena and political agency of (wild) weather in.

The windows showed erratically spots of burning fire,

the elbow of one branch,

and then

some tranquil space of pure clarity.

The blind hung red at the window's edge

and within the room daggers of light fell on the chairs and tables making cracks across their lacquer and polish.

The green pot bulged enormously,

with its white window elongated in its side.

Light driving darkness before it spilt itself profusely

upon the corners and bosses;

and yet heaped up darkness

in the mounds of unmoulded shape.[30]

Watching from within

The weather watching station is not the only form of a constructed interior built for observation in the wilderness. Designed to blend into the landscape, hunting and bird watching structures known as blinds, stands and hides provide cover from the elements and afford key opportunities for viewing prey.[31] A blind, used for hunting ducks, often consists of a woven mat of local plant material configured as a camouflage screen. It is frequently left open to the sky.[32] A stand, typically used in hunting deer, is a makeshift perch for one person situated in a tree. While it does not offer much enclosure or area in which to move about, it provides exceptional overhead viewing while reducing the chance of detection by scent. Bound by minimal size, material and aesthetic considerations, each of these forms of observatory demonstrates a basic condition of an interior: to support the power of vision emanating from the inside out.

Hides, on the other hand, sequester bird watchers in a fully enclosed interior space immersed within the environment. Usually roofed and fitted with seats for patient waiting, hides are often blended into the foliage by using materials gathered from the immediate site or paint colours approximating the local palette.[33] I sought out and tested my observation skills at a hide nestled into the grasses of a local New Zealand tidal inlet. (Fig 9)

This experience enunciated a slight shift in my understanding of the relationship between weather-watching and *LOW TACK/LOW TECH/HIGH TACT GLARE.* As a hut set apart from other dwellings, as a shelter from climate, and as a disguise that facilitates immersive observation, this hide suggested more than fortuitous viewing. It welcomed interior occupation by a commemorative plaque adorning its lintel, the accoutrements of its internal furnishings (latches, benches, ledges, ventilation flaps), and the smooth and oily surfaces demonstrating use – marred only by graffiti carved into the timber's salt-leached patina. The hours I spent alone in that hut – sometimes

Fig 9. J. Preston (2009). Interior and exterior views of a bird watching blind located at Patahanui Inlet, Porirua, New Zealand.

with the viewing flaps up but mostly leaving them down – broughtme to a mute state of interiority; my audible voice was silent, my thought voice was active but a slave to sounds and smells permeating through and from the timber cladding. I knew then what the impulse to cover my mouth, to not speak out loud, in the performative installation affected: Editing (my) noise in order to blend in (to the walls, inhabit the margin); to listen.[34] (Fig 10)

Before applying the tape to the windowpane I had never really heard the walls belch, the electric outlet hum or the girls in the studio giggle. It was just environmental chatter, easily ignored, even dismissed, I suppose, because the large window commanded my attention to view out, like every picture window is geared to do. Would it pay to remember that the glass surface was implicated in the picture window and the glass curtain wall façade as modernist architectural elements? Much of twentieth century architectural practice has adhered to the tenets of modernist theory canonised by the International Style exhibition held at the Museum of Modern Art (MOMA) in New York City in 1931. As a primary principle, the concept of transparency bestowed material surfaces with the responsibility of honestly expressing the space of architecture (the interior) through direct experience; i.e. vision. Architectural volumes were to be "enclosed by thin planes or surfaces as opposed to the suggestion of mass and solidity."[35] Volumes were to be surfaced in a homogenously manner, "unbroken in effect, like a skin tightly stretched over the supporting skeleton" and yielding textile-like surface tensions stretched in all directions.[36] These qualities underscore the power of glass: to see in and to see out, to be smooth, clear, uniform and (almost) seamless. No more hiding inside. My neighbour's house or office is as accessible to me as I am to them. All is made intelligible through virtues of float glass. In which case, material is bound up with aesthetic and political democratic space.

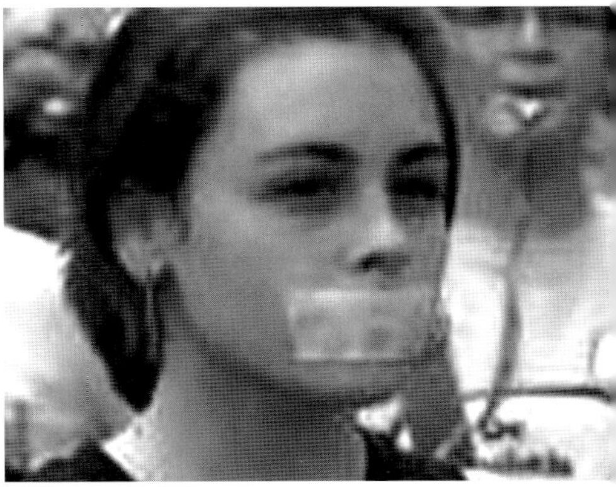

Fig 10. Taping one's mouth is not a new feminist protest strategy. A 2007 female protester demonstrates the adage "See no evil, Hear no evil" as a challenge to Venezuela's President Chavez's decision to close down the television network that dared to criticize his government. http://www. artdiamondblog.com/archives/2007/06. In public domain.

The red curtains and the white blinds

blew in

and out,

flapping against the edge of the window,

and the light which entered by flaps

and breadths   unequally   had in it some brown tinge, and some abandonment

as it blew through the blowing curtains in gusts.

Here

it browned a cabinet,

there a reddened chair,

here it made the window

waver in the side of the green jar.[37]

Letting in

There is one exquisite site-specific interior installation that helped me follow what I would admit started as an intuitive process. I came upon it by accident when considering how acts of editing – crossing out, over-writing, replacing, patching, red-lining, erasing – could be generative and affirmative rather than critical, judgmental or corrective in a disciplining sort of way. When so much of the rhetoric and actions associated with freedom from oppression are geared towards more or louder vices, and greater presence, exposure and transparency, how could acts of covering up, filling in, and blocking out the view given by a glazed window enable a feminist interior practice?

In the late 1960s, artist James Turrell transformed an abandoned hotel in the small seaside town of Ocean Park, California, into a studio and exhibition space. In an effort to master the art of light projection, he painted over and covered all windows on the outside with gypsum board walls, insulated all spaces with acoustic deadening material, and surfaced everything in a pure white plaster finish. These efforts effectively severed all spatial and temporal ties between the inside and outside. Upon realising that the external environment was an untapped resource of fine grades of light experience, Turrell set out to mine the interior space of the hotel as a spatial instrument. As a site-specific orchestration of temporal values, *Mendota Stoppages* existed as a progression of ten night spaces and two-day spaces on either side of the 1970 equinox. A musical score was produced to annotate the performance to reflect small shifts in sunlight angles and light intensities.[38] External events were filtered through apertures created in the body of the building and cast upon the walls, floors and ceilings surfaces.

Mendota Stoppages was significant because it was a site-specific sensing space: a space where the visual qualities within such space – its density, grain, tone, sense of surface, and where vision lost its distinction of being 'out there' and 'in here' – were explored.[39] Both of Turrell's biographers, Noever and Adcock, credit the installation as a founding work of Turrell's continuing re-conceptualisation of space as something that could be felt and generated by merely closing one's eyes.[40] Mendota Stoppages lends credence to understanding interiors as vessels for receiving, observing and appreciating exterior environments, especially those spatial factors associated with weather. It highlights the manner in which interiors harbour a threshold: weather in the form of wildness is cajoled across the sill and transformed by the process of falling upon an interior surface.

Turrell's signature is an infusion of light around, upon and against a surface, such that the edge of what is concrete vaporises. This poetic technique is reminiscent of the luminists, a group of late nineteenth century landscape painters known for inducing silence and stillness into a perfect, miniature universe that triggered monumentality through scale rather than size.[41] As a sequence of scenes couched in spatial duration, *Mendota Stoppages* is an introspective re-conceptualisation of interior. More phenomenal than political, more sensual than technological, it is a work more intimate and immersive than a large glass window could possibly offer.[42]

The performative installation *LOW TACK/LOW TECH/HIGH TACT GLARE* officially began on 9 September 2009 at 8:00 am New Zealand time. I had used several days leading up to this one to apply the tape. A web cam mounted to my computer and set on a desk in the middle of the room recorded this process. During these initial days I worked at the desk and watched the window through the web cam. (Fig 11) For some inexplicable reason, the web cam picked up a wider spectrum of light, and therefore colours. I was able to capture glaring moments in a time-stamped image. My back was to the window, full glare on the computer screen and I faced the door to anyone that might enter. This part of the installation was kept private except to those watching from the apartment building across the street. On the day of the public portion of the performative installation, I turned the computer around on the desk and sat facing the window, which was now fully surfaced with tape. I used the web cam to watch the door, the corridor and studio behind me and selectively photographed that view throughout the day. A computer monitor and keyboard were positioned in front of me. They served as my technological writing pad, which I used to record my observations and communicate with visitors who came through the door. A piece of the green tape stretches across my mouth as well as the window; two forms of deprivation.

Even with the din of pre-dawn street lamps, the room was aglow in an indescribable green hue. Many of my observations tried in vain to describe it. It just was. The expressions on people's faces offered the best description. As the observational notes attest, my thoughts migrated from pondering on close-at-hand details to contemplation on abstract issues. I was surprised at how the colour green induced people who entered the room to be quiet. It prompted the materials of the room, the people outside of the room, the building, the city to become resoundingly more present. The office felt larger than ever even when there were people coming and going, standing at the door, leaning against the wall or sitting on the floor watching with me. What they could not see though was the way that the web cam saw more, or differently. Somehow more sensitive and yet more pixelated, it harvested an image of wildness into exotic fields of colour. The edges that typically define the difference between body and environment became spots of colour indiscriminately migrating across the human: non-human divide to favour of tonal vibration over cultural hegemony. The door served as a threshold through which many chose to venture and others walked past. For some the wildness was too great to cross the threshold; I saw them looking from the safe distance of the studio, its strangeness within the Architecture School's setting and culture too much to risk.[43] I was reminded of the many visitors who were welcomed into Henry David Thoreau's humble cabin on a cold winter evening in the wilderness of Walden, Massachusetts amongst spirited company and politically charged conversation:

> I had three chairs in my house; one for solitude, two for friendship, three for society ... One inconvenience I sometimes experienced in so small a house, the difficulty of getting to a sufficient distance from my guest when we began to utter the big thoughts in big words ... If we are merely loquacious and loud talkers, then we can afford to stand very near together, cheek by jowl, and feel each other's breath; but if we speak reservedly and thoughtfully, we want to be farther apart, that all animal heat and moisture may have a chance to evaporate. If we would enjoy the most intimate society with that in each of us which is without, or above, being spoken to, we must not only be silent, but commonly so far apart bodily that we cannot possibly hear each other's voice in any case ... As the conversation began to assume a loftier and grander tone, we gradually shoved our chairs farther apart till they touched the wall in opposite corners, and then commonly there was not room enough.[44]

Here Thoreau not only speaks to the virtues and ideals of wilderness as a philosophical and practical inoculation to all things that he deems ail mid-nineteenth century society, he also offers a simple spatial model that links the cabin's interior volume and dimensions with the sociability of spatial experience and liveliness, a sociability that he extended to all woodland creatures, materials, sounds and weather phenomena.[45] A small domestic interior gives rise to public and civic space. This schema to 'let things in' served as a modus operandi to the project and this chapter.

As if Thoreau's cabin and my office were not already amply occupied by visitors, wild and not so wild, I am indebted to two other scholars for inspiring this boundary-crossing activity. In an essay that traces the affects of weather on healthy living in early eighteenth century Britain, Vladimir Jankovic calls for a form of virtual citizenship between indoors and outdoors. As a historian in atmospheric sciences, Jankovic reminds us that weather is a private and public condition, not a measurable entity.

> One learns important things about the historical meanderings of meteorological interests if one sees them as related to social and somatic attitudes towards the weather as a milieu … Seeing the weather before it is assembled and appropriated as a subject of a shared discourse based on rational discussion and exchange of comparable data – as in some way a boundary object straddling conceptualizations – is like seeing a soil before it is cultivated. What is cultivated depends on the nature of the soil.[46]

Jankovic's investigation of intimate climates via medicine, health and social preconceptions around dampness, draughts, fresh and stagnant air is an inquiry on domestic atmosphere, a subject which he notes is marginally addressed in historical research. "We possess no studies on bathroom monsoons, attic drizzles or the oven Sirocco."[47] *LOW TACK/LOW TECH/HIGH TACT GLARE* took his challenge to heart. I found interior weather in one of the most unlikely places of all: a twenty-first century cellular workplace office fitted with common interior materials and finishes on the dark side of a renovated warehouse building (trying hard to be a modernist international style piece of architecture) in the middle of a densely populated and developed urban landscape.

The idea of 'letting in' is one that I developed through the creative process of preparing and performing *LOW TACK/LOW TECH/HIGH TACT GLARE* informed by my reading of contemporary British social scientist and geographer Doreen Massey's philosophy on space and place. Her works have become touchstones within what is known worldwide as the spatial turn; they are recognised as pivotal to geography's central role in imagining and giving action to spatial politics focused on contingent forces forming, not patterns or flat representational surfaces mistaken for space, but space in its lived capacity. For Massey, place is neither essential nor static: places have multiple identities, places are the continuous effect of dynamic processes, and places are not enclosures with definitive insides and outsides. Her empirical research offers a critique of globalisation and defends hanging on to the specificity of places but only if understood through a spatial lens which acknowledges mutual co-production across scales, continents, governments and historical events. As a strong advocate for relational theory, Massey rethinks the territorial as a philosophical and conceptual issue that gravitates towards the political rather than the economic.

This project presents a conundrum for me in terms of Doreen Massey's philosophy, a philosophy I hold dear, at least intellectually. Throughout my study I have held to the importance of three notions: 1) That interiors are not discrete objects or mere volumetric residue of an external structural envelope; 2) That the material that presumes to enclose an interior is but thickened live surface participating in the dynamic processes of life; 3) That the coincidence of 1) and 2) could imagine an interior as an active political geographic territory. 'Letting in' registered a desire to bring interiors, interior design and interior design theory into a larger field of concern, not with the aim to adopt any sort of grand narrative but, as Massey says, to engage the big stories of the moment. In this way, I am participating as a speculative force exploring how the world might shed its cloistered assumptions about interiors as domesticated environments. Dispelling wilderness as a locale free from human intervention and recognising that its inhabitant is a qualitative state of wildness, in an interior, was a finding I could not have predicted when I set out to mediate glare with low tack decorator's masking tape.

But, there is a reason that this is the third of five chapters and there are unresolved matters at hand. The fact that the performative installation used time-stamped still photography to record the event and then play it back as a segmented history, a representation of space as time, raises a question about the extent to which I have fully ingested and translated my understanding of Massey's *For Space* through the creative work.[48] This self-critique exposes the experimental aspect of this project but underscores how paramount it is to explore what the role of 'surface' means even if to abandon it as a fashionable folly within recent architectural discourse and practice. Though I consistently work at full scale employing materials and processes in concrete ways, the matter of bringing you, the visitor, to the work after its intensity has waned has only repeated the representational surface as space that Massey's works disavow and I dream of transcending. If anything, *LOW TACK/LOW TECH/HIGH TACT GLARE* revealed a way that boundaries (especially those defended by the solidity of concrete, glass and steel) are as permeable to transgression and migration, and in the end, putting into doubt surface as a hard and fast edge that divides world and things.

[1] Virginia Woolf, *The Waves*, ed. with an introduction and notes by Gillian Beer (Oxford: Oxford University Press, 2008), xiii-xviii.

[2] Earlier versions of this essay have featured as a keynote presentation and conference paper at *Atmospheres Symposium* 2009, University of Manitoba, Canada and then as a full-length peer-reviewed journal article "The Great Outdoors'" in *IDEA 2010* (http://idea-edu.com/journal/2009-idea-journal/).

[3] Woolf, *The Waves*, 21.

[4] Woolf, *The Waves*, 60.

[5] Thoreau reports that the cabin was approximately 10 x 15 feet. This has serendipitous coincidence; the office was very nearly the same size.

[6] Henry David Thoreau, *Walden, or Life in the Woods* (New York: Thames & Hudson: 1854), 73.

[7] Linda Pollack, "American Ground: Four Kinds of Disturbances," *Lotus International* 100 (1990): 127.

[8] J. B. Jackson, "Anthorphobia, or the Death of Landscape," *Modulus* 20 (1991): 109.

[9] Jackson, "Anthorphobia," 111.

[10] John Shultis, "Social and Ecological Manifestations in the Development of the Wilderness Area Concept in New Zealand," In *The State of Wilderness in New Zealand*, ed. by Gordon Cessford (Wellington, New Zealand: Department of Conservation, 2001), 59.

[11] Gregory Aplet, Janice Thompson & Mark Wilbert, 'Indicators of Wildness: Using Attributes of the Land to Assess the Context of Wilderness,' in *USDA Forest Service Proceedings* RMRS-P-15-VOL-2 (2000): 89

[12] P. H. C. B. Lucas, Preface to *The State of Wilderness in New Zealand*, ed. by Gordon Cessford (Wellington, New Zealand: Department of Conservation, 2001), xi.

[13] John Shultis, "Social and Ecological Manifestations in the Development of the Wilderness Area Concept in New Zealand," In *The State of Wilderness in New Zealand*, ed. by Gordon Cessford (Wellington, New Zealand: Department of Conservation, 2001), 3.

[14] Hugh Barr, "Establishing a Wilderness Preservation System in New Zealand - A User's Perspective," in *The State of Wilderness in New Zealand*, ed. by Gordon Cessford (Wellington, New Zealand: Department of Conservation, 2001), 17.

[15] Woolf, *The Waves*, 89.

[16] Thoreau, *Walden*, 243-244.

[17] Ministry of Culture and Heritage, *Te Manatu Taonga* (2005-2008). Te Ara Encyclopedia of New Zealand, www.teara.govt.nz.

[18] Thoreau, *Walden*, 248.

[19] Woolf, *The Waves*, 123.

[20] Benarthur Castle Haynes, *Techniques of Observing the Weather* (New York: John Wiley & Sons, 1947), 11.

[21] Haynes, *Techniques of Observing*, 80-98.

[22] W. N. Shaw, *Forecasting Weather* (London: Constable & Company Ltd, 1933), 3-4.

[23] George Teysott, "Mapping the Threshold: A Theory of Design and Interface," *AA Files: Annals of the Architectural Association School of Architecture* 57 (2008): 57.

[24] Robert Kunzig, *The Physics of Glass*, http://www.glasslinks.com/newsinfo/physics. htm (1 of 3) [13/05/2012 12:16:13 p.m.]

[25] Robert Kunzig, *The Physics of Glass*, http://www.glasslinks.com/newsinfo/physics. htm (1 of 3) [13/05/2012 12:16:13 p.m.]

[26] Philip Gibbs, October 1996. http://math.ucr.edu/home/baez/physics/General/ Glass/glass.html (8 of 8) [13/05/2012 12:14:41 p.m.]

[27] John Ruskin, *Storm-Clouds of the Nineteenth Century*, Two Lectures Delivered at the London Institution, 1884, Project Gutenberg, http://www.gutenberg.org/ etext/20204.

[28] John D. Rosenberg, *The Genius of John Ruskin: Selections from his Writings*, (London: Allen and Unwin, 1964), 321.

[29] Brian J. Day, "The Moral Intuition of Ruskin's 'Storm-Cloud'," *Studies in English Literature*, 1500-1900, 45(4) The Nineteenth Century (Autumn 2005): 928.

[30] Woolf, *The Waves*, 137.
[31] Phil Bourjaily, "The Invisible Hunter," *Field and Stream* 111(6) (2006): WF6-WF7.
Kirk Deeter,
[32] "Duck Luck," *Field and Stream* 113(6) (2008): WF11-WF13.
[33] "Using Hunting Blinds," *Field and Stream*, 90(12) (1986): 58.
[34] There is a future essay to write solely focused on having a piece of tape over one's mouth. I originally thought that the greatest political impact of the installation was to turn a highly sought after office space into a "green" space, an electronic yet natural garden. Instead what I found was that not being able to speak to me directly made people uncomfortable, alarmed, and put off as well as more likely to touch me, want to write to me rather than speak themselves, or just ignore me all together. This presents a form of non-violent civil disobedience of a next degree. (However, some of my visitors told me that they thought to take away my spoken voice is not only antifeminist, but very self-violent!)
[35] Alfred Barr, "Preface" in Henry-Russell Hitchcock and Philip Johnson, *The International Style* (New York and London: W. W. Norton & Company: 1966), 13.
[36] Henry-Russell Hitchcock and Philip Johnson, *The International Style* (New York and London: W. W. Norton & Company: 1966), 45.
[37] Woolf, *The Waves*, 152.
[38] Peter Noever, ed., *James Turrell: The Other Horizon* (Germany: Cantz Verlag, 1999), 88.
[39] Noever, ed., *James Turrell*, 90-91.
[40] Noever, ed., *James Turrell*, 90.
[41] Gina Crandell, *Nature Pictorialized: 'The View' in Landscape History* (Baltimore and London: The John Hopkins University Press, 1993), 146-147.
[42] All of these facets reinforce what landscape theorist Jacqueline Labbe describes as the gendered condition of the (male) prospect view –legitimate, authoritative, abstract – in contrast to that of the (female) detailed view – low, confined, concrete. Labbe further distinguished the detailed view with that of the landscape, as if in the landscape rather than standing above it looking down from a summit. See Jacqueline Labbe, *Landscape, Gender and Romanticism* (New York: St. Martin's Press and London: MacMillan, 1997).
[43] Outside the door next to the poster, a notice read: "Welcome, come in! Please be aware that this event is being photographically recorded."
[44] Thoreau, 111-112.
[45] Jane Bennett's book, *Thoreau's Nature: Ethics, Politics, and the Wild* (Rowman & Littlefield, 2002) offers an expanded view of this notion.
[46] Vladimir Jankovic, "Intimate Climates: From Skins to Street, Soirées to Societies," in *Intimate Universality: Local and Global Themes of Weather and Climate*, ed. by J.R. Fleming, V. Jankovic and D.R. Coen (Sagamore, Massachusetts: Science History Publications/USA, 2006), 3.
[47] Jankovic, "Intimate Climates," 3.
[48] Doreen Massey, *For Space* (Los Angeles, London, New Delhi, Singapore: Sage Publications, 2005).

Chapter 4

making note(s) *OF* **surface**

sexuate subject 11
I was here

Imagine venturing amongst the folds of a dark, worn and crumpled wrapping to find Luce Irigaray's book *This Sex Which Is Not One*. (Fig 1) Its volume is amply enhanced by the insertion of many notes, sketches, photocopies and material samples, including glossy photographs of an artist's installation. (Fig 2) You notice that the book's internal pages, in particular, Irigaray's essay "The 'Mechanics' of Fluids" have been renovated.[1] (Fig 3) A textual narrative in the form of a small pamphlet modestly printed on plain bond paper and bound by staples in its gutter has been shunted into the middle of the book, which is also the middle of the essay. The pamphlet, this text, the very text you are now reading, offers varying degrees of connectivity between all of these multifarious nodes. A pervasive sense of porosity envelops the experience.

Before I go much further, let's get something out in the open: this text will not explain or tell you how to interpret what is in your hands, on your lap or lying sprawled on the table; it is not a puzzle or an algebraic equation to be solved. It invites you into a condensed, compressed and fluid version of my studio and the site of making a performative installation entitled *No Fixed Seating*. In order to proceed further, some readers may find that they need to set aside an exegetical mode of thinking and inquiring along with much of the rhetoric associated with 'frameworks', 'platforms', 'criticality' and other language signifying power and allegiance to 'rigour.'[2]

Abdicating such modes of normative research discourse method does not mean that this chapter lacks an argument or intent beyond descriptive interpretation or archival documentation; it is more than detritus swept off my studio floor. This text was assembled as a space as close as possible to my practice short of bringing you into the studio room and putting you to work. As well as deploying a tactic that Irigaray

Fig 1 (p.133, 163). J. Preston, *inertia: interiors, surface, matter* [doctoral exegesis (2013)]. This section of my exegesis literally inhabited a copy of Irigaray's book as a housing, critique and supplement. Several editions were created. Each book was cloaked in a building construction material. In this case, the material was tar paper, a material used to prevent water from entering an interior space. Having been distressed through hand manipulation for several hours, the tar paper lost its stiff platelike constitution and gained a leathery suppleness.
Fig 2 (p.134, 162). J. Preston, *No Fixed Seating* (2010). A collection of images that chronologically document the performativity of seat covers inscribed and fused by a re-writing of Irigaray's text and furthermore, another form of re-writing as seats are occupied.
Fig 3. A copy of Luce Irigaray's book *This Sex Which is Not One* became the surrogate context for images, sketches, hand written notes and samples of filtration materials pertinent to the development of *No Fixed Seating*. Tucked between pages, these interventions literally expanded the volume and of Irigaray's book, at points interfered with the legibility and offered a critical response to its text.
Fig 4. The text on each page of Irigaray's essay "The 'Mechanics' of Fluids" was made more porous by piercing each full stop, "o", or any letter or number that formed an enclosed figure.

uses to employ the written word as a textual medium to lash out against logic, reason, scientific method and patriarchy embedded in language, *making note(s) OF surface* practices Irigaray's use of metaphors as a material medium to migrate amongst an open-ended and non-hierarchical field: rugs, feminist philosophy, chairs, architectural theory, flashings, fine arts photography, slip covers, rules of grammar, weather proof membranes, building envelopes, upholstery and art installations. (Fig 4) The ability to make your own sense of the work points to this project's adaptation of Andrew Benjamin's strategy of 'decontextualization,' a strategy he crafts relative to architectural theory and surface effects. For him, theory is understood as an engagement with design practice, whereby practice is broadly interpreted and inclusive of many ever-changing means of representation. Benjamin points to theory's speculative role in relation to history: "What occasions the introduction of theory is the presence of a space opened by a relationship whose formal presence cannot be determined in advance" and necessitates "an iterative reworking of the elements of history."[3] Benjamin asserts that theory's core concern is the destruction of the field of meaning in order that another potential can be realised. This approach runs in tandem with my own conviction that theory can be constructed thru material practice, i.e. both the process of working with or upon a material and the material objects are theoretical constructs in themselves.

Some readers may recognise a resemblance here to Paul Carter's notion of 'material thinking' or Mieke Bal's close reading practice of 'focalization.'[4] In much the same manner as the wedge/shim introduced in Chapter 1: *The Yield Principle*, I am employing decontextualisation to incite destruction in its generative mode as well as drawing on creative license associated with open interpretation of a work, a practice common in fine art. Hence, I am engaging you as a user and viewer, a maker and critic, in the book's performance in the same way that the participants, the chairs, the lecture room, the weather and the student political rallies 'made' *No Fixed Seating*. I recall telling a woman sitting in front of me at the symposium about how the project was inspired by Irigaray's essay "The 'Mechanics' of Fluids." She nodded politely, took off her coat and after sitting on the covered chair for twenty-minutes, she turned, smiled at me as if we shared a secret and said, "I get it." It is my aim to bring you to that same corporeal-knowing state with this object/space.

In the same space, this chapter muses on the subject of 'surface' and its productive value to the entire research project — a project initially motivated by an ambiguous question: What can an interior surface do? This concern prompted research into what surface has been understood to be and what special circumstances arise when an interior is understood through issues of surface or, more specifically, as a surface. It was my intention to embrace the nature of surface associated with superficiality (inclusive of its negative connotation) connected to interior design's professional practices which serve to furnish inhabitation through various modes of aesthetic material assemblage, appliqué, and decoration, all of which carry a well-known, criticised and yet entrenched identity marker as frivolous and inconsequential. The links between issues of surface and the superficial extend to a gendered association with the female sex and femininity. Effectively, the research set out to find the depth in surface and, like every heroic journey, something else, something unintended, was discovered. That other matters arising out of the research eclipsed initial concerns leaves me undaunted; this potential is not a risk but inherent to speculative fluid thinking and creative practice research.

Of Whirlwinds and Fluids

No Fixed Seating was a performative and site-specific installation featured in a group exhibition and panel *Whirlwinds* (curated and convened by Dr Jane Rendell, Dr Ana Araujo and Dr Penelope Haralambidou) which was part of the larger international conference *Sexuate Subjects: Politics, Poetics, Ethics* (convened by Dr Peg Rawes). This event occurred during the first week of December 2010 at University College of London, most notably at Wates House, which is the home of the Bartlett School of Architecture and the Slade School of Art, which hosts the Woburn Gallery. While the conference drew responses to French philosopher Luce Irigaray's theory of sexual difference for enabling critically-aware global formations of self-identity and community, art, architectural and spatial practices, ecology, environmental care and sustainability, health and biomedically assisted life, the *Whirlwinds* panel considered issues of sexual ethics and difference raised by Irigaray's essay "The 'Mechanics' of Fluids" and Irigaray's understanding of the experimental, material and conceptual construction of space. This event drew my attention because in its call for creative practice contributions it demonstrated a conviction that poetic practice matters as an active politically charged force.

Producing a synopsis of "The 'Mechanics' of Fluids" is a challenging task because its poetic and forceful eloquence has inspired many interpretations and actions over the years, which deliberately evade a singular canonical reading. It is a text that stands ready for first-person digestion. What lured me into Irigaray's text is its rejection of logical discourse in favour of what she calls *parler femme* and the manner in which "speaking (as) woman" questions logic as the most neutral of all practices, in fact, how it questions the very possibility of neutrality, especially in language.[5] Her title for the essay critiques the field of fluid mechanics as an emblem of a dominant patriarchal system that applies super-rationalisation to the point of annihilating woman from symbolic logic. (Fig 5) Irigaray scholar Marjorie Hass puts forward:

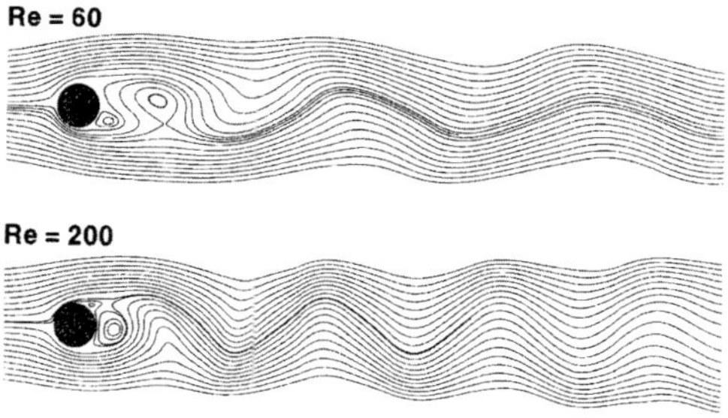

> "...Irigaray's work rests on the premise that the generative sense-giving structures of Western culture (e.g., law, language, logic and economy) provide no representation of feminine existence, except insofar as it is commensurable with masculinity. More problematically, these structures are such that it is impossible to fully represent feminine otherness within them. All that is available is the small space of representation assigned to women's bodies: the symbolic images of flow, fluidity, indefiniteness. In her work, Irigaray uses these images as a lever, encouraging us to push our thinking and speaking in new directions and bring about a transformation in consciousness. She acts as both a prophet and muse urging us to a land just out of reach, just beyond the next horizon. And it is in just this mode that Irigaray returns again and again to the logic of negation, identity and generality to illustrate the monosexuality of our theoretical paradigms, to gesture toward new paradigms, and to reconstruct relationships."[6]

No Fixed Seating materially transformed "The 'Mechanics' of Fluids" text in the indeterminate form of thirty-three plastic slipcovers draped over a section of seating

Fig 5. Fluid mechanics flow diagrams and microscopic imaging. Image in public domain. I faithfully followed Irigaray's instructions to review textbooks on fluid mechanics. Though well educated as an architect and landscape student in algebra, geometry, chemistry, physics, structural engineering and water run-off, the pages of these volumes filled with long equations appeared as hieroglyphics, a foreign language with an elegant aesthetic. Most every equation equalled zero as if all things coming to nought was ideal. I find it difficult to reconcile a phenomenal state of nothing.

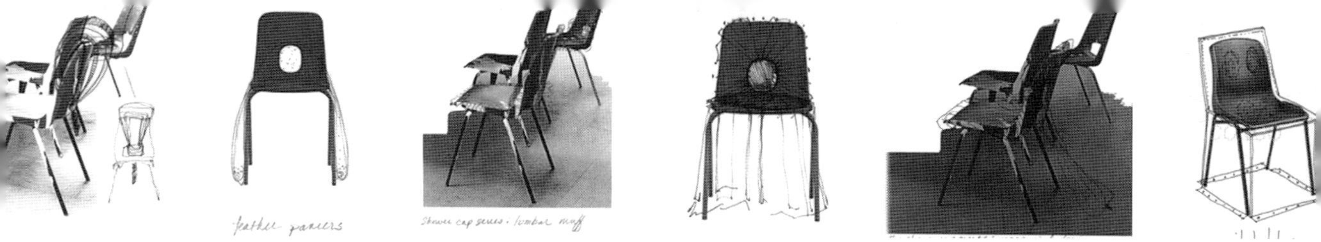

in the main conference venue. (Fig 6) Each slip cover donned a surface-effect created when thermal technologies were used to fuse, scar, perforate and punctuate Irigaray's text onto two layers of thin plastic films simultaneously. (Fig 7) What was two became one. Throughout the three-day event, the slip covers honoured and publicised Irigaray's presence, adorned the mass-produced injection-moulded chairs, affirmed occupation and participation through identity tags, mediated a porous relation between body and seat, and acoustically softened the concrete surfaces of the room. During this event, the external world entered the venue in predictable and also unexpected fashion: Women and men, each scholars in their own way on Irigaray's works, feminism and creative practice, travelled from all over the world to work on the question: "What kind of response is feminism capable of making today?"[7]

Before the conference even began, a certain degree of tension was building. This event took place the very same weekend that snow and ice shut down airports, trains and streets across northern Europe and UK students occupied the University College of London campus to practice their rights to free speech and demonstration over the raising of tuition, the closure of study programmes and their general discontent over the state of the nation and its negation of their futures. Prior to my arrival in London, my proposal to cover the lecture venue chairs and also to separate the linked rows into individual chairs drew considerable concern from the university health and safety officer, a curious political development I had not anticipated. Upon entering the exhibition venue for the first time, I shook my head in surprise; fields of chairs were set up in each of the legs of the 'L' shaped room, each facing a projection screen. At

Fig 6. Julieanna Preston, *No Fixed Seating* (2010). Slip cover and chair developmental studies. Image in public domain. My initial ideas for the exhibition included the use of various materials such as sand, feathers, butter, milk, water, oil and salt to fill out a sculptural response to the existing chair, to comment on its unresponsiveness to any specific body let alone a female body. I observed that these fluid materials were substitutes for actual visceral matter such as semen, blood, tears, saliva, mucous, faeces, all of which I had been warned were not viable materials to use in this context. That withstanding, I veered away from using them because I knew I could rely on live bodies full of fluids to be present and actively engaged instead of represented.
Fig 7. Plastic and cloth slip covers. Image in public domain. http://www.estampeinc.com/auto-seat-covers/auto-seat-coversdisposable-slip-grip-id96.html Most people have had the dubious pleasure of sitting on a couch coverec in thick protective plastic. My first experience was in Charleston South Carolina where the summers are relentlessly hot and humid and the air conditioner units are always in a state of repair. The sweat collected at the back of my neck, tailbone, thighs and knees and in rivulets so profuse that I felt I might be swept away by my own fluids in comic relief.

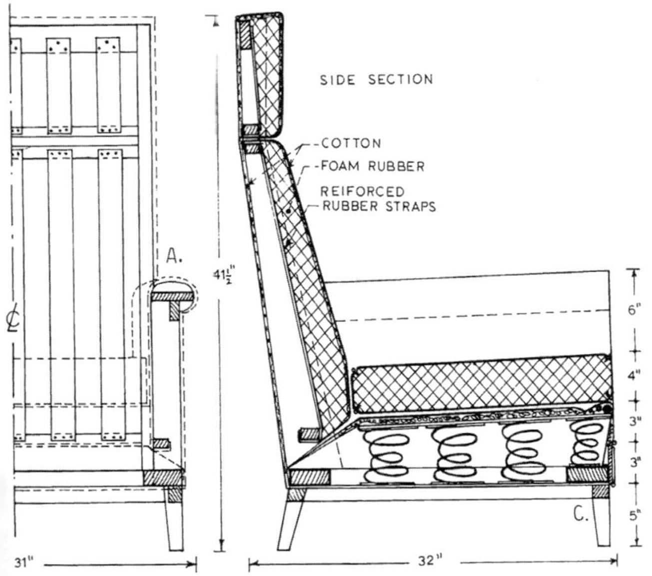

first glance it seemed a functional and instrumental response to seating as many people as possible. That it would split the audience in two parts unable to see the other seemed fitting to the conference's focus on Irigaray's works. I quickly segregated the chairs according to their design styles and adorned a sector of the chairs that showed a likeness to Robin Day's famous canteen design with the protective slip-covers. (Fig 8) My creative work operated at a very local level upon the same issues at play in the university, the city and the country. We, the audience of the conference, were sitting on Irigaray's text, an inhabitation of bodies and the chairs that reconstructed the textually-inscribed upholstery through an occupational weathering of tears, stains, rips, wrinkles, stretches, and not least of all, knots. (Fig 9)

Fig 8. Traditional upholstery details and images in Dal Fabbro, Mario, Upholstered Furniture, Design and Construction. New York: McGraw-Hill Book Company, 1969, 167. These detailed drawings reveal the craft and technology invested in supporting a posture and the weight of a body as much as they speak to the immense effort to conceal a supporting frame and all the seams and edges in the fabric. There is a certain metaphoric exchange at play here between a human body and the hard timber frames, medium density foam, soft padding and the fabric stretched taut across their surface, as if an ironic conundrum is set up between two skeletons wrapped in flesh and fat.

Fig 9. Injection moulded chairs similar to those used in *No Fixed Seating:* Image in public domain. Day's Poly Chair: "The poly chair was produced in 1962 and to this day has sold over 14 million in 23 countries. This injection moulded polypropylene seat is supported by an enamelled bent tubular steel base. This invention is not plainly a staple in advanced canteen design, but has been touted as one of the most democratic advanced designs of the 20th century. The poly chair may be seen in schools, in the village hall, in bistros, cafes and canteens - nearly everyplace because it's one of the most versatile and low-priced design classics available and likewise one of the most lasting. It is favoured in school cafeteria settings because it may take in many years' worth of tossing around and endure abuse from school age children of various ages. Day's poly chair is still so successful today that it's developed at the rate of 500,000 per year." (http://interpret.zar.vg/art/Business/Sales/canteen_furniture__great_designs_from_famous_designers.php).

Of knots

While reflecting on *No Fixed Seating*, I recall another seat draped in a textile surface fraught with meaning and intents of comfort — a ryijy rug at Hvitträsk House outside of Helsinki, Finland, a dwelling most notably occupied by the Saarinens, Eliel and Loja, in the early and mid 1900s. (Fig 10) Hvitträsk House was fitted with ryijy rugs as a matter of invoking a nationalist (Finnish) identity and infusing an Arts and Crafts ethos central to the house's architects/ occupants Gesellius, Lindgren, and Saarinen. Despite being credited to Eliel Saarinen, there is evidence to suggest that his wife Loja, an accomplished textile artist in her own right, was involved with their design execution in association with the Friends of Finnish Handicraft. According to Saarinnen historians Hvitträsk House is an "integral work of art: [it takes] control of the aesthetic elements in our environment so that all internal and external details are treated as one entity, from the trees of the forest to the most unobtrusive interior ornaments."[8] Such sentiment is born in the rugs' patterns, which elicit a pivotal political and cultural moment in Finland's battle for independence.[9]

As a traditional Scandinavian textile, the ryijy (pronounced ru-i-you), or rya rug, is as much a blanket as it is a floor covering or a wall hanging tapestry. As a home furnishing, the rug forms a single continuous surface draped across wall, couch and floor to exceed their normative and segregated purposes. The rugs are made using a unique knotting technique where long individual wool strands are woven to encase and flesh out a flexible structure such that the space between the warp and weft is filled up.[10] This process strengthens the rug overall, increases its weight and has the tendency to reduce pliability in the short direction. Importantly, this rug has two sides; one with long pile and one with a short decorative pile.[11] These factors accentuate the rug's draping attributes making it less supple than a curtain but more agile than

Fig 10. Hvitträsk House living room, 1902, architects, Gesellius, Lindgren, Saarinen. Photo Rauno Träskelin. Courtesy of the Museum of Finnish Architecture. There is a modest version of this hung-draped carpet-couch in the main living room of the Saarinen House at Cranbrook nAcademy of Fine Art. As a student, I occasionally had access to this room. To sit on this piece of furniture was not as anguishing an experience as the image suggests; the textile's bristles irritated my skin and my feet did not touch the floor nor did my back have support. However, the winter draught was stifled. The exceptionally heavy tapestry was tacked to the wall, which fixed the couch in place, a consequence that I felt increased the level of formality in the room.

a typical floor covering. The ryijy rug in Hvitträsk House's main living room, the largest and most famous of the two rugs, supplements a room whose internal surface is merely the back face of the building's log structure. In this case, the rug reiterates a custom of using woven textiles to spatially distinguish external from internal domains yet relate them aesthetically. Appearing to cascade from wall to floor, it is one of the only soft surfaces in the dark voluminous medieval-like space. The rug's swelling topography tempts one to ponder what it is like to sit on this hybrid furnishing. What empathetic discussion between body posture and tufted surface does it affect? According to ryijy rug lore, one is meant to crawl under the heavy tapestry-blanket where one's body would interface directly with inward-facing coarse woollen fibres knotted in a narrative of symbolic pattern and figures. Ah, what haptic poetry — to imagine body, material and knots mingling as inter-surfaces! But wait, one does not have to imagine — Cristina Iglesias' art work *Untitled* (1993- 1997) installed at the Whitechapel Gallery presents the potential of entering an interior space figured by a reflective aluminium sheet mounted to the gallery wall and a tapestry adhered to a concrete panel. The tapestry panel suggests that it is in a state of transition — in the process of being pried off the wall or being pressed up against the wall. This raises questions about the wall and the concrete panel's state of plasticity and pliability. Where the metallic reflection and the knotted tapestry meet, a vertical form of horizon extends a virtual potential for going into the surface. (Fig 11)

Posing a tapestry as an interior and interiorising surface draws immediate reference to Gottfried Semper's treatise *The Four Elements of Architecture* where the art of textiles and the knot is heralded as the oldest technical symbol and the origin of architecture.[12] Semper speculates on architectural enclosure evolving from the knot to the woven wall and further to architectural decoration. The plaiting of sticks and branches used to make a woven fence or animal pen produced a visual and structural pattern as the first vertical enclosure and led to the weaving of grasses.[13] Experimentation with colour, sequence, arrangement and form eventually developed the artificial processes of dying

Fig 11. Cristina Iglesias, *Untitled* (1 993-1997). Fibrocement, iron, aluminium, tapestry 245 x 365 x 0.7 cm. Courtesy of the artist. I think this artwork prompts some curious plays on gravity. For certain the rug is too heavy in mass to stand on its own edge and too pliant to curl back off the face of the wall of its own accord. The fibrocement though cast and rigid yields a duplicitous role as both master to the tapestry and servant to its hanging — "I will hold you up, but press you flat!" Its weight is a mighty force that exceeds that of the thinner aluminium whose soft surface is vulnerable to dings and scratches but more impervious to the salts that leach from concrete. Are the two walls in cahoots to force the tapestry to see its own pattern or to make multiple copies as a printing press?

and knitting to forecast the inventions of colourful carpets used as wall dressings, floor coverings and canopies. Semper cites this as "a means to make the 'home,' the inner life separated from the outer life, and as the formal creation of the idea of space..."[14] According to architectural historian Joseph Rykwert, late nineteenth-century Viennese architect Adolf Loos is responsible for crafting the well-familiar narrative regarding Semper's woven walls:

> You need carpets ... to cover the floors of your room, and woven stuff to cover its walls and make your room inhabitable. But carpets and tapestries cannot stand on their own. They need a framework of some kind to support them — something solid, rigid. Walls and frames are therefore the essential but secondary part of architecture secondary both historically therefore, but also logically since they have no essential relation to the way a building is occupied and used. The true architect concerns himself in the first place with rooms and their surfaces, with the interior; and only after that with structure.[15]

Elvis Richardson's 2009 artwork *HOUSED* at the VCA Margaret Lawrence Gallery, University of Melbourne tested architectural structure as a trace given by an assemblage knots forming a household carpet. She installed a carpet excised from a Melbourne housing unit into the large voluminous exhibition space to demonstrate the power of these textile interior surfaces to reflect critically on interior inhabitation so woefully out of the public eye and so obviously marginalised from the concern of architectural form. The simple shift of an interior lining from one private and hidden locale to another public and publicised locale politicised an architectural problem of housing, poverty, affordability and economies of scale. I pocketed this tactic that I saw catalysed change through insertion into a new context. Re-writing Irigaray's text on plastic sheets, traveling with them from New Zealand to London and facilitating their interaction amongst the audience showed potential to invoke transformational change more than simply the slip-covers' material surface. (Fig 12)

Fig 12. Elvis Richardson's, *Housed* (2009) consists of carpet retrieved from a two bedroom unit located in South Eastern Melbourne and owned by the Department of Housing. 16.5 x 8 meters installation Margaret Lawrence Gallery, VCA. Image courtesy of the artist.

Andrew Benjamin also advances Semper's theory, albeit in a more conventional theoretical method: "[T]he creation of surfaces (interior walls or facades and so on) organizes a programme which allows for a reading of the space of architecture."[16] Benjamin's allusion to Semper is both fruitful and limiting in light of the many ways that Semper's text has been interpreted and Semper's own commitment to genitive theory as a form of "interpretive taxonomy."[17] As architectural theorist Adrian Forty points out, Semper's theory is pivotal, perhaps even to blame, in establishing space as a condition of enclosure, and as a result, prompting a didactic relationship between inside and outside that resides in a direct apprehension of physical form over a perceptual or psychological saturation of images.[18] And yet, quietly residing in Rykwert's introduction to Semper's book, I find the necessary fuel to override a century of misreading:

> The use of the term "elements" (Elemente) in this regard is misleading. As it is clear from his later theory, Semper conceived of them as not material elements or forms, but as "motives" or "ideas," as technical operations based in the applied arts.[19]

What an impact this change of word stimulates! As elements, the objectified signs of hearth, mound, roof and wall are transformed into motives for building industriously. Working with fire, earth, timber and fibre stimulates temporal spaces of action instead of mere industrial building products. Such a small shift in emphasis makes room for reconsidering all that has been written about surface via Semper and shines light on the act of making enclosure as a performance of building with intent and collective agency. The active tense of these verbs is what directs it as spatial endeavour.[20] More so, what becomes immediately apparent is the role of a decorative woven surface to differentiate a spatial condition. And in doing so, the surface shapes an aesthetic identity through second or third degree abstraction of a material joining via the detail and the first-hand intimate experience of bodily comfort.

Of body

The thought of occupying in, under or on the ryijy rug surface is not simply a cosy one; it is a virtual occupation of interior surface not unlike a provocation seeded by Gins and Arakawa's philosophical and political call for an architecture that risks understanding our reason for being in the world by challenging the mortality of our own destiny. Theirs is a plea to recast "Why?" with "What if and how?" which figures the body, our body, my body as the resistant agent and builder/maker in a contingent world. Gins and Arakawa's book *An Architectural Body*, a textual hypothesis, describes something that feels like a surface behaving as a building, something called a landing-site:

> ANGELA: How do you expect me to get into something this totally flat to the ground?
> GINS: You have to go under it. Pick it up and insert yourself into it.
> ROBERT: I can't get a hold of it. There's nothing to hold onto.
> ANGELA: Wow, it's so light! What material is this?
> GINS: A new material developed by NASA.
> ANGELA: Is it fireproof?
> ARAKAWA: Definitely, and waterproof. It's flexible, durable, and, to our delight, it happens to provide great insulation as well. ANGELA: That's unbelievable.
> GINS: Take that section of material you are holding in your left hand and push it up a little higher. Bring it up to at least waist level.
> ANGELA: Oh, here's somethizng that looks like a handle. If I hold onto it to slide the material ...
> ARAKAWA: You need to slide it to the left at the same time you push it upwards.
> ANGELA: Yes, it opened. This is scary. It keeps changing … volumes open with my every motion ... With each push … it's changing right in front of my eyes, with each push … pushing open ... opening. How I spread my arms to push it open ... It takes shape from how ... If I push it to one side...[21]

Their book provides a convincing case for critical consciousness around building as an act invested with an ethical charge; to reach for what appears impossible, or in other words, to defy the assumption of death through means of reimagining life. Declaring their architecture as "tentative constructings toward holding in place," Gins and Arakawa's text brings issues of surface into a political arena linked to practice, ethics, and sustainability.[22] The surface of architecture, in their case, is one of meta-thought and material potential grounded within an experiential framework. In my reading of their work, body is an interior surface-informing procedural force, a force that they call ambient kinaesthesia.[23] Because of sheer numbers of bodies, the world is formed as "a concatenation of partial procedures or procedural-like occurrences, diffuse or defused procedures, incomplete or bedevilling ones".[24] This is a call to build – not simply as a design or construction service – but as an affirmation of collective effort and consciousness motivated by a provocation to wonder. To wonder under the ryijy rug: I would be roused to consider the many hours and female bodies that tied those many knots, how their hands, backs and eyes might have ached with strain, and how and if they were paid. I would lay in observation of how laboured my breathing became with the weight of the textile and once stable, how it induced a dark mottled space humid with exhales and tainted by all those many sheep that gave up their fleece. I would curse as my partner's movement realigned the coarse fibres or my daughter's entry contaminated the space with a cold draught. I would consider the rug's worth in this new downturned economy, recalling the rug's value as a tax payment or wedding present in the eighteenth century.[25] Might this rug offer any practical benefit to current urban street dwellers?

Of membrane

If Gins and Arakawa's topographical roof-space-blanket is purposed to mediate the temperature, moisture, airflow, visibility and accessibility between human bodies and celestial climatic bodies and operate kinetically, what kind of flashing details would it require? For flashing is a first layer of protection against leaks; in building construction, they mitigate the joins where two or more materials meet, change direction and are susceptible to movement. (Fig 13) They are the sites of Irigaray's fluid mechanics in architecture! Perhaps that is another virtual dimension of Gins' and Arawaka's speculative philosophy — a dwelling made of a continuous multi-functioning responsive surface, one with no joins, and hence no leaks, no flows, no porosity, or

more interestingly, one that is completely permeable as Irigaray imagines.

Siegfried Ebeling offered the world a similar futuristic interior surface in the form of a design called a space membrane. As a German architect in the early part of the twentieth century, Ebeling was associated with the Bauhaus and more significantly with Hugo Junkers and his airplane factory in Dessau, a place dedicated less to manufacturing than to developing research for the latest technologies. As part of his dream of biologically-determined architecture, Ebeling designed a breathing wall-skin for productive exchange between internal and external space, a concept that set his design apart from the stiff and rigid concrete edifices of early modernism.[26] (Fig 14) The house was a conducting medium capable of "channelling a continuous stream of forces — a stream of forces that is refracted several times in its trajectory, flowing from a ground surface that in geophysical terms is variously defined, and then back again in the reverse direction".[27] Claiming space as the new prosthesis, Ebeling's membrane was conducting and filtering electrical current through metal and glass prisms in an effort to induce physical comfort and protect against harmful radiation. Further to his utopian vision, Ebeling worked on an avant-garde proposal for the membrane to assume the form of an inorganic extension of the human skin that shifts the living subject from being surrounded by space to becoming space. He writes in *Extra Muros: An Introduction to a Theory of the Free House* (1947), "This time there were no walls, only a radiating field — space or a 'sea' ... of physical and psychological forces that could expand on the free landscape of the earth and (self) sustain the autarchic 'architecture of tomorrow'."[28] This calls to mind the 2005

Fig 13. Copper flashing construction details and images in *Copper Flashings and Weatherings* (Kendals Hall, Radlett, Herts: Copper Development Association, 1947), 57. Image in public domain. The craft of flashing is fascinating — the way that the edges of pliable flat sheets curl up amongst each other to further extend the surface that much further. Whenever I see them drawn in section I think they are just about to sprout as they suck moisture up into the maze of their folds. And drawing them is so very different than installing them; In building, the metal is sharp. Either extreme of hot or cold sets the tone of disciplining them into corners and around corners in the spirit of three-dimensional continuity. I learned the hard way on my first house renovation how important they are to channelling water away from the inside. Rot was not all that romantic when I had to install new window sills three years later. Image in public domain.
Fig 14. Siegfried Ebeling, *Space as Membrane* (1926), In *Space as Membrane* (1926), Siegfried Ebeling, ed. Spyros Papapetros, trans. Pamela Johnston (London: Architectural Association, 2010), cover image. Image in public domain.

site-specific installation by Roger Hiorn entitled *SEIZURE* (2008, London) where an abandoned apartment was propagated with copper sulphate crystals which grew as effervescent blue shards, far from comfortable in the normative sense but fascinating as a live site-specific forming surface. (Fig 15)

Ironically, the beauty bestowed by this surface installation is inversely proportioned to its toxicity; copper sulphate is typically used as the active ingredient for fungicides, insecticides, snail bait, pig and chicken fattener, sheep and cattle foot rot remedy, timber preservative, and prevention from malaria amongst other alarming uses. If he had been alive to visit *SEIZURE*, Ebeling would have been interested in the crystals' ability to draw light deep into the dark interior of the building. I could only wonder that he may have also seen the crystal coating as an alternative to the rigid and inflexible geometric shell he assigned to his house design.

Of code

Though these descriptions of Ebeling's space membrane sound more technological than philosophical, and his drawings register a strong resemblance to the conventions of built space as we still know it, his 1926 designs emerged well before smart textiles, nanoengineering or computer-numerically-controlled manufacturing techniques were even conceptualised. Herein lies the link to contemporary architectural surface works predominantly developed through parametric design, modelling and digital fabrication as well as innovations in material science and engineering. Of those actively engaged in this contemporary field of architectural design thinking, practice and production, Mark Burry, Bernard Cache, Alecia Imperiale, George Liaropolous-Legendre and Mark Taylor contribute significantly to critical and reflective theory specific to surface.[29] From early hypothetical projects to recently completed built works, I observe a certain tendency to cast surface in an almost exclusively instrumental light.

Fig 15. *Seizure,* Roger Hiorns, 2008. Comissioned by Artangel and the Jerwood Charitable Foundation, supported by the National Lottery through Arts Council England, in association with Channel 4. Image courtesy of the artist.

"To ask the question – what is a surface in architecture? – is to ask as much about the practical implications of how surfaces are used and materials are deployed to create them, as it is to ask about the generation of surfaces on computer screens."[30] Such contemporary architectural projects tend to realise surface's abstraction in the form of overtly exterior and structural responses. In this case, surface effect, the material and tectonic manifestation of surface as architectural envelope, is privileged over the affect or impact of surface(s) on inhabitation or political and/or cultural encounters. Mark Burry credits computationally-assisted design as the means to work outside of an orthodoxy, towards the creation of perplications which "are neither surface or substance yet appear to be both at once, and represent what we can do today that could not be done tomorrow."[31]

I continue to look for interpretations upon these kinds of contemporary technologically-driven works; looking for someone to ask the hard questions about what these works might affect, how they might change the way we think or dwell. Some of the built works have now been in existence long enough for these questions to be tested. Though the impetus to engage industrial building economies is predictably understood, and it might explain the vacuity of works and discourse specific to interiors, I am heartened by Benjamin's reasoning "that surface should be understood neither as a merely structural, nor as merely decorative aspects of building."[32] Granted, the creative works I have led you to thus far have not been guided and fabricated by computer-aided design ideation and production. Yet their contribution towards developing a sensibility of surface has effect beyond the consequence of the process of their own creation.[33] What they do affect in terms of interior surface is an investment into labour practices, collective economies and sustaining philosophy as critical motives for imagining and developing spatial occupation. That they do it outside of contemporary computational technologies only suggests there may be other means to probe surface in relation to building. That issues of materiality and performativity are common amongst all of these approaches to surface is notable. My consideration of surface from an interior point of view is fuelled by the wealth of these works rather than a criticism of them. These works make possible the inclusion of another approach to surface that is neither oppositional nor confrontational, just another dermal layer detected deep in the ectoderm, as Mark C. Taylor might say.[34]

Of matter

Boyd Webb's photography is one of the dermal layers to my research project where surface operates as a spatio-political site. The politics of his work lean towards sustainability but with a wry sense of humour and sharp criticism of local and global economies, particularly consumer capitalism and what lies in its wake. My interpretation of these works is informed by a personal encounter I had with his early works at the Museum of Contemporary Art, Los Angeles in 1988. That exhibition included a collection of large format colour photographs as well as a display of the photographic scene spatialised at full scale. I recall how this exhibition opened my sensibilities towards realism and how factual data, things and stuff had possession of their own materiality. The installation coupled with the photographs started a long process that disintegrated my assumptions about image and surface as flat, static, immaterial and fixed in time, a transformative process I am obviously still grappling with in my own creative projects more than two decades later.

I am intrigued by his photographs for the way that they act as the residue of theatrical performance scenes, interior sets, which propagate several dimensions of meaning as a result of manipulating lighting and material, most specifically, materials found in everyday interiors such as polyethylene plastic film, tufted carpet, linoleum, foam underlay and resin-coated flooring paper. This material palette is noticeably artificial and synthetic in nature, a sign of their receptivity to human modification as modern materials emerging as "autonomous forces within an overarching modernist prosopopeia … they become protagonists and heroes endowed with powers and properties of agency and moral value, capable of sharing in the particular and universal attributes of human subjects and/or serving as prosthetic extensions of humanity."[35] I am in awe of how, in the staging of these materials, he makes them live: he overrides their banal and inert qualities with simple techniques of hanging, draping, puncturing, bundling and folding. Webb's frank approach to these non-organic materials appears to transcend their history as domesticated and stylised imitations of more precious natural materials, a trait in Webb's work that reinforces their inclusion as the artificial flora of a 'fourth kingdom' of chemical synthesis capable of creating an abundance of ephemeral waste and infinite transformative proliferations.[36] As early works in Webb's career, they foreshadow his more recent and explicit concerns over consumption, pollution and ecological balance. Boyd Webb's photographs are made entirely without the aid of digital imaging software and therefore if any illusions are perceived, they would be for the sake of the craft of setting the scene in three-dimensional, gravity-obeying space. With no disrespect to his work, these scenes are the exquisite elaboration of props empowered by simple decontextualising techniques. As seen in Webb's photographs, the basic technology of pulleys, guide wires, box-cutters and multiple lighting gels measure the difference between a common domestic scene and that of a political consciousness on human occupation and ecology. (Fig 16)

Not subscribing to illusion, Webb's work instils a pregnant realism that allows us to see the membranes of inside and outside as tactile, spacious and transgressive without abolishing their distinctive functions. In and out, under and above are reordered as this face and another face, a constant signal of the potential for another surface to become un-obscured or surface's depth to be mined. (Fig 17- 18) Such hidden depth recalls the superficiality attributed to surface and surface's expression of the inner, which as Mark C. Taylor reminds us, is a condition of skin at a local body and global culture scale. Since the organism as a whole is formed by a complex layer of dermal layers, the body is, in effect, nothing but a strata of skin in which interiority and exteriority are thoroughly convoluted ... As such the skin is forever doubled and hence unavoidably duplicitous. Hide hides hide, which hides nothing ... nothing but other hides.[37]

Such infinite folds of flesh introduce the intriguing yet slightly abhorrent photographs by visual artists Aziz + Cucher who grafted the human (skin) onto the inhuman (interior environments) in order to model the artificial as an organic, interiorised phenomenal state. (Fig 19) Like Webb's images, these images are also not digitally

Fig 16. Boyd Webb *LUNG* © Boyd Webb 1983. Image courtesy of the artist.

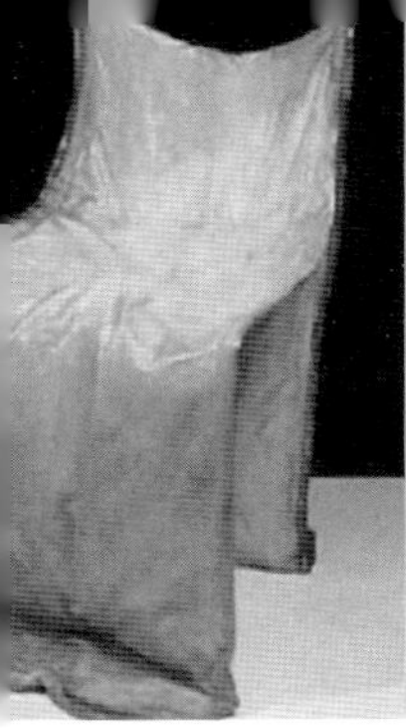

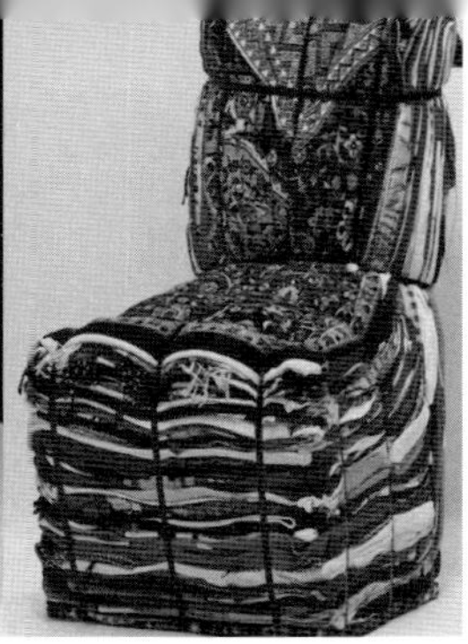

corrected to remove the blemishes, a paradoxical contradiction that enmeshes the exterior within; the (human) body becomes camouflaged within the immensity of its surroundings, effectively lost by virtue of a depth of surface.[38] As in Webb's image *Lung* (1983) where depth is plainly insinuated by the faux-ness of swirling pale blue flooring material, the surface in Aziz + Cucher's work yields appearances in a successive process of unhiding whereby depth and surface are one and the same – all is revealed, one surface after another - then surface is a process of transitioning from one interior to the next.

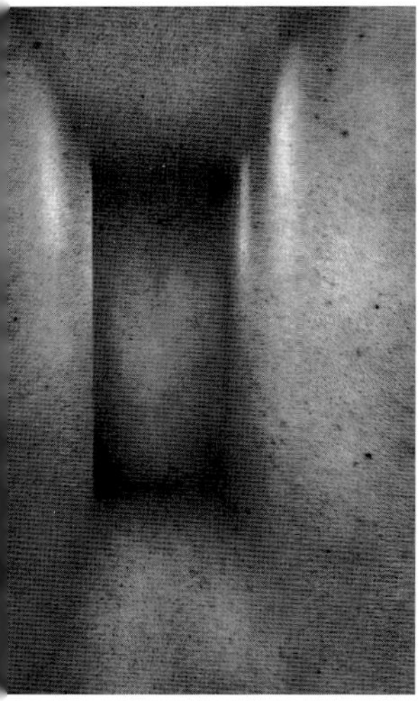

Of depth

Conceptualising surface as having infinite depth as Mark C. Taylor suggests above is an activity that would attract the attention of Avrum Stroll, a philosopher who asks the question "What are Surfaces?"[39]

Two major models of surface with accompanying variations emerge from Stroll's inquiry. Each model is probed via the perception of everyday objects and the "geometry of ordinary speech."[40] Physical and abstract readings of concepts such as 'margin', 'boundary', 'limit' and 'edge' assist to formulate a topological system distinct from mathematics and physics. For example, Stroll's model "The Leonardo Conception" offers surface as a boundary without substance, a common join of two media. Indeed, his example of a lake where the limit of air and water meet exposes assumptions about air's 'nothingness' and a boundary's depthless and abstract identity. In this model, surface "belongs to neither of the two contiguous media it separates", which negates the possibility of an intermediary of 'between'; surface is a non-material entity, an abstract interface.[41] A variant of the Leonardo model adopts a higher degree of abstraction whereby the interface is possessed by the dominant of the two media. This model leaves surfaces susceptible to the same power struggles rampant in boundary line disputes. For example, if posed in the context of the ryijy rug: Who

Fig 17. Gaetano Pesce, *Golgotha,* 1972-1973. Dacron, Fiberglass, Polyesterharz Dacron, fiberglass, polyester resin. In public domain. http://www.chairblog.eu/2010/03/23/golgotha-chair-by-gaetano-pesce/ accessed 1 June 2010.
Fig 18. Tejo Remy, *Rag Chair* Vienna, 1991/2008. Lumpen, Stahlbänder Rags. steel bands. Courtesy of Atelier Remy & Veenhuizen.
Fig 19. Aziz + Cucher, *Interiors* (1999-2002). www.azizcucher.net. Courtesy Aziz + Cucher.

owns the rug? When both sides are front sides, i.e. useable, which one possesses the surface? Does it belong to the wall, the couch or the floor? What bio-security hazard does it bring as it travels from one continent to the next?

Stroll's 'PS' model proposes surfaces as a physical part of physical entities. It offers additional insight to surface occupation. Within the perspective of the ordinary, surfaces maintain a sensory stimulus that can be described in such ways as "rough, smooth, wet, dry, slippery, sticky, chipped, pitted or damaged; and one can speak about sanding, polishing, painting, wiping and waxing such surfaces."[42] In this model, to have surface is to be something made and be made of material stuff. Surface belongs to material and its manipulation for spatial effect is at the core of design activity. I borrow and amend Stroll's PS model to suggest that surface includes a successively remaking (and unmaking) as invocation of the active form of the verb 'to do' or 'to be'. In this way, I am underscoring Gins and Arakawa's sense of procedure and highlighting an exchange between the body and that which is made in the process of building. This concept of surface brings objects, materials and actions into a contingent interface where surfaces meet, merge and circulate; surfaces are neither static nor objectified. They are spatialise material relations.

Of relation

Sometimes that which is made in the process of building is greater than the building itself. Artist Ann Hamilton's piece *tropos* offers additional dimensions to this proposition of interior surface, in particular an expansion of the role of labour and collective consciousness latently embodied in material and its means of affecting spatial experience. Between 7 October 1993 and 19 June 1994, the main gallery of DIA Center for the Arts, New York was host to a carpet of horse hair monitored by a single sitter diligently focused on the task of burning a book's text in the same process as its reading. Needing the institutional authority of the gallery and the density of its painted white masonry walls to bound the scene as a situation withdrawn but actively linked to social space, Hamilton forged economies of exchange between labour, material and sentience in the form of a sanctuary or preserve.[43]

The power of this scene to unify interior surfaces relied on latent calibrations amongst the staunch and rational inside of a warehouse gallery. The sinister but erotic swirls of large quantities of animal hair and the silent aloofness of a woman absorbed in peculiar work served as actors in a spatial network. Images of this installation exceed simple representation to elicit corporeal response as if I was there. The detritus of beast mingling with charred words inhabit a zone of acridity in the back regions of my mouth. Like a beacon, like a docent, like a guardian angel, she sits there uninterested in my presence but confirming it even as she destroys a book. (Fig 20) I cannot see the name of the book, so this may not be such a sacrifice. We are in this sea of stuff together, she on her chair and me stepping tentatively hoping not to trip or fall through. If hair is above, what lies below but a fetid gelatinous soup of bones, blood and sinew? Its surface draws me into eddies of a repulsive elixir drawn between the implied slaughter and the security and warmth of deep fur. She is still there, not watching me struggle to find my feet. In the short time since entering this space, the sun's brilliance has vacated the whitewashed brick wall. The wall and the floor-covering now whisper through surface appearance of the many gestures invested to secure their different formal structures at the same time the book relinquishes its own. If I stayed through the night, would she proceed to comb this flooring and rewrite the book as acts of reparation? Complicit with Webb and contrary to Stroll, Hamilton's installation *tropos* assists in reconsidering the shallowness attributed to superficiality where the surface, readily apparent through its own material opacity, i.e. the horse hair floor or the book-burning protagonist, is imbued with the power to secrete other surfaces through selective modes of phenomenal transparency. This is only made possible by virtue of the installation's spatial extension, duration and occupation.

Fig 20. Ann Hamilton, *tropos* (1993). Photo Jeanson courtesy Ann Hamilton Studio. Credit to Thibatoult.

Of "OF"

'Of' is a very big word. For such few letters, 'of' serves the huge task of designating place and time, motion, direction and distance. Despite being credited as a weak and derivative preposition, it has expansive powers across spatial dimensions. (Such weakness is audibly understood when compared to its half-sister, the word 'off', a word with explicative force.) The Oxford English Dictionary defines 'of':

> From its original sense, *of* was naturally used in the expression of the notions of removal, separation, privation, derivation, origin or source, starting-point, spring of action, cause, agent, instrument, material, and other senses, which involve the notion of 'taking, coming, arising, or resulting from.'[44]

Employing the word 'of' is like applying grease to a rusty hinge; as an accessory to a door, a hinge enables variable forms of occupation and possession. This is not simply a manner of playing with words, nor is it a post-modern argument couched in language. Famous for her experimental 'misuse' of language to affect new sensibilities that fused knowing, feeling and thinking, Gertrude Stein considered prepositions as one of her favourite parts of speech because they are lively, 'on the move', easily mistaken, shifting and flexible.[45] In her poem "Patriarchal Poetry" she protests against rational logic embedded in language by exposing its disruptive potential in a text composed almost completely out of prepositions:

> For before let it before to be before spell to be
> before to be before to have to be to be for before to
> be tell to be to having held to be to be for before to call to be for to be
> before to till until to be till before to be for before to be until to be for
> before to for to be before will for before to be shall to be to be for to be
> for to be before still to be will before to be before for to be to be.[46]

I am one of the many people in the world that (often unintentionally) keep things moving by my misuse of prepositions. In my written works and even in speech, this is the most frequent error I make which copyeditors are quick to highlight. Stein makes the case that there is something much more at stake in such mistaken-ness that takes apart the discourse of patriarchal culture: objectification, definition, possession through cognition, erasure of difference, linear progression, propositional forms of language linked to modern rationality's discourse of objectification. Stein calls this the "poetry of nouns" which operates in terms of the definition, the name, the proper, property, identity and substance to effectively annihilate the encounter of experience and any emerging subjective (emotions) and deny the "intense existence" of things and the world: "I had to feel anything and everything that for me was existing so intensely that I could put it down in writing as a thing in itself without necessarily using its name."[47]

In this chapter I have employed the word 'of' for its genitive and transitive attributes but, most significantly, 'of' is being used to unhide another surface of surface. Surface, for me, has always been prefaced by prepositions such as on, in, under or upon which offers up the surface as if it belongs to something else more mighty or substantial, or alternatively, as if surface is only appearance and not the force knitting a spatial and material relationship between bodies, human and other. In this way, while speaking to surface as of surface, I am signalling a reverence and respect for it as something other than me, something apart but reciprocally involved and related to me, and other things. As Jane Rendell expresses, "A shift in preposition allows a different dynamic of power to be articulated..."[48]

And so it has. Throughout this chapter I have made reference of many other artists, architects, thinkers and writers and their works, thoughts and theories. I have offered them up to you as morsels constituting the field of concerns that came under consideration as part of my creative development and reflection on the performative installation *No Fixed Seating*. Sixty-six sheets of flimsy plastic, joined in pairs, over 72 hours of heat, rubbing together and being thrown casually over a set of iconic chairs brings new meaning to Irigaray's famous phrase "two lips touching" and its reference to female labia and the secretions that lubricate sensibility and sensation.[49] (Fig. 21-24) Their purpose as protective slip covers is ambiguous; the perforations that form the text confound the virtue of plastic to serve as a protective barrier, a non-permeable membrane, and it is not clear if the seat or the sitter is the body to be protected. No Fixed Seating suggests there are other relationships to be fostered between human bodies and thing bodies. As a materialisation of Irigaray's philosophy, it both practices her message and critiques it. Like the building envelope details, Irigaray's text maintains a separatist boundary, a two-ness, if you will, that demonstrates a dependence on binary constructions. No Fixed Seating operated as a contingent interface between the furniture, participants, the events of the conference, the weather and the urban upheaval.

The legibility of Irigaray's text was never stable or fixed from the moment it was scanned as an image, translated into vector-based code, inscribed by a laser beam, transported halfway across the world, stretched, worn and torn to fit a multitude of body shapes and postures, folded neatly and transported back to New Zealand to the moment it now lays draped across a chair, languishing and dishevelled in my studio. The interior surface is not this object. Its value is not in its material or the labour invested in its making or the almighty power it affected on its users or the site. The interior surface is what it afforded — the modest realisation that comes with "I get it" and the transmission of fluid thinking through material interaction. In a practice that binds the philosophical to the material through the use of metaphor, surfaces are regarded as agents of 'OF' and the forces that set things in motion. This work proved to have a profound impact on my practice: it granted me a view of a way of working that was site-specific yet responsive to unforeseen or unknowable factors; it saw me take a woefully common throw-away material and bring it into an aesthetic state that recognised its own expressive capacity; and it saw my work become interactive – a part of the social fabric. Chapter 5: *utter matter* is where I will put Irigaray's urge to listen and Stein's call to write in "intense existence" into full scale spatial and material action and where the 'surface' is regarded as the ever-shifting matrix of relations reconstituted into the singularity of its occurrence. Though perhaps not as central to the research as I thought initially, and bound up with spatial relations, issues of surface nonetheless remain a vital force in this research project.

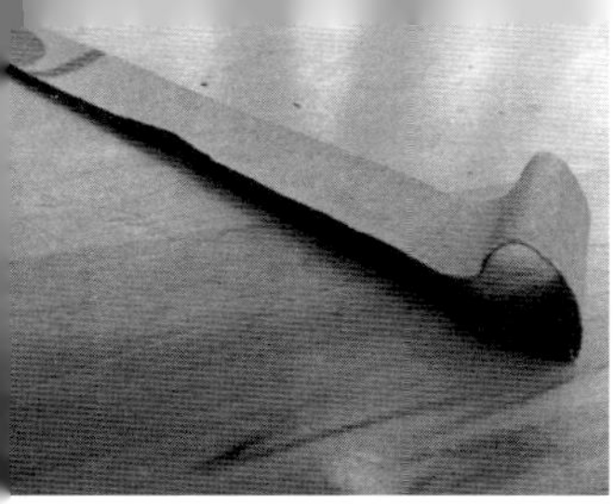

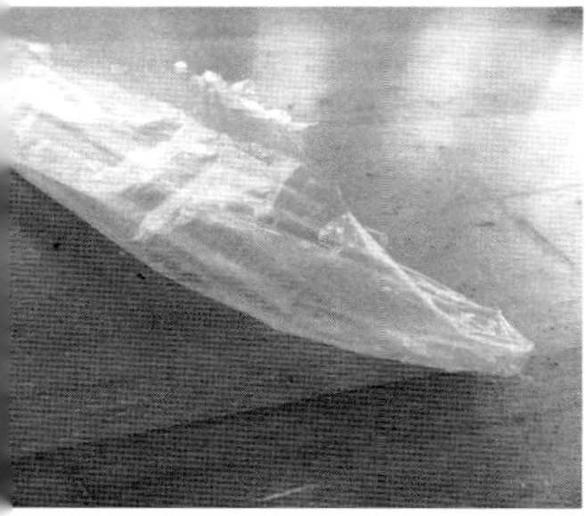

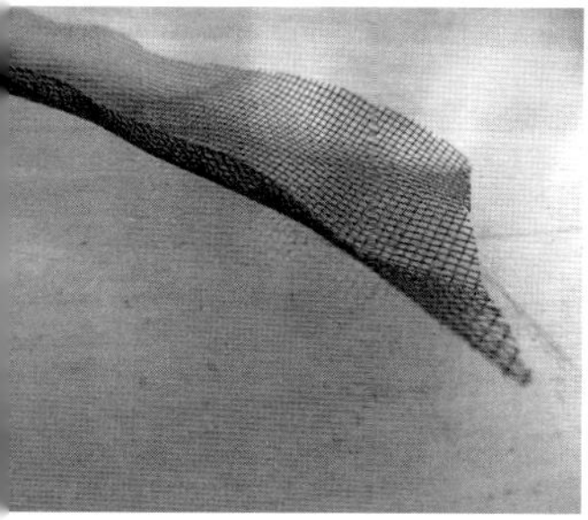

Fig 21. J. Preston, *No Fixed Seating* (2010). Material sample. Building paper is used as a water-resistant membrane on roofs and walls. It gets its water resistance from bitumen (tar) impregnation. Flame retardant building paper is primarily designed as a damp-proof course under roofs as a waterproof seal against water, moisture and draughts. It has an added value of resisting fire.
Fig 22. J. Preston (2010). *No Fixed Seating.* Material sample. Plastic sheeting or film is typically used as protective water-proof covering when storing or transporting goods. It is frequently used in 1.5 or 3 mm sheets as a drop cloth when renovating interior rooms. Technically, this material is called polyethylene, "which is just one ingredient used to produce plastic products. But there are several different types of polyethylene, including high-density polyethylene (known as HDPE) and low-density polyethylene (LDPE). Also there is polyethylene terephthalate (known as PET and PETE). These types of plastics vary in hardness and softness and can be used for making other products besides drop cloths or drop cloth backings." http://www.ehow.com/info_8651925_type-plastic-paint-drop-cloths.html#ixzz2w66RIDl2 accessed 2 January 2012.
Fig 23. J. Preston, *No Fixed Seating* (2010). Material sample. Tyvek. Trademarked by Dupont, Tyvek is a non-woven 'flash-spun' synthetic material made with high-density polyethylene fibres. It is applied as a "house wrap" to the exterior face of a building's substructure to ensure a breathable envelope. It can also allow for a micro space between structure and cladding to encourage weeping as opposed to wicking. http://www2.dupont.com/Tyvek/en_US/index.html.
Fig 24. J. Preston, *No Fixed Seating* (2010). Material sample. Window screen is made of finely woven plastic or metal wire and used to filter out insects such as mosquitoes and flies from the interior. It is used more in the Northern Hemisphere than New Zealand.

[1] Luce Irigaray, "The 'Mechanics' of Fluids," in *This Sex Which is Not One,* trans. Catherine Porter with Carol Burke (New York: Cornell University Press, 1985).

[2] Michael A. R. Biggs and Daniela Büchler, "Rigor and Practice-based Research," *Design Issues* 23 (3) (2007): 62-69.

[3] Andrew Benjamin, "Surface Effects: Borromini, Semper, Loos," *Journal of Architecture* 11(1) (2006): 2.

[4] Paul Carter, *Material Thinking: The Theory and Practice of Creative Research* (Carleton, VIC: Melbourne University Publishing, 2004). Mieke Bal demonstrates this practice most explicitly in her book *Louise Bourgeois' Spider: The Architecture of Art-writing* (Chicago: University of Chicago Press, 2001).

[5] Luce Irigaray, "When Our Lips Speak Together" and "The 'Mechanics' of Fluids," in *This Sex Which is Not One*, trans. Catherine Porter with Carol Burke (New York: Cornell University Press, 1985). See Luce Irigaray, *i love to you: Sketch of a Possible Felicity in History,* trans. by Alison Martin (New York and London: Routledge, 1996).

[6] Marjorie Hass, "Fluid Thinking: Irigaray's Critique of Formal Logic," in *Representing Reason: Feminist Theory and Formal Logic*, ed. Rachel Joffe Falmagne and Marjorie Hass (Lanham, Boulder, New York, Oxford: Rowman & Littlefield Publishers, 2002), 72.

[7] Sexuate Subjects Conference Call for Papers 2010, accessed 4 June 2012, http://www.ucl.ac.uk/sexuate-subjects/

[8] Gutheim, Frederick, "Hvitträsk: exploring the roots of Saarinen," *Inland Architect* 32 (1) (1988): 59.

[9] Anna-Lisa Amberg et al, "Hvitträsk: koti taideteoksena = Hvitträsk: the home as a work of art," in Anna-Lisa Amberg et. al and Juhani Pallasmaa, Juhani ed., *Hvitträsk: koti taideteoksena = Hvitträsk : the home as a work of art* (Helsinki: Suomen Rakennustaiteen Museo/ Museum of Finnish Architecture, 1987), 87.

[10] Amberg et al, Hvitträsk, 32.

[11] Lesley Jackson, "Finnish carpets and textiles," *Modern Carpets + Textiles* Spring (2006): 36.

[12] Uuno Taavi Surelius and Alex Maeson, *The Ryijy-rugs of Finland: A Historical Study* (Helinski Finland: Otava Publishing Company, 1926), 23.

[13] Semper, *Four Elements*, 254.

[14] Gene Kangas. *Maine Antique Digest*, (2007), accessed 1 March 2009, http://maineantiquedigest.com/articles_archive/articles/may07/ finnrug0507.htm

[15] Gottfried Semper, *The Four Elements of Architecture and Other Writings*, trans. Harry Francis Mallgrave and Wolfgang Hermann, ed. Francesco Pellizzi and Joseph Rykwert (New York, Melbourne, Sydney: Cambridge University Press, 1989), 254.

[16] Benjamin, *Surface Effects*,1.

[17] Joseph Rykwert, "Architecture is All on the Surface, Semper and Bekleidung," *Ressegna* 20 (93) (1998): 20.

[18] Adrian Forty, *Words and Buildings: A Vocabulary of Modern Architecture* (New York: Thames and Hudson, 2000), 256-275.

[19] Joseph Rykwert, "Gottfried Semper: Architect and Historian," in *The Four Elements of Architecture and Other Writings*, trans. Harry Francis Mallgrave and Wolfgang Hermann, ed. Francesco Pellizzi and Joseph Rykwert (New York, Melbourne, Sydney: Cambridge University Press, 1989), 32.

[20] Forty, *Words and Buildings: A Vocabulary of Modern Architecture*, 257.

[21] Madeline Gins and Arakawa, *Architectural Body* (Tuscaloosa and London: The University of Alabama Press, 2002), 25.

[22] Gins and Arakawa, *Architectural Body*, 21.

[23] Gins and Arakawa, *Architectural Body*, 69.

[24] Gins and Arakawa, *Architectural Body*, 52.

[25] Kangas, *Maine Antique Digest*, 2007.

[26] Walter Scheiffle, "Membrane and Ecological Architecture," in *Space as Membrane* (1926), Siegfried Ebeling, ed. Spyros Papapetros, trans. Pamela Johnston (London: Architectural Association, 2010), II and V.

[27] Siegfried Ebeling, *Space as Membrane* (1926), ed. Spyros Papapetros, trans. Pamela Johnston (London: Architectural Association, 2010), 32.

[28] Spyros Papapetros, "Future Skins," in *Space as Membrane* (1926), Siegfried Ebeling, ed. Spyros Papapetros, trans. Pamela Johnston (London: Architectural Association, 2010), XX.

[29] Mark Burry, "Between Substance and Surface," in *AD: Surface Consciousness*, ed. Mark Taylor (London: Wiley-

Academy, 2006), 19.
[30] Benjamin, *Surface Effects*, 3.
[31] Mark Burry, *Between Substance and Surface*, 19.
[32] Benjamin, *Surface Effects*, 3.
[33] Benjamin, *Surface Effects*, 3.
[34] Mark C. Taylor, *Hiding* (London: The University of Chicago Press, 1997), 18.
[35] Jeffrey T. Schnapp, "The Fabric of Modern Times," *Critical Inquiry* 24(1) (1997): 192.
[36] Jeffrey L. Meikle, "Into the Fourth Kingdom: Representations of Plastic Materials, 1920-1950," *Journal of Design History* 5(3) (1992): 174 and 179.
[37] Mark C. Taylor, *Hiding*, 12.
[38] Cay Sophie Rabinowitz, "Aziz+Cucher: Landscapes and Interiors" exhibition catalogue (Sydney: Artereal Gallery, 2006), accessed 4 June 2012, http://www.azizcucher.net/critical-text/aziz-cucherlandscapes-and-interiors-catalog-essay-by-cay-sophie-rabinowitz/
[39] Avrum Stroll, *Surfaces* (University of Minnesota, Minneapolis, 1988). For a succinct overview of Stroll's book, Surfaces, refer to Mark Taylor's essay 'Surface-Talk' in *AD:Surface Consciousness*, 2006, 30-35.
[40] Stroll, *Surfaces*, 4.
[41] Stroll, *Surfaces*, 45.
[42] Stroll, *Surfaces*, 51.
[43] Lynne Cook, "The Viewer, the Sitter, and the Site: A Splintered Syntax." in *Ann Hamilton, tropos*, ed. Lynne Cook and Karen Kelly (New York: Dia Art Foundation, 1994), 59-88.
[44] *Oxford English Dictionary*. http://www.oed.com/24 Feb 2009 11:06 am
[45] Gertrude Stein, "Patriarchal Poetry," *The Yale Gertrude Stein*, intro. Richard Kostelanetz (New Haven, CT: Yale University Press: 1980), 106.
[46] Gertrude Stein, "Poetry and Grammar," in *Lectures in America* (Boston, MA: Beacon Press, 1985), 212.
[47] Stein, *Poetry and Grammar*, 242.
[48] Jane Rendell, *Site-writing: The Architecture of Art Criticism* (London and New York: I. B. Tauris, 2010), 7.
[49] Luce Irigaray, "When Our Lips Speak Together," trans. Carol Burke, *Signs* 6 (1) *Women Sex and Sexuality Part 2* (Autumn 1980): 69-79.

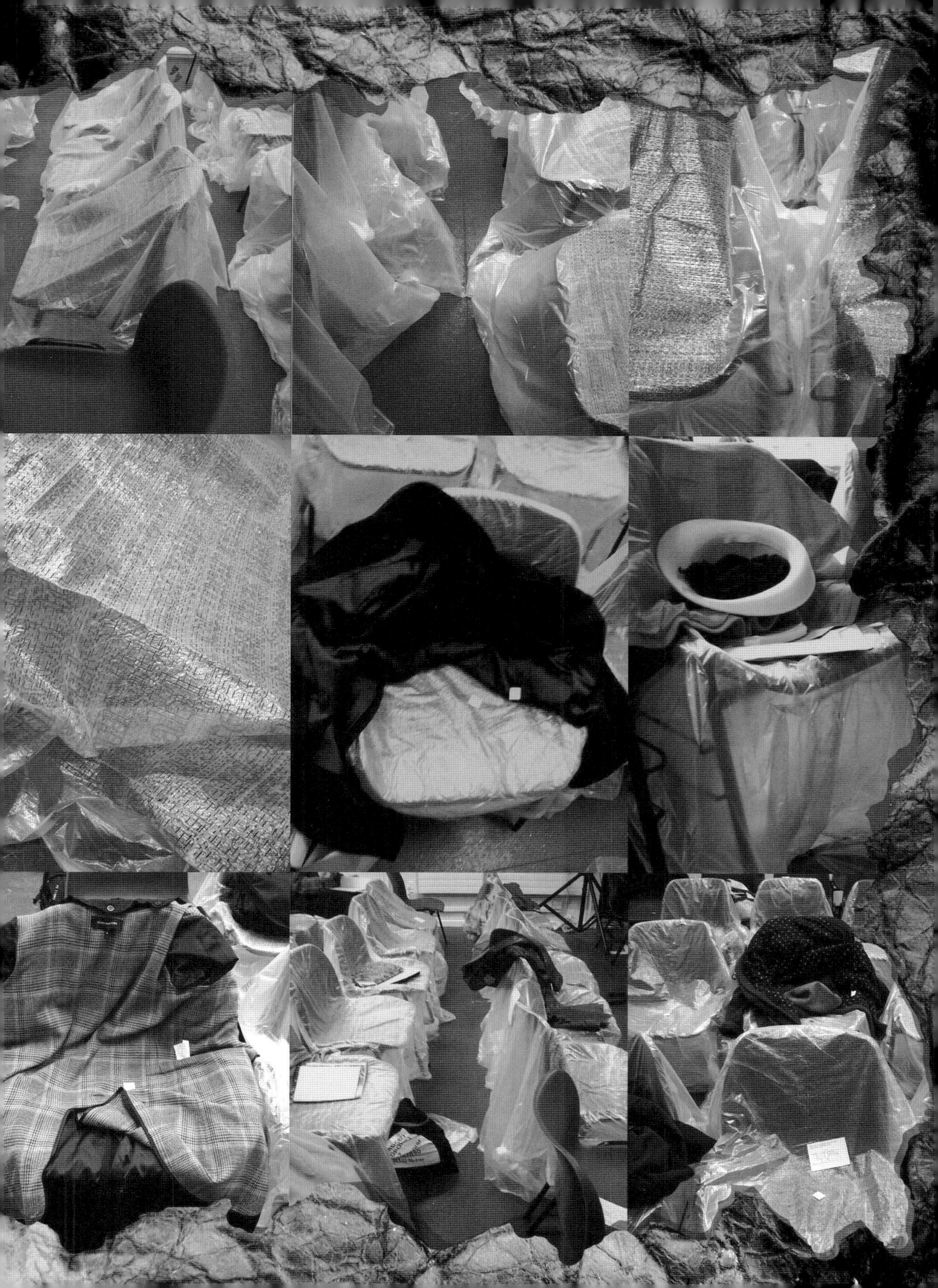

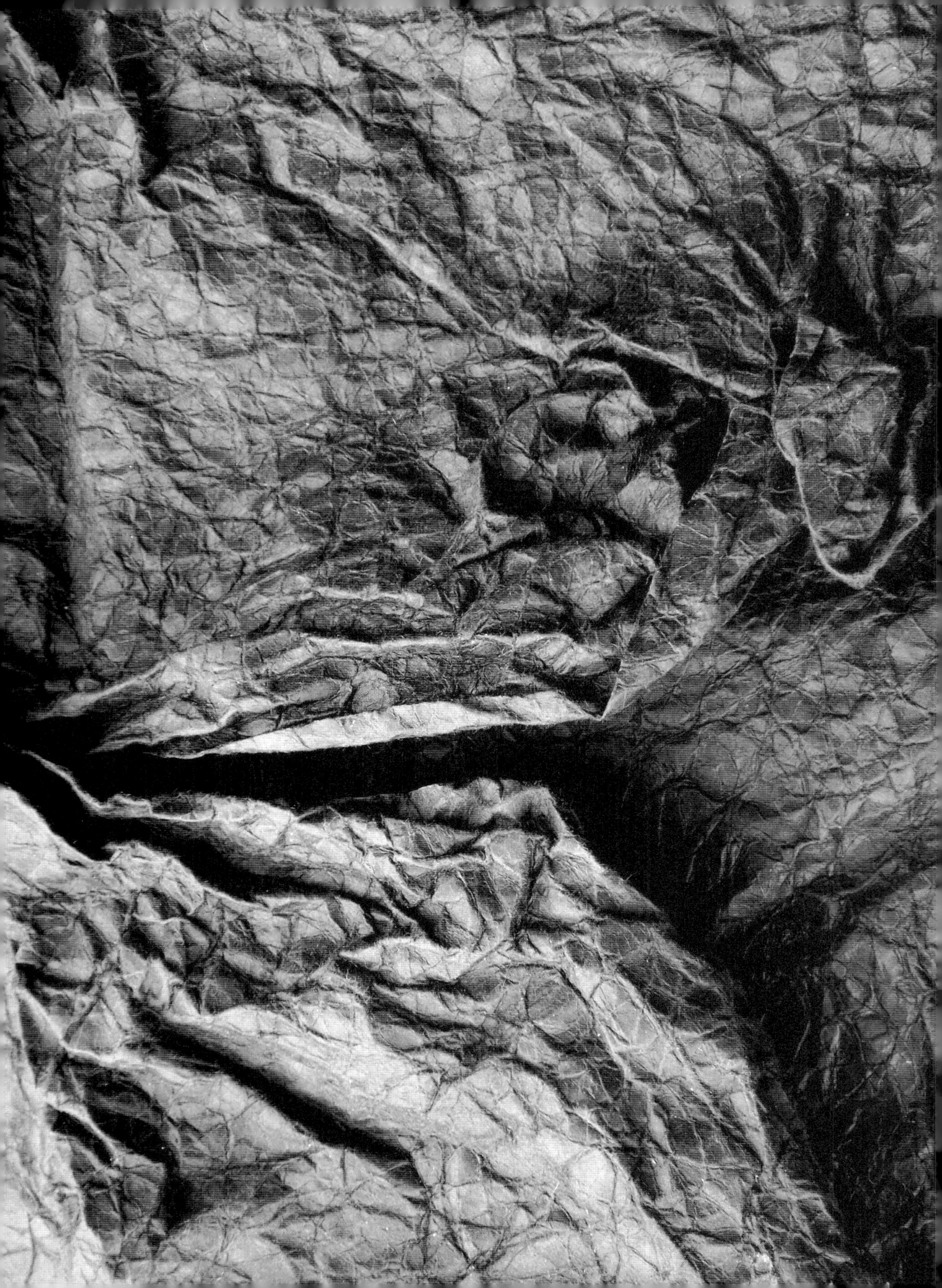

Chapter 5

utter matter

001-1124
SNOWWHITE
Monday to Friday 9am - 4pm

The Back Story

Chapters 1, 2, 3 and 4 expose the use of an affirmative feminist agency to emancipate seemingly inert interior finishing materials from an oppression I attribute to building construction systems, patriarchal paradigms and political economies promulgating neutralization, homogeneity and uniformity. Chapter 1: *The Yield Principle* introduces the wedge/shim as a conceptual, methodological and physical tool capable of liberating material expression suppressed by standardized industrial manufacturing processes. Chapter 2: *Voice Lessons* pries open the power of oration and do-it-yourself renovation to expose the political bias of neutrality, including neutral colours. Chapter 3: *IN wildness* tampers with phenomenal and conceptual states of transparency to move beyond the interior as a bounded, domesticated and private territory. *Chapter 4: making note(s) OF surface* articulates 'surface' as a relational encounter catalyzed by material and spatial forces. Building on the trajectory of these texts and the creative works presented within them, this chapter, *utter matter,* tracks a significant shift in the intellectual and practical concerns of my project; I change from a researcher who seeks to liberate interior materials to one who engages with materials (and objects) as like matter. This adjustment to the project's emphasis was probed in a performative installation entitled *BALE* where an interior space (Snowhite Gallery), a bale of greasy wool (identified by the sack it arrived in as Tenderden Downs 49) and I inhabited for three days. *BALE* was an experiment that extended Luce Irigaray's notion of respectful engagement between women and men enunciated in her essay "i love to you" to material objects.[1] I sought to find wildness, the animal and the animate in material objects, and in me, through the interaction that brings to bear the kind of democracy that Bruno Latour suggests lies beyond the subject-object/ figure-background/ nature-culture binaries that assert power over that which is fluid, connected and relational.[2] Without a prescribed set of outcomes, *BALE* eventuated as a sequence of spatial and material encounters that collectively called into play Joseph Beuys' 1974 installation *Coyote: I Like America and America Likes Me*, Francis Ponge's proems *The Voice of Things* and Jane Bennett's advocacy for vibrant materiality.[3]

Fig 1 (p.163, 189). J. Preston, *BALE* (2011). An up close and personal experience with a bale of greasy wool proves to engender a tangled, fibrous network of human and non-human relations.
Fig 2 (p.164, 187). J. Preston, *BALE* (2011). The gallery space was closed to the public during the performative installation except for the view provided by a CCTV camera displayed outside the gallery.
Fig 3. Floor plan of Snowwhite Gallery, Auckland, New Zealand.
Fig. 4-13 (p.165–184). J. Preston, *BALE* (2011). Selection of still images taken over the course of the three day performative installation.

What follows is a text that reflects on the perfomative installation *BALE* as it imagines what might happen if the script was not a prescribed set of directions but instead, a catalyst to set things in motion. *utter matter* considers *BALE* in more than an after-the-fact description and visual representation; listening-to rather than looking-at, *utter matter* registers a metamorphosis in my understanding of what it might take to engaged all things material— humans, animals, vegetation and objects— with respect for their specific energies and constitutions.[4] *BALE* revealed to me how challenging it was/ is to cast off ingrained and habitualised assumptions, behaviors, gestures and language riddled with human domination including a privilege granted to thinking over feeling or sensing. It follows that *utter matter* is an attempt to expose the pedagogical underbelly of *BALE*.

At the same time, *utter matter* is a script to a play that could happen, a script that might assemble a cohort of actors and prompt a range of interior surface encounters, effectively, or rather, affecting, a performance of actor-network theory (ANT). The script's collapse of what happened and what could happen adopts a notion of time put forward by Michelle Serres and Bruno Latour: "...time does not flow according to a line...nor according to a plan but rather according to extensive complex mixture, as though it reflected stopping points, ruptures, deep wells, chimneys of thunderous acceleration...all sown at random, at best in a viable disorder."[5] My approach draws actor-network theory out of its mode as an analytical method serving the social sciences into an aesthetic creative practice context. While *BALE* and *utter matter* add to the large and burgeoning community gathering around ANT, they belong to a small group of artists, designers and architects probing the implications and affects of ANT in performative and material works.[6] These works do not represent ANT, they practice it spatially, and more so, bear a vital connectivity between philosophy, politics and creative practice.

Folding reflective and the speculative modes of written expression together affords me the means to introduce a litany of human and non-human actors in this state of play: Luce Irigaray, Joseph Beuys, Bruno Latour, Francis Ponge and Jane Bennett have leading roles billeted alongside objects such as pink wool blanket and graphite pencil. All these things make themselves present through their actions. Their voices are aired as forces to *BALE*'s conception and more importantly, to what *BALE* generates.

Inspiring me from the sidelines is Brazilian dramaturge Augusto Boal who developed *The Theatre of the Oppressed* in Rio de Janiero in the 1970's.[7] Boal's method of

performative theatre takes improvisation to its limits; often guided by an open-ended script or scenario, audiences are transformed into active participants in the theatrical experience to enable a socially liberating collaboration. While Boal's performances challenged the passive state of spectators and increased the theatre as a site of political discourse, *utter matters* extends these liberating tactics to a conscious-raising state of performativity amongst things that are assumed to be even more passive than spectators, and I suggest, equally oppressed, as seemingly inert objects. Towards the same purpose, *utter matter* also employs the same experimental material principles to textual language as those used by Francis Ponge: "...letters and words are concentrations of energy: dynamic, material beings that have the power of speech, that dance across the page, that reveal different characters (depending on their typography), that can be seen as well as heard, that possess a history as well as a pre-history, and that disclose forceful, idiosyncratic personalities."[8] Written as a script for a play without dialogue, *utter matter* veers away from the role that speaking lines have to direct a specific narrative and ending to a performance. The absence of spoken voice leaves a space open for the audience (the reader) to interpolate and participate in the exchange —to invoke change. Structured as three scenes, one for each day of the performative installation, the text takes liberties with the conventions of punctuation, grammar, paragraph formation and possessive pronouns as a means to explore non-verbal communication between things.

SCENE ONE

enter snowhite[9]

a gallery
a ground floor space consisting of two rooms connected by a doorway
one door welcomes
and locks out the foyer
the other sneaks in through a back corridor

snowhite is hemmed in by a dull chalky white coat blistered by an overly absorbent brick structure

to an architect, snowhite looks like this

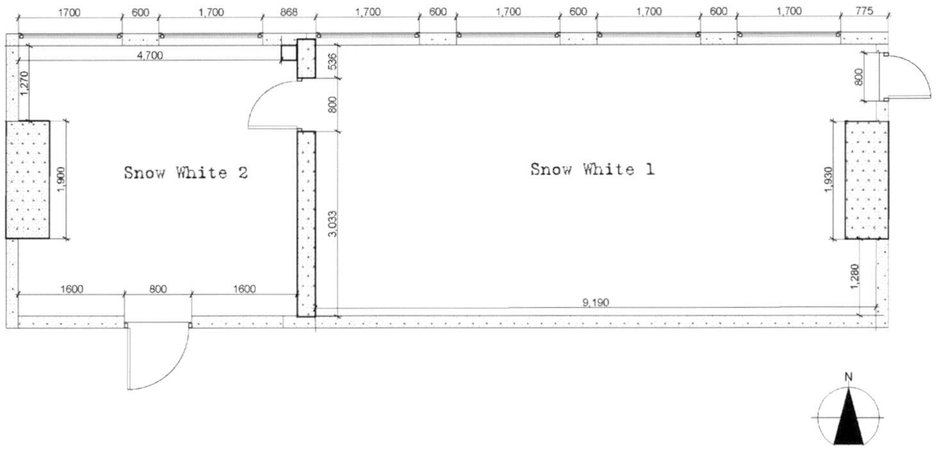

isolated
bifurcated
misnamed
empty
emaciated

enter panasonic and sony
a button on panasonic
a video camera perched
on an internal ledge
inside snowhite 1
confirms that transmission to sony
the LCD screen mounted

outside the gallery entrance
is receiving a signal
green to red
going live to an audience
merely passing by
if there at all
watching from the outside
an indeterminate number of other yous
casual engagement
possible surveillance
of the vicissitudes
of a three day encounter
sony is confused by the stillness of the image on screen
pixels vibrating
expectant
anxious for action

49 meets snowhite

A wide girth stalls the ceremonial entry but the momentum of the volume finds 49 in equilibrium with a luminous puddle conveniently in full view of panasonic
watching persistently
voyeuristically

49 reeks of the shearing shed outside hamilton
grieves over being severed from the host
a ewe
bulges with pride
testing the woven sack
to hold it all in
waiting with baited breathe for the right moment to escape
to expand an interior volume exponentially

snowhite and 49 meet julieanna

sony grants julieanna a first glance of snowhite and 49 entwined
napping
she enters snowhite from the back door
shoes in the threshold
shades drawn
julieanna succumbs to horizontality
to the floor
to 49 and snowhite
on their own terms
grey hair and clothing fall into shadow
present in a pump profile
waiting for something to else to move

something like the eyes of the cat that stalked the darkened
studio in front of the camera
left running by bruce naumann[10]
a flash of retinal disturbance overtaking the interior pregnant moment
insulated from the urgency of life
on the other side of the door

enter luce
luce slips julieanna a small thin book under the back door
gift to
of to
liberation from the shackles of language that enslave one to another
segregating a sentence into active and passive tense
symbolizing the ownership of one person to another
even in the
throes of communicating
the ultimate profession
confession
i love you
luce renounces love as a possessive trap

julieanna finds several passage in the book underlined,

i love to you says there are no strings attached to my love, no contracts, no promises, just a gift that acknowledges us as equals; i love to you means I maintain a relation of indirection to you. I do not subjugate you or consume you. I respect you (as irreducible). I hail to you: in you I hail. I praise you: in you I praise. I give you thanks: to you I give thanks for...I bless you. for...I speak to you, not just about something; rather I speak to you. I tell you, not so much this or that, but rather I tell to you.[11]

...can we construct a temporality?[12]
If I am attentive to your intentionality, to your fidelity to yourself and to its/your becoming, then it is permissible for me to imagine whether there can be anything long-lasting between us, whether our intentionalities can come into accordance.[13]
And so, you do not know me, but you know something of my appearance. You can also perceive the directions and dimensions of my intentionality. You can not know who I

am but you can help me to be by perceiving that in me which escapes me, my fidelity or infidelity to myself. In this way you can help me get away from inertia, tautology, repetition, or even from errancy, from error. You can help me become while remaining myself.[14]

julieanna touches 49 and snowhite with luce's words

Thus: how am I to speak to you? And: How am I to listen to you?[15]

enter joseph

joseph is hauled in by the sound of an ambulance siren
carving a path
through a new york city night
a spectacle wrapped in wool felt
on a gurney
to a gallery divided into two parts by a chain link fence
on one side
coyote paces
the other
an entourage watches

joseph meets coyote
donning the signature hat and vest
actions oscillating between hieratic figure and ordinary man
wielding a shepherding staff
tap tap tap   tap

laying down a stack of newspapers
smoking a cigarette
making a nest of the felted wool
chiming a triangle
chiming a
chiming
ting ting ting ting

in harmony with the animal
in the animal
rekindling a connection
to the animal
with the possibility of freedom[16]

sony sees none of this
blind to history
legend
posterity

joseph makes art happen
an art happening
actioning
art in action
actionism
the drama of material acting in and against itself[17]
social sculpture includes the everyday man
mankind
maybe even
woman-kind
certainly animal
coyote-kind

reciprocity, fluid communication, never a one way flow[18]

the stakes are high
a healing act uniting material
spiritual
human
animal
vegetal worlds
ensuring survival in its fullest most creative freedom[19]
immaterial acts of shaping ideas
freeing creative energies
instating human universality rather than reifying capital
the affliction that is
making our world the
ultimate rigor
mortis
a fixation
an obsession
an addiction on the inorganic
production of physical goods
a destructive
misinterpretation of
value.[20]

the goal
freedom
the ideal
self-determination

julieanna meets joseph

joseph proclaims himself a shaman
a mystic figure
wages protest to the secular thrust of modernism
worldly all the same
because of the currency that joseph attributes to materials
wax
fat
lead
felt
soap
storehouses
of energy
full of potential
batteries of warmth
more than physical warmth
spiritual warmth
evolutionary warmth

coyote
i like america and america likes me
a political campaign
a warning shot fired over the bow
of western
european culture
a heed to listen
to act with empathy
to embrace human frailty

coyote
an environmental symbol
a powerful deity for the north american indian[21]
yet a wild animal plucked out of the desert
caged
taunted by domesticating techniques
clickety click clickety clickety click
joseph demonstrating his cultish powers
a whisperer to animals
a preacher to students
an ability to reinstall an aura that
walter benjamin had declared lost[22]
proposing nature as the organic alternative
infiltrating the animal kingdom in order
bringing its secrets to the surface
of blackboards and watercolour washes

bringing nature so close that humans fall
back into it
like thales who fell
into a well while
watching the sky[23]

a hire car drops julieanna off in front of snowhite
not long after a farm ute delivers 49
no fanfare
no fans
no media other than sony
a witness
49 has been rescued
temporarily
from the fate of a long stormy boat ride to china
to be graded
combed
bleached
spun
to journey back again
to New Zealand
to be felted
woven
wound
the animal in 49 extracted
dags of sheep excrement
staining the fibres
pungent shades
yellow ochre
mustard green
ashen brown
industrial
bleaching
julieanna touches the ewe
with gratitude
for sacrificing a coat
in circumstances less than noble
more than humiliating
thrown down
held down
shorn down
stripped bare
bearing
underbelly
private parts

to the camera
the audience

julieanna actions a redemptive
reconciliatory agenda
healing a relationship between human and material
all matter
utter matter
a mutual expanded way of thinking
thinking that sets matter free
open ended making
keeping it free
material actions that set thoughts free
binding creativity and life through action
self-affirmation
self-creation[24]

49 is free to exit at any time
as is snowhite

julieanna pondering

How is an interior an object or thing? That implies edges, definition, limits. Does being a thing, having a name, thus being named by a noun, imply any kind of mastery? What is not owned, possessed or belong to something else. Might Luce join me in banishing apostrophes? Am I part of snowhite, one of its kinetic accessories or an animated surface? Where does 49 begin and snowhite end? Why do they each have to end and begin?

enter jessica
visual interpreter
jessica circumnavigates snowhite
an awkward invasion
disrupting a trance
sets off an impulse to move
to act
a prosthetic eye
nikon
roves about opportunistically
shutter snapping
consuming
gobbling up the view
trespasses and translates

interactions are minimal
no talking ensues

enter pink wool blanket bees wax candle matches bottled water cake of soap ball of twine a jar of honey sewing shears stainless steel bowl cotton towel electric kettle gingernut biscuits finely ground coffee beans coffee plunger ceramic cup mandarin oranges and solid graphite pencil[25]
an army of props and acting accessories
adopting a stoic stance
bundles of energy
assigned an empty geometric form and function by Plato
before they are filled with a material substance

long overdue for a coup
the revolution of things
the commodious revolt
consumptive gout

enter francis
francis shuffles in
unnoticed
taking in the scene
chewing on the details
sniffing matter
ears pulled close
to the plethora of things acting up
mute objects of expression
a silent symphony to anyone seeking gratification
giving voice to ordinary objects
finding the profound in the secular
exalting the trivial[26]
pulling the inalienable rights of things
to the surface
soap
snail
door
wasp
meadow
glass of water
mud
orange crate
restoring the power and purity to language
avoiding the stereotype
steering clear of emotion and symbolism

francis writes essays that look like poems
poems behaving as essays
proems
exhausts the thing through intense

ferocious
observation
finds the visual equivalence between writing
matter
finds no privilege or status too high
or
too low
an existentialism of things
universally equal
but different
makes sense of the things through the senses
the object senses
real
concrete
visceral
a material constitution
and life in the world
without the heavy overlay
of human imposition
the object direction
an independence
interfacing with human history
mythology
biology
geology
humour
puns
lots of french puns
performing
lively
showing little hesitation to play with words
thoughts as they emerge[27]

with a prod from francis
the transparency of the glass door to snowhite 1 is obscured by soap

> a [m]agic stone! The more it forms, with air and water, clusters of scented grapes, explosive. Water, air and soap overlap, then, play leapfrog, form bombastic and slight combinations which a breath, a smile, the least interior vanity, the slightest exaggeration cause to explode...[28]

francis makes notes about snowhite
the specifics of heat
air

art
light
water

scratches in a small notebook
turned away from panasonic

shy
introspective

a pinch of 49 wanders with francis
to the back room
in a pocket
a sanctuary
out of view

sighs
shuffling
scratches
a rhythm expelled by graphite consorting with coarse paper
giving its self up
as a soft cursive trail
to the subjects of blanket
candle
matches
bottle
soap
twine
shears
bowl
towel
kettle
biscuits
coffee beans
plunger
cup
oranges
of course pencil
sitting with things
noticing the life of things emerge in their stillness

julieanna opens the flaps of the sack that bind 49
reading
noticing
peeling back
stripping
unwrapping
undressing
finding more sacks

laying out
opening up
woven details
wearing details
repairing details
travelling data
puncture wounds
oily residue
thick
tacky
rank

enter bruno
the outside world whirls
twirls
swirls
breaks the soliloquy
bruno is out on the lawn
hands waving
eyebrows knitting
twitching
orchestrating a storm that washes away modernism as nothing more
than a fanciful misguided construct
a very persuasive marketing campaign by those claiming
to know
know what they
don't know
know that they have
it all under control
know that
everything can be
known

rap rap rap window glass rants
bruno points to the ants ants ants
they are everywhere
those agents
those actants
those actors
those forces
go go go
go towards the richness
the realness of the world
get moving
associate

assemble
migrate
circulate
connect
negotiate
be social
socialize as things

free things
things that matter
thing matter
things with concerns not mere facts
be free as things to mingle
collaborate
join forces
fuse
incorporate
multiply with other things
things that might not have heartbeats
or mammary glands
but things fertile all the same
thinking
reasoning brains aside
reconsider the networks between things that make other things happen
the connective tissue
the current
the currency

francis peaks around the corner
waving a text on electricity[29]
bees wax candle ignites a wick
a koha
an offering
bottled water strikes a transparent pose
waiting for thirst or smoke
just in case
because 49 is frothing
steaming
spewing
coming apart at the seams
escaping the sack as anticipated
things are heating up
49 topples over

julieanna runs from all corners of snowhite
flinging corporeal mass into fibre mass
again again again
once more with abandon

heaving flesh into the air
into fleece
trusting 49 to soften the fall

all colour drains from snowhite
except for two tiny dim red lights
panasonic transmitting
with the glowing ember of a torch
beuys warding off the
prospect of becoming
a victim of the wild in
coyote
jessica retreats to consort with sony

luce exits
slight scowl
perfume linger

francis grins as frail wisps of 49 catch air currents
lofting
eddies
julieanna dreams into the thick surface of pink wool blanket and 49
overcome by the pungence of sensing

SCENE TWO

enter jane
saunters in courageously
daring to play at the edges of animism
fetishism
anthropomorphism
brave enough to use plain english
to speak to
to speak of plain things
plain things that play havoc
have a life of their own
not gremlins
fairies
pixies
taniwa
borrowers

angels or
nymphs
but lively matter
deeply entangled
in the matters of humans

so much so that the matter of humans
the body
might be just a transformative host
a compost accelerator to
minerals
nutrients
fluids

challenging a modern definition of
nature as mechanistic and lifeless
which acts to demystify the messy and
unruliness of bodies and world as well
as perpetuate a seemingly insatiable
state of consumption

francis makes bubbles with soap in stainless steel bowl
having stood vigil throughout the night

jane hangs the wool sacks
to filter the exuberance of bruno
who is still outside making a racket
telling stories about how relations do
or do not assemble

ANT is better understood as a toolkit for telling interesting stories about, and interfering in, those relations.
More profoundly, it is a sensibility to the messy practices of relationality and materiality of the world.
Along with this sensibility comes a wariness of the large-scale claims common in social theory: these usually seem too simple[30]

julieanna stirs
dances a jig
herds 49 towards the edges of snowhite

1 2 3 4
1 2 3 4
left stomp right swing swing swing
left stomp right kick kick swing
stomp kick swing swing

stompswingswingkick

49 accruing at the boundary
an island converted to a meadow
of floor
coffee
cup
gingernuts invited to a picnic in the meadow

francis applauds with pleasure[31]

all pause
heavy breathing

joseph
bruno lecture to the public
outside

democracies are not all equal

julieanna 49 blanket agree to go horizontal
lounging in wool sown field
distributed evenly
basking freely
yielding
defiant to art history
the floor
as opposed to the orthogonal
verticality of the canvas is
debased and uncultured[32]
jane hovers overhead
in the heat
rising from the beach

snowhite quiet

SCENE THREE

unwrapping julieanna
migrating 49 to the passage
towards the door

throw lob toss pitch hurl

snowhite stopping the draft

squeeze clasp clutch

julieanna fitting soft mass

roll stuff compress pile push stack press tuck
presstuckpress
topple
once more pilepresstuck

shore
pilepresstuck
bolster

49 fills
sate
slake
insulate

hueeeemp

snowhite plugs
sucks
seals

swaaaaaaup

blanket props
leans
slumps

aaaghghghhhh

breath taking
holding

whoooooooou

49 exhales
vacates
evacuates

heh heh heh hey hee

sacks cut free
falling flat
splat

smaaacck flumppf

49 fills
stuffs
exhausts one sack
another sack
another sack

sweissssh shusush

three ripe bales ready
still
temporarily

not THE END

[1] Luce Irigaray (1932-) is a Belgian continental feminist philosopher, linguist, psychoanalyst, sociologist and cultural theorist most notably known for Speculum of the Other Woman (1974) and *This Sex Which Is Not One* (1977). See also Luce Irigaray, *i love to you: Sketch of a Possible Felicity in History*, Trans. Alison Martin (New York and London: Routledge, 1996).

[2] This text has been informed primarily by Bruno Latour, "On recalling ANT," in *Actor Network Theory and After*, ed. John Law and John Hassard, 15-25. Oxford: Blackwell, 1999. Bruno Latour, *We Have Never Been Modern.* London: Harvester Wheatsheaf, London, 1993. Bruno Latour (1947-) is a French anthropologist and sociologist of science and and an influential theorist in the field of Science and Technology Studies (STS). His influential books *We Have Never Been Modern* (1991/1993) and *Science in Action* (1987) have served to bring ANT to an international and interdisciplinary audience.

[3] Joseph Beuys (1921-1986) was a German post-war sculptor, art theorist and performance artist active in the FLUXUS movement and developing the concept of social sculpture to effect change in society and politics at a metaphysical scale. The exhibition *Coyote* occurred at the René Block Gallery, New York, May 1974. Francis Ponge (1899-1989) was a prominent figure in French literature credited as being influenced by Surrealism and best known for his close and intimate examination of everyday objects in his work *Le parti pris des choses* (1942) and *Le Savon* (1967). Jane Bennett, *Vibrant Matter: A Political Ecology of Things* (Durham and London: Duke University Press, 2010). Jane Bennett is Professor of Political Theory and Chair of the Department of Political Science at Johns Hopkins University. In addition to *Vibrant Matter*, she is the author of *The Enchantment of Modern Life: Attachments, Crossings, and Ethics* (2001) and *Thoreau's Nature: Ethics, Politics, and the Wild* (2002).

[4] Luce Irigaray and Mary Green, ed., *Luce Irigaray: Teaching* (New York: Continuum, 2006), 231.

[5] Michel Serres and Bruno Latour, *Conversation on Science, Culture and Time* (Ann Arbor: University of Michigan Press, 1995), 57.

[6] For example see the work of Albena Yeneva, 'When a Bus Met a Museum: Following Artists, Curators and Workers in Art Installation', *Museum and Society* 1/3 (2003): 116-31.

[7] Augusto Boal, *Theatre of the Oppressed* (London: Pluto Press, 1979).

[8] Richard Stamelman, "The Object in Poetry and Painting: Ponge and Picasso," *Contemporary Literature* 19/4 (1978): 410.

[9] Snowhite is a peer-reviewed gallery housed in the Department of Design and Visual Arts, Unitec, Auckland, New Zealand curated by Mary-Louise Brown and Penny Thomson, 24 June 2012, http://www.unitec.ac.nz/unitec/snowhite/?page_id=5

[10] Bruce Nauman, "Mapping the Studio I (Fat Chance John Cage)" (2002), 23 June 2012 http://www.diaart.org/exhibitions/main/29

[11] Irigaray, *i love to you*, 109.

[12] Irigaray, *i love to you*, 110.

[13] Irigaray, *i love to you*, 112.

[14] Irigaray, *i love to you*, 112.

[15] Irigaray, *i love to you*, 113.

[16] Arthur C. Danto, "Foreword: Style and Salvation in the Art of Beuys," in *Joseph Beuys: The Reader,* ed. and trans. Claudia Mesch and Viola Michely (Cambridge, MA: MIT Press 2007), xiii-xviii.

[17] Valie Export, "Aspects of Feminist Actionism," *New German Critique* 47 (1989): 70.

[18] Carin Kuoni, ed., *Joseph Beuys in America: Energy Plan for the Western Man* (New York: Four Walls Eight Windows, 1990), 22.

[19] Kuoni, *Joseph Beuys in America*, x.

[20] Kuoni, *Joseph Beuys in America*, 143-144.

[21] Kuoni, *Joseph Beuys in America*, 14.

[22] Kuoni, *Joseph Beuys in America*, 2.

[23] Thales of Miletus, Internet Enyclopedia of Philosophy, 22 June 2012. http://www.iep.utm.edu/thales/

[24] Export, *Feminist Actionism*, 70 citing Weibel, "Material Thinking as Freeing People's Products From Their Thing-Characteristics." Kritik der Kunst.

[25] All of these things are a part of my daily life: For example, an inheritance from my Croatian grandmother Rosalia Thelin, pink wool blanket usually serves as the first layer in my bed linens. Because my partner is a beekeeper, bees wax candles and jars of honey are staples in my household. My two Labradors Te Hine Poché and Raison d'Etre lent their stainless steel water bowl to this installation. There are few pleasures better than dipping a gingernut biscuit into a fresh cup of coffee.

[26] W. G. Regier, (no title), *Prairie Schooner* Spring (1975): 90.

[27] Donald Sutherland, "Wonderful Things," *Parnassus: Poetry in Review* Spring/Summer (1973): 60-8.

[28] Francis Ponge, *Soap*, trans. Jane Dunlop (Stanford, CA: Stanford University Press, 1989).

[29] Francis Ponge, *Text on Electricity, ~e; Text on Electricity* (Ponge), 20 June 2012. http://archives.openflows.org/electronetwork-l/msg00273.html

[30] John Law, "After ANT: Complexity, Naming and Typology," in *Actor Network Theory and After*, ed. John Law and John Hassard (Boston and Oxford, UK: Blackwell Publishers; Keele: Sociological Review, 1999), 2.

[31] Francis Ponge, *The Making of the Pre: La Fabrique Du Pre*, trans. Lee Fahnestock (Geneve: Albert Skira, 1971).

[32] Rosalind E. Krauss, "Horizontality," in *Formless: A User's Guide*, ed. Bois Yve-Alain and Rosalind E. Krauss (New York: Zone Books, 1997), 93–103.

Epilogue

THIS SEX WHICH IS NOT ONE

There is an established body of knowledge associated with material performance that is core understanding for designers, architects, builders, engineers and material scientists. This knowledge veers towards an essentialist perspective of materials based on an assumption that there are inherent properties to every type of material influencing how a material behaves to environmental conditions, reacts to other materials and responds to tried and true processes. Often understood as general or common knowledge, it is disseminated with an air of truth that underpins a matter-of-fact conception of materials. In contemporary craft, fabrication, construction and manufacture, these properties shape how things are made, assembled and constructed. They factor reliability that lends to repeatability; we can depend on them to perform in specific ways and hence make units and products over and over again with an assurance of consistency. How a material performs is typically documented in fact sheets bearing product specifications, the results of regulatory testing and parameters for installation or use. Such data often plays a prominent role (second to improper installation or maintenance) in any legal issues arising out of a failure to perform as intended. With the exception, perhaps, of allowances for tolerance, changes due to thermal gain or loss, and calculated degradation over time, each material type is defined as unquestionably stable, forever constant, dead stuff. So, for example, a log of pinus radiata is always prone to check and the sticks milled from it are very likely to twist, bow or buckle because of its quick growth rate. It will also burn quickly too due to a high level of resin flowing in its vascular system. A bale of wool will always reek of dung and the sweat of the ewe until it is bleached and combed. A chunk of basalt thrown up from the bowels of the earth by volcanic eruption will always hold heat longer and deeper than a sheet of slate. And as American Cultural Historian Jeffrey Meikle points out, it is the fourth kingdom of plastic materials, the non-organic species, that because of their chemical bonds appear so dead and so insusceptible to decomposition.[1]

In many ways, the creative works and text in this book operate with and yet against the status quo of this body of knowledge; they take affirmative actions on material surfaces as a point of resistance to these dominant ways of thinking. Chapters 1, 2, 3 and 4 expose the use of a form of feminist agency to emancipate seemingly inert

Fig 1 (p.189, 210). J.Preston, *all that matters* (2012). Piles, heaps and stack of materials spatialised in the course of an exhibition at THE HUB, Victoria Street, Melbourne, AUS.
Fig 2 (p.190, 209). J.Preston, *all that matters* (2012). Grease, oil, clay and ice waiting to escape white porcelain on a trestle table of bespoke booklets.

interior finishing materials from an oppression I attribute to building construction systems, patriarchal paradigms and political economies promulgating neutralization, homogeneity and uniformity. Chapter 1: *The Yield Principle* introduces the wedge/shim as a conceptual, methodological and physical tool capable of liberating material expression suppressed by standardized industrial manufacturing processes. Chapter 2: *Voice Lessons* pries open the power of oration and do-it-yourself renovation to expose the political bias of neutrality, including neutral colours. Chapter 3: *IN wildness* tampers with phenomenal and conceptual states of transparency to move beyond the interior as a bounded, domesticated and private territory. Chapter 4: *Making note(s) OF surface* articulates 'surface' as a relational encounter catalysed by material and spatial forces. Chapter 5: *utter matter* builds on this trajectory to track a significant shift in the intellectual and practical concerns of my practice; what started as a protest and demonstration to liberate interior materials from the oppressive clutches of industrial processes, emerged as a transformative practice centred on relational engagements with materials (and objects) as like matter, performing matter.

Material performance to performing matter: a simple reconfiguring of terms draws attention to each individual matter's quality, difference and capacity to act on its own accord and to form confederations with other matter. Resistance, any force that slows or stops movement or keeps movement from happening turns into a practice that embraces stillness, slowness, slowing down, listening closely, hesitating before acting, yielding – all hinged to a new materialist philosophy advocating ethical material practices. At some basic level, this research bears hope that forming respectful relationships with materials will realise a greater liberation than that of interior surfaces in an architectural realm or women in a man's world. The stakes are much greater when dead things are found to be live.

The spatial experience and encounter of *BALE* is the closest I have come to realizing an ethical engagement with matter inclusive of the matter of language; I am sure that there is still more to be done on this front. The process of writing *utter matter* lends crucial evidence and wonderment to the final stage of the research project. It expands the concepts and actions driving a performative installation such as *BALE*. To use the writing process as a parallel state of play and experimentation, underscores what I have professed all along: language is material and as susceptible and resistant to hard edged tools and metaphors as concrete, or wool. Together, *BALE* and *utter matter* clearly cross a threshold of achievement because the works took me out of my comfort zone, pressed me to own up to what I was 'on' about, helped me shed some of the detritus of other ways of thinking and practice. Most of all, they were cathartic; they left me standing in front of a (new) door (or better, lying on the floor) in a heap of questions, material, and zeal for where the practice can journey. I have never experienced this so profoundly.

utter matter also made clear to me that material is matter is material, to borrow a ploy from Gertrude Stein. In an immersive experience that trialled the animate constitutions and capacities of things human and nonhuman, standard modes of communication such as speech, writing and gesture were quickly replaced with modes of exchange (acting upon and with each other) and then further, shifting to states of sensing and feeling. Words had no place in the end; language was too mental, too systematic, too articulate. Even Ponge's sense of speech as a faculty of elocution proved more intellectual than animal. I believe this becomes all too evident at the (not) end of *utter matter* as I struggle to write sounds as words, and not just as onamonapias, but sounds that rest in your gut or mouth. Language, even spoken, is/was getting in the way of making contact. Beuys' work with the coyote highlights that primal and visceral sensibility. I had to learn this myself nearly forty years after his performance in the context of performing with matter and motivated by different causes and concerns. It is still too soon to say whether or not this revelation will curtail my spatial writing or performative installation practice or merely shift me into the realm of sound art, phonetics, visual poetry or even actual script writing. What is certain is that that the feminism I applied towards the emancipation of interior materials as vibrant, vital and forceful stuff has absorbed me into a liberating assemblage.

For this I am indebted to political theorist Jane Bennett's scholarship on vibrant material, Thoreau and wildness and the enchantment of the modern world; each work opening the door to a philosophical view linking matter and ethics.[2] In *Vibrant Matter* Bennett dwells on commonplace things and physical phenomena including electricity, rubbish, stem cells, landfills as stuff imbued with vital materiality running through and across bodies, human and not. Her political analysis of public events reveals the potential to develop an ethical and more ecologically responsible politics that acknowledges humans and non-human as matter embroiled in a web of force-affecting situations. Philosopher Bryan Bannon's review of *Vibrant Matter* highlights its relevance to my project:

> Building on her previous book, *The Enchantment of Modern Life* (Princeton, 2001), where she argues for a renewed attention to the ethical value of affects in addressing human malfeasance toward the material world, *Vibrant Matter* turns its attention toward the "thing power" that produces these affects. In this sense, Bennett's vital materialism is akin to theories such as Val Plumwood's "weak panpsychism" from *Feminism and the Mastery of Nature* (Routledge, 1993) and David Abram's terrestrial animism from *The Spell of the Sensuous* (Vintage, 1997). What these three positions have in common is their sincere attempt to provide a materialist philosophy that does not rely upon traditional definitions of matter as passive, inactive, and unitary… Following Deleuze, Bennett defines life as "an interstitial field of non-personal, ahuman forces, flows, tendencies, and trajectories" (61). To establish matter as vital, Bennett creatively synthesizes Latour's work with Deleuze and Guattari's. Those familiar with these thinkers will find themselves on recognizable terrain: material bodies are taken to be "assemblages," aggregates of interacting bodies and forces, which interact with other assemblages to form larger networks of agency. By revealing how human agency is only possible within larger assemblages of bodies, Bennett claims to be "raising the status of the materiality of which we are composed…"[3]

The gentle but persuasive force that Bennett uses to reason matter's agency and hence its liveness proved significant in framing *BALE* and *utter matters*. Though I am aware of the dangers of translating philosophy into concrete material form and actions, I feel that Bennett's works welcomed bringing conceptual and abstract thoughts into a physical presence especially since her own examples demonstrated virtuosity through real world circumstances. And thus throughout this research, I have consistently asserted that my practice crossed out or crossed over artificial divides between theory and practice, and writing and making. I have engaged spatial writing practice to reflect, position and tease out the issues of concern in the sculptural, exhibition and performative work and vice versa. Even the preparation of this manuscript has not been more than the mere "writing up the research"; it is a re-working of the original creative projects carried out with a firm conviction that language is a pliable material as susceptible to shimming, prying and wearing processes as wood, or even — bless you Ponge — soap.[4]

Spatial writing is related to 'art-writing' which was developed by cultural critic Mieke

Bal to bring one closer to art by placing it at the centre of attention. Bal's close reading of the visual work as a structured narrative reveals to me a relational intimacy between the matter of me as an art viewer, the matter of the space of encounter and the matter of the objects.[5] 'Site-writing' is a practice articulated by architectural theorist and art critic Jane Rendell to prioritise the sites of engagement with art. "These include the sites — material, emotional, political and conceptual — of the artwork's construction, exhibition and documentation, as well as those remembered, dreamed and imagined by the artist, critic and other viewer."[6] For the time being, I hold on to calling my own practice spatial rather than site-writing simply because of the project's focus on the spatiality of surface and the connotations 'site' has to an architecturally-bound place. But for all intents and purposes my spatial writing practice follows Jane Rendell's lead, without perhaps the same deep knowledge and command of art and architectural theory and psychoanalytic interpretation. Where Rendell has invested in site-writing to position the critic in relation to art objects, architectural spaces, theoretical ideas and the act of writing itself, I have devoted spatial writing to the artist, a special kind of art user, who is seeking to discover what materialises in the work before words.[7]

As the previous pages make evident, I am not bound by proper academic discourse; I am at ease using a full array of writing voices, tactics and alternative forms of communication etiquette including the use of the subjective pronoun 'I' and sentences that are written with emphasis on aurality and, at times, laden with emotion. In addition, this project engages the autobiographical, a tactic employed frequently in feminist works to reinforce and acknowledge the specifics of the individual as much as to avoid generalisations that reify essences. 'I' is never neutral or disinterested. The five chapters present a full spectrum of spatial writing experiments that parallel the research's maturation and my own skill and understanding of what this practice can yield and how it can also behave as matter.

Performing Matter: interior surface and feminist actions is a gift to the discipline of interior design. It rethinks what an interior is, how it is practiced, how it is performed and how it is gendered. It exposes where the discipline is thought to be fragile, weak and seemingly superficial only to find an alternative mode of power, another kind of strength, within all those attributes which have for centuries placed interiors, women, material and surface on the back side of a slash: '/'- a sign use in mathematics for fractions, a violent cutting action, a line demarcating a boundary or a binary relationship, and as my colleagues at the University of Brighton told me after a big laugh, to urinate - the backside of a slash is not a good place to be.

The research set out on a voyage to explore what an interior surface could do. The creative projects and spatial writing practice make evident that interior surfaces can wage a protest, support a feminist agenda, deploy a campaign, deny entry, prompt boundary-crossing, facilitate sensibilities, and, perhaps most of all, act as agents against oppression as well as actants for positive change. In the midst of probing interior furnishings and finishes, the research revealed how industrial products and building processes partner with modernist paradigms to support smooth, white, uniform and homogenous surfaces. These interiors are now suspect for the way they hide behind shades of neutrality sustaining spatial (and racial) indifference. While offering a point of resistance to the forces of consumerism, convention and standardization brandish in many everyday interiors, *Performing Matter: interior surfaces and feminist actions* bears evidence of an interior's capacity to be vibrant and expressive in its own material muteness. As one interior conspired with its inhabitant to wage an amplified protest against inequity, another interior bestowed a polychromatic experience of wildness in the stillness and quietude of a non-verbal exchange. These exercises serve to pry the interior loose from assumptions about an interior's domestic and domesticated state, its onus to provide comfort, its confinement to architectural structures and its role as a retreat from the realities of a supposed external world.

Throughout the research, interiors have shun assumptions about their identity as the mere consequence of material objects arranged in a room and they have withstood the temptation to be deferred to an insular state of interiority couched in subjectivity and stimulated by phenomenon. In the process, interiors link to an expanded notion of surface as spatial encounters between things i.e. human, organic, synthetic, vegetal, non-human matter. Such disruption of the normative Western social pecking order reconfigured the primary aim of the project from one that used an interior to champion a feminist cause to one that employed feminist values towards the development of a material ethics. An interior changed from being the centre of concern to the site where an issue was performed, and in doing so, an interior was entangled with issues well beyond the physical borders of the room.

As such, the research contributes to interior design's emergence as a contemporary, speculative and experimental spatial enterprise and part of a growing international effort to expand the practice of interior design through new media, modes of inquiry and intellectual scholarship.[8] Again, with an affirmative outlook, this research looks at what the practice of interior design could be given its history concerned with domesticity, consumer goods, social status and built enclosure yet with an urge to leap out of the margin and participate in the questions and challenges of the twenty-first century. It does so with confidence in an interior's capacity to be political, to support difference, to be a mobile assemblage. My creative work and spatial writing practice launches a future for interior design that capitalises on its rich history, its existing links with many other disciplines, practices and industries as well its embrasure of many ways of thinking that integrate empirical processes with poetic conceptualisation.

Performing Matter: interior surface and feminist actions' critical and experimental exploration of building construction, material details and methods and processes of making space bring interior design's normative practices to decorate, assemble, apply and arrange into a broader field of discourse and engagement with contemporary issues that are both philosophical and political. Rather than abandon them – to take flight, as Rosi Braidotti would say – the project invests in them intellectually and creatively; to mine what is *OF* the surface rather than look on it or below it, acts which reinforce subservience or superficiality.[9] This aspect of the gift is by no means exclusive to interior design. As the creative works reveal, the divide between humans and things, live and dead matter, is <u>the</u> site of oppression. This project calls upon me to expand that ethical efficacy in future works; to guide my feminist values and female body to the ethics of matter, especially those of materials.

While this research has successfully transformed my creative practice, it has also propelled me towards a far more proactive and transdisciplinary engagement that is pointed at the nexus of the practical and the conceptual. All I can see, think about and act upon are the multiple avenues that the work introduced me to. There is enough to sustain a lifetime of creative activity and research. I am prepared to embrace transdisciplinarity with greater vigour; to give up sovereignty to any one discipline, to form — out of difference and diversity — new insights from emergent properties; to be a "generic rebel".[10] And as such, I will proceed to be fluid, to assemble, associate and circulate as a live force amongst others.

[1] Jeffrey L. Meikle, "Into the Fourth Kingdom: Representations of Plastic Materials, 1920–1950," in *Journal of Design History* 5 (3) (1992): 173-182.

[2] Jane Bennett: *Vibrant Matter: A Political Ecology of Things* (a John Hope Franklin Center Book), Durham: Duke University Press Books, 2010. / The Enchantment of Modern Life: Attachments, Crossings, and Ethics, Princeton, NJ: Princeton University Press, 2001. / *Thoreau's Nature: Ethics, Politics and the Wild*, Thousand Oaks, California: Sage Publications, 1994.

[3] Bryan E. Bannon, "Vibrant Matter [book review]", *Environmental Philosophy* 8(1) (2011): 121-124.

[4] An excerpt from Ponge's proem *Soap*: "Saturated with soap, the water froths at the least movement. Wants to join the air, climbs in the assault of the sky. Grabs the air's arm, climbs the sky's knees ... throws itself into the sky's arms ...throws itself onto the sky's neck ... Displays even a sort of aerostatic pretention. Displays a sort of exaltation, and even an aerostatic pretension. Sometimes achieves, in this respect, miraculous, brilliant short-lived success." Francis Ponge, *Soap*, trans. Lane Dunlop (Stanford, California: Stanford University Press, 1998), 75.

[5] Mieke Bal, *Looking In: The Art of Viewing*. Amsterdam: Overseas Publishers Association, 2001, 46.

[6] Jane Rendell, *Site-writing: The Architecture of Art Criticism* (London and New York: I. B. Tauris, 2010), 1.

[7] Rendell, *Site-writing*, 2.

[8] In the past five years this expanded field has been fuelled by an unprecedented collection of conferences, exhibitions, symposiums and book publications aimed at international audiences. The authors, designers, artists and writers featured in these venues represent concerted efforts to see the interior design practice, including its theoretical explorations, link to contemporary discourse, media and modes of engagement. The following is a short list; I am a leader in this field of concern. Lori A. Brown, ed. *Feminist Practices: Interdisciplinary Approaches to Women in Architecture*. Surry, England: Ashgate, 2011. (Including an international touring exhibition) Fleming, Hay, Hollis et.al, eds., Interior Tools, *Interior Tactics: Debates in Interiors Theory and Practice.* Interiors Forum Scotland, Oxfordshire: Libri Publishing, 2011. Gigli, Hay, Hollis et. al., eds. *Thinking Inside the Box: A Reader in Interiors for the 21st Century*, London: Middlesex University Press, 2007. Kent Kleinman, Joanna Merwood-Salisbury and Lois Weinthal, eds., *After Taste: Expanded Practice in Interior Design*, New York: Princeton Architectural Press, 2011. Gini Lee, ed. "Interior Territories: Exposing the Critical Interior." *IDEA Journal* (2009). Julieanna Preston, ed. *Interior Atmospheres*, Chichester: Wiley, 2008. Mark Taylor, ed. "Interior Spaces and Other Places," *2010 IDEA Symposium*, Brisban, AUS, 2010.

[9] Braidotti, *Nomadic Subjects*, 77.

[10] Margaret Somerville and David J. Rapport, *Transdisciplinarity: Recreating Integrated Knowledge*. Oxford, UK: EOLSS Publishers Co, 2000, XV-7.

Bibliography

__ . "Ryijy rugs." *Form Function Finland* 73 (1999): 61.

__. "Using Hunting Blinds." *Field and Stream* 90(12) (1986): 58.

Actup. Accessed 22 April 2008. 12:38p.m. http://www.actupny.org/documents/CDdocuments/ACTUP_CivilDisobedience.pdf

Adcock, Craig. *James Turrell: The Art of Light and Space*. Berkley, Los Angeles, Oxford: University of California Press, 1990.

Alaimo, Stacy and Susan Heckman, eds. *Material Feminisms*. Bloomington and Indianapolis: Indiana University Press, 2008.

Allen, Edward and Joseph Iano. *Fundamentals of Building Construction Materials and Methods Fourth Edition*. Chichester: John Wiley and Sons, 2004.

Amato, Ivan. *Stuff: The Materials the World is Made Of*. New York: BasicBooks, 1997.

Amberg, Anna-Lisa and Juhani Palaasma, eds. *Hvitträsk: koti taideteoksena = Hvitträsk : the home as a work of art*. Helsinki: Suomen Rakennustaiteen Museo/Museum of Finnish Architecture: 1987.

Aplet, Gregory, Janice Thompson and Mark Wilbert. "Indicators of Wildness: Using Attributes of the Land to Assess the Context of Wilderness." In *USDA Forest Service Proceedings* RMRS-P-15-VOL-2 (2000): 89-98.

Aranda, Benjamin and Chris Lasch. *Pamphlet Architecture 27: Tooling*. New York: Princeton Architectural Press, 2006.

Attfield, Judy & Pat Kirkham, eds., *A View from the Interior: Women and Design*. London: Women's Press, 1995.

_____. *Wild Things: The Material Culture of Everyday Life*. Oxford and New York: Berg, 2000.

Bal, Mieke. *Looking In: The Art of Viewing*. Amsterdam: Overseas Publishers Association, 2001.

_____. *Travelling Concepts in the Humanities: A Rough Guide*. Toronto, Buffalo, London: University of Toronto Press, 2002.

Barber, Daniel. "Militant architecture: Destabilising Architecture's Disciplinarity." *The Journal of Architecture* 10 (3) (2005): 245-253.

Barr, Alfred. "Preface." in Henry-Russell Hitchcock and Philip Johnson, *The International Style*. New York and London: W. W. Norton & Company: 1966.

Barr, Hugh. "Establishing a Wilderness Preservation System in New Zealand -A User's Perspective." *In The State of Wilderness in New Zealand*. Edited by Gordon Cessford, 16-21. Wellington, New Zealand: Department of Conservation, 2001.

Baxter, Paula. "Thirty Years of Growth in the Literature of Interior Design." *Journal of Design History* 4 (4) (1991): 241-250.

Beecher, Catharine and Harriet Beecher Stowe. *The American Woman's Home*. Edited by Nicole Tonkovich. Hartford, Conn.: Harriet Beecher Stowe Center; New Brunswick, N.J.: Rutgers University Press, 2002.

Belenky, M Field, B. McVicker Clinchy, N. Rule Goldberger & J. Mattuck Tarule. *Women's Ways of Knowing:*

The Development of Self, Voice and Mind. New York: BasicBooks, 1997.

Benjamin, Andrew. "Surface Effects: Borromini, Semper, Loos." *The Journal of Architecture*, 11(1) (2006): 1-35.

Benjamin, Walter. *The Arcades Project*. Edited by Rolf Tiedemann. Translated by Howard Eiland and Kevin McLaughlin. Cambridge, MA: Belknap Press of Harvard University Press, 2002.

Bennett, Jane. *The Enchantment of Modern Life: Attachments, Crossings, and Ethics*. Princeton and Oxford: Princeton University Press, 2001.

_____. *Thoreau's Nature: Ethics, Politics, and the Wild*. Rowman & Littlefield, 2002.

_____. *Vibrant Matter: A Political Ecology of Things*. Durham and London: Duke University Press, 2010.

Bieri, David et al. *Gypsum Wallboard and Method for Producing Same*, Patent 3,389,042. United States Patent Office, 1968. Accessed 21 June 2010. http://news.google.com/patents/about?id=VbdsAAAAEBAJ

Biggs, Michael A. R. and Daniela Büchler. "Rigor and Practice-based Research." *Design Issues* 23 (3) (2007): 62-69.

Blackwell, Mark. *The Secret Life of Things: Animals, Objects, And It-narratives in Eighteenth-Century England*. Lewisburg, PA: Bucknell University Press, 2007.

Bloomer, Jennifer. "Big Jugs." In *Gender Space Architecture: An Interdisciplinary Introduction*. Edited by Jane Rendell, Barbara Penner and Iain Borden, 371-384. London: The Althone Press, 2001.

Boal, Augusto. *Theatre of the Oppressed*. London: Pluto Press, 1979.

Bolt, Barbara. "Materializing Pedagogies." *Working Papers in Art and Design* 4 (2006). Accessed 1 February 2010. sitem.herts.ac.uk/artdes_research/papers/wpades/vol4/bbfull.html

Bonsieppe, Gui. "Visual/Verbal Rhetoric." *Ulm* 14/15/16 (1965): 30.

Bourjaily, Phil. "The Invisible Hunter." *Field and Stream* 111(6) (2006): WF6-WF7.

Braidotti, Rosi. *Metamorphoses: Towards a Materialist Theory of Becoming*. Malden, MA: Polity, 2002.

_____. *Nomadic Subjects: Embodiment and Sexual Difference in Contemporary Feminist Theory*. New York: Columbia University Press, 1994.

Brown, Lori A. *Contested Spaces Abortion Clinics, Women's Shelters and Hospitals: Politicizing the Female Body*. Surrey, England: Ashgate Publishing Company, 2013.

Brown, Lori A. ed. *Feminist Practices Interdisciplinary Approaches to Women in Architecture*. Surrey, England: Ashgate Publishing Company, 2011.

Brunsson, Nils and Bengt Jacobson. *A World of Standards*. New York: Oxford University Press Inc., 2000.

Buckley, Cheryl. "Made in Patriarchy: Toward a Feminist Critique of Design." *Design Issues* 3 (2)(1986): 3-14.

Build (BRANZ, October 1991).

Burry, Mark and Julieanna Preston. *Construction Primer*. Wellington, NZ: VUW Press, 2000.

Burry, Mark C. "Between Substance and Surface." In *Architectural Design: Surface Consciousness*. Edited by Mark Taylor, 9-19. London: Wiley Wiley-Academy, 2006.

Cache, Bernard. *Earth Moves: The Furnishing of Territories*. Cambridge, Massachusetts: MIT Press, 1995.

Carter, Paul. *Material Thinking: The Theory and Practice of Creative Research*. Carleton, VIC: Melbourne University Publishing, 2004.

Ching, Francis D. K. and Catherine Adams. *Building Construction Illustrated* Third Edition. New York: John Wiley & Sons, Inc., 2001.

Clegg, Sue and Wendy Mayfield. "Gendered by Design: How Women's Place in Design Is Still Defined by Gender." *Design Issues* 15 (3) (1999): 3-16.

Code, Lorraine. *What Can She Know?: Feminist Theory and the Construction of Knowledge*. Ithaca, NY: Cornell University Press, 1991.

Cogdell, Christina. "Product or Bodies: Streamline Design and Eugenics as Applied Biology." *Design Issues* 19 (1) (2003): 36-52.

Coleman, Debra, Elizabeth Danze and Carol Henderson, eds. *Architecture and Feminism*. New York: Princeton Architectural Press, 1996.

Colomina, Beatriz, ed. *Sexuality and Space*. Princeton, NJ: Princeton Architectural Press, 1992.

Cook, Lynne. "The Viewer, the Sitter, and the Site: A Splintered Syntax." In *Ann Hamilton, tropos*. Edited by Lynne Cook and Karen Kelly, 59-88. New York: DIA Art Foundation, 1994.

Coole, Diana and Samantha Frost, eds. *New Materialisms: Ontology, Agency and Politics*. Durham and London. Duke University Press, 2010.

Crandell, Gina. *Nature Pictorialized: 'The View' in Landscape History*. Baltimore and London: The John Hopkins University Press, 1993.

Dal Fabbro, Mario. *Upholstered Furniture, Design and Construction*. New York, London, Toronto: McGraw-Hill Book Company, 1969.

Danto, Arthur C. "Foreword: Style and Salvation in the Art of Beuys." In *Joseph Beuys: The Reader.* Edited and Translated by Claudia Mesch and Viola Michely, xiii-xviii. Cambridge, MA: MIT Press 2007.

Daston, Lorraine and Peter Galison. *Objectivity*. New York: Zone Books, 2007.

Day, Brian J. "The Moral Intuition of Ruskin's 'Storm-Cloud'." In *Studies in English Literature, 1500-1900*, 45(4) The Nineteenth Century (Autumn 2005): 917-933.

Deeter, Kirk. "Duck Luck," *Field and Stream* 113(6) (2008): WF11-WF13.

De Landa, Manuel. *A Thousand Years of Nonlinear History*. New York: Zone Books, 1997.

Deleuze, Gilles. *Essays Critical and Clinical*, trans. Daniel W. Smith and Michael A. Greco. Verso, New York, 1998.

Department of Building and Housing/ Te Tari Kaupapa Whare, Residential Tenancy Agreement (Wellington: New Zealand Government, 2005), 4. Accessed 23 June 2010. www.dbh.co.nz

Deutsche, Rosalyn. *Evictions: Art and Spatial Politics*. Cambridge, Massachusetts and London: MIT Press, 1996.

Ebeling, Siegfried. *Space as Membrane* (1926). Edited by Spyros Papapetros, Translated by Pamela Johnston. London: Architectural Association, 2010.

Edwards, Clive "'Home is Where the Art is': Women, Handcrafts and Home Improvements 1750-1900," *Journal of Design History* 19: 1 (2006) 18, 19.

Export, Valie. "Aspects of Feminist Actionism." *New German Critique* 47 (1989): 69-92.

Ferry, Emma. "'Decorators May be Compared to Doctors': An Analysis of Rhoda and Agnes Garrett's Suggestion for House Decoration in Painting Woodwork and Furniture (1876)." *Journal of Design History* 16 (1) (2003): 15-33.

Forty, Adrian. *Words and Buildings: A Vocabulary of Modern Architecture*. New York: Thames and Hudson, 2000.

Friedman, Alice T. *Women and the Making of the Modern House: A Social and Architectural History.* New York: Abrams, 1998.

GIB SITE CODE For Residential and Commercial Installations: CBI 5113, May 2006, New Zealand: Winstone Wallboards LTD, May 2006), 92. Accessed 24 June 2010. http://www.gib.co.nz/assets/Uploads/Gib-SiteGuide-2003.pdf

Gibbs, Philip. October 1996. Accessed 1 June 2012. http://math.ucr.edu/home/baez/physics/General/Glass/glass.html (8 of 8)

Gibson, J. J. *The Ecological Approach to Visual Perception*. New Jersey and London: Lawrence Erlbaum Associates, 1986.

Gill, Alison. "Deconstruction Fashion: The Making of Unfinished, Decomposing and Re-assembled Clothes." *Fashion Theory* 2 (1) (1998): 25–50.

Gins, Madeline and Arakawa. *Architectural Body*. Tuscaloosa and London: The University of Alabama Press, 2002.

Gordon, Beverly. "Woman's Domestic Body: The Conceptual Conflation of Women and Interiors in the Industrial Age." *Winterthur Portfolio*, 31 (4) (1996): 281-301.

Graham, Stephen and Nigel Thrift. "Out of Order: Understanding Repair and Maintenance." *Theory Culture Society* 24 (1) (2007): 1-25.

Grosz, Elizabeth. *Architecture from the Outside: Essays on Virtual and Real Space*. Cambridge, MA: MIT Press, 1995.

_____. *Volatile Bodies: Towards a Corporeal Feminism*. Bloomington and Indianapolis: Indiana University Press, 1994.

Gutheim, Frederick. "Hvitträsk: Exploring the Roots of Saarinen." *Inland Architect* 32 (1) (1998): 54-60.

Hale, Jonathan. "Signs of Resistance: Remembering Technology." *The Journal of Architecture* 5 (2000): 94-5.

Hamilton, Ann. *tropos*. DIA Center for the Arts, New York, 1993.

_____. *Present-Past*, 1984-1997. Milan: Skira, 1988.

Haraway, Donna. "Situated Knowledges: The Science Question in Feminism and the Privilege of Partial Perspectives." *Feminist Studies* (1988) 575–599.

Haraway, Donna. *When Species Meet*. Minnesota: University of Minneapolis, 2007.

Harding, Sandra. *Feminism & Methodology*. Bloomington: Indiana University Press, 1987.

Hausen, Marika. 'Hvitträsk: koti taideteoksena = Hvitträsk : the home as a work of art,' in Amberg, Anna-Lisa et a (ed team) and Pallasmaa, Juhani (ed), *Hvitträsk : koti taideteoksena = Hvitträsk: the home as a work of art*. Helsinki: Suomen Rakennustaiteen Museo/ Museum of Finnish Architecture, 1987, 10-69.

Havenhand, Lucinda Kaukas. "A View from the Margin: Interior Design." *Design Issues* 20 (4) (2004): 32-42.

Haynes, Benarthur Castle. *Techniques of Observing the Weather*. New York: John Wiley & Sons, 1947.

Hellman, Mimi. "Furniture, Sociability, and the Work of Leisure in Eighteenth-century France." *Eighteenth Century Studies* 32(4): 415–45.

Heynen, Hilde. *Architecture and Modernity, A Critique*. Cambridge, MA and London, England: MIT Press, 1999.

Hitchcock, Henry-Russell and Philip Johnson. *The International Style*. New York and London: W. W. Norton & Company: 1966.

Hodges, Richard. "Cruel and Unusual Treatment to Fabrics." In *BORO BORO*. Tokyo: NUNO Corporation, 1997.

hooks, bell. *Yearning: Race, Gender, and Cultural Politics*. Boston, MA: South End Press, 1990.

Howes, David, ed. *Empire of the Senses: The Sensual Culture Reader*. Oxford, New York: Berg, 2005.

Imperiale, Alicia. *New Flatness: Surface Tension in Digital Architecture*. Basel, Boston and Berlin: Birkhauser, 2000.

Ingraham, Catherine. *Architecture, Animal, Human: The Asymmetrical Condition*. London and New York: Routledge, 2006.

Irigaray, Luce and Mary Green, ed. *Luce Irigaray: Teaching*. New York: Continuum, 2006.

_____. *i love to you: Sketch of a Possible Felicity in History*. Translated by Alison Martin. New York and London: Routledge, 1996.

_____. *The Sex That is Not One*. Ithaca, NY: Cornell University Press, 1985.

_____. *To Speak is Never Neutral*. Translated by Gail Swab. London and New York: Continuum, 2002.

Jackson, J. B. "Anthorphobia, or the Death of Landscape." *Modulus* 20 (1991): 109.

Jackson, Lesley. "Finnish carpets and textiles." *Modern Carpets + Textiles*, Spring (2006): 36-41.

Jankovic, Vladimir ."Intimate Climates: From Skins to Street, Soirées to Societies." In *Intimate Universality: Local and Global Themes of Weather and Climate*. Edited by J.R. Fleming, V. Jankovic and D.R. Coen, 1-34. Sagamore, Massachusetts: Science History Publications, 2006.

Jessup, Philip C. and Francis Deák. *Neutrality: Its History, Economics and Law, Volume 1: The Origins*. New York: Octagon Books, 1976.

Kangas, Gene. *Maine Antique Digest* 2007. Accessed 1 March 2009. http://maineantiquedigest.com/articles_archive/articles/may07/finnrug0507.htm

Kirkham, Pat, ed. *Women Designers in the USA, 1900-2000* (New York: Yale University Press, 2000).

_____. *The Gendered Object*. Manchester, UK and New York: Manchester University Press, 1996.

Krauss, Rosalind E. "Horizontality." In *Formless: A User's Guide*. Edited by Bois Yve-Alain and Rosalind E. Krauss, 93-103. New York: Zone Books, 1997.

Kullack, Tanja. *Architecture: A Woman's Profession*, Berlin: Jovis, 2011;

Kunzig, Robert. *The Physics of Glass*. Accessed 13/05/2012. Accessed 13 May 2012. http://www.glasslinks.com/newsinfo/physics.htm (1 of 3)

Kucni, Carin, ed. *Joseph Beuys in America: Energy Plan for the Western Man*. New York: Four Walls Eight Windows, 1990.

Labbe, Jacqueline. *Landscape, Gender and Romanticism*. New York: St. Martin's Press and London: MacMillan, 1997.

Latour, Bruno. "On recalling ANT." In *Actor Network Theory and After*. Edited by John Law and John Hassard, 15-25. Oxford: Blackwell, 1999.

_____. *We Have Never Been Modern*. London: Harvester Wheatsheaf, London, 1993.

Latour, Bruno. *What is the Style of Matters of Concern?*. University of Amsterdam: Van Gorcum: 2008.

Law, John. "After ANT: Complexity, Naming and Typology." In *Actor Network Theory and After*, ed. John Law and John Hassard, 2-14. Boston and Oxford, UK: Blackwell Publishers; Keele: Sociological Review, 1999.

Lebovici, Elizabeth. "This is not my Body." In *Spheres of Action: Art and Politics,* edited by Éric Alliez and Peter Osborne, 65-77. London: Tate Publishing, 2013.

Lees-Maffei, Grace. "Introduction: Professionalization as a Focus in Interior Design History." *Journal of Design History* 21 (1) (2008): 1-18.

Liaropoulos-legendre, George. *ijp: the book of surfaces*. London: AA Publications, 2003.

Lippard, Lucy R. *The Pink Glass Swan: Selected Essays on Feminist Art*. New York: The New Press, 1995.

Lloyd-Thomas, Katie, ed. *Material Matters; Architecture and Material Practice*. London and New York: Routledge, 2007.

Lucas, P. H. C. B. *Preface to The State of Wilderness in New Zealand*. Edited by Gordon Cessford, ix-x. Wellington, New Zealand: Department of Conservation, 2001.

Marjorie Hass, "Fluid Thinking: Irigaray's Critique of Formal Logic." In *Representing Reason: Feminist Theory and Formal Logic.* Edited by Rachel Joffe Falmagne and Marjorie Hass. Lanham, Boulder, New York, Oxford: Rowman & Littlefield Publishers, 2002, 71-89.

Massey, Doreen. *For Space*. Los Angeles, London, New Delhi, Singapore: Sage Publications, 2005.

_____. *Space-time and the Politics of Location In Architecturally Speaking: The Practices of Art, Architecture and the Everyday*. Edited by Allan Read. New York: Routledge, 2000.

McDowell, Linda *Gender, Identity & Place Understanding Feminist Geographies*. Minneapolis: University of Minnesota Press, 1999.

McKellar, Susie and Penny Sparke, *Interior Design and Identity*. Manchester: Manchester University Press, 2004.

McMullin, Ernan, ed. *The Concept of Matter in Modern Philosophy*. Notre Dame, London: University of Notre Dame Press, 1978.

Meikle, Jeffrey L. "Into the Fourth Kingdom: Representations of Plastic Materials, 1920-1950." *Journal of Design History* 5 (3) (1992): 173-182.

Melchionne, Kevin. "Living in Glass Houses: Domesticity, Interior Decoration, and Environmental Aethetics." *Journal of Aesthetics and Art Criticism* 56 (2) (1998): 191-200.

Messer, Thomas M. (no title). *Arts* 45 (8) (Summer 1971).

Ministry of Culture and Heritage, Te Manatt Taonga (2005-2008). *Te Ara Encyclopedia of New Zealand*, www.

teara.govt.nz.

Miriam Webster Dictionary, Accessed 9 April 2012. http://www.merriam-webster.com/dictionary/tolerance

Muir, John. *Wilderness Essay*. Salt Lake City: Gibbs-Smith Publisher, 1980.

Naa Norle Lokko, Lesley. *White Papers, Black Marks: Architecture, Race, Culture. London*. The Athlone Press, 2000.

Nauman, Bruce "Mapping the Studio I (Fat Chance John Cage) (2002)." Accessed 23 June 2012. http://www.diaart.org/exhibitions/main/29

Noever, Peter, ed. *James Turrell: The Other Horizon*. Germany: Cantz Verlag, 1999.

Oldershaw, Barbara et. al., "Gender and Design." *Design Book Review* (1992): 7-45.

Oxford English Dictionary. Accessed 24 February 2009. http://www.oed.com

Petrucsa, Doina, ed. *Altering Practices: Feminist Politics and Poetics of Space*. London and New York: Routledge, 2007.

Pollack, Linda. "American Ground: Four Kinds of Disturbances." *Lotus International* 100 (1990): 104-128.

Ponge, Francis. *Le parti pris des choses/The Voice of Things*. Paris: Gallimard, 1942.

_____. *Soap*. Translated by Jane Dunlop. Stanford, CA: Stanford University Press, 1989.

_____. *Text on Electricity, ~e; Text on Electricity (Ponge)*. Accessed 20 June 2012. http://archives.openflows.org/electronetwork-l/msg00273.html

_____. *The Making of the Pre: La Fabrique Du Pre*. Translated by Lee Fahnestock. Geneve: Albert Skira, 1971.

Praz, Mario. *An Illustrated History of Interior Decoration from Pompeii to Art Nouveau*. London: Thames and Hudson, 1964.

Preston, Julieanna. "A Fossick for Interior Design Pedagogies." In *After Taste: Expanded Practices in Interior Design*, edited by Kent Kleinman, Joanna Merwood-Salisbury and Lois Weinthal, 92-109. New York: Princeton Architectural Press, 2011.

Preston, Julieanna ed., Interior Economies, IDEA Journal (Australia and New Zealand, 2011). http://idea-edu.com/journal/2011-idea-journal/

_____. "Into After." In *The Proceedings of Interior Space and Other Places*, IDEA 2010 Symposium, Brisbane, AUS. http://www.idea-edu.com/Symposiums/2010-Interior-Space-in-Other-Places

Pringle, Patricia. "Scampering Sofas and 'Skuttling' Tables: The Entertaining Interior." *Interiors: Design, Architecture and Culture* 1 (3) (2010): 219-243.

Rabinowitz, Cay Sophie. "Aziz + Cucher: Landscapes and Interiors." (Sydney: Artereal Gallery, 2006). Accessed 4 June 2012. http://www.azizcucher.net/critical-text/aziz-cucher-lancscapes-and-interiors-catalog-essay-bycay-sophie-rabinowitz

Rancière, Jacque. *The Politics of Aesthetics: The Distribution of the Sensible*. Translated by Gabriel Rockhill. London and New York: Continuum, 2004.

Reed, Christopher. *Bloomsbury Rooms: Modernism, Subculture, and Domesticity*. New York: Bard Centre, 2004.

Regier, W. G. (no title), *Prairie Schooner*. Spring (1975): 90.

Rendell, Jane, Barbara Penner and Iain Borden. *Gender Space Architecture: An Interdisciplinary Introduction.* London and New York: Routledge, 2000.

_____. "Undoing Architecture." In *Occupying Architecture: Between the Architect and the User*. Edited by Hill, Jonathan, 135-145. London and New York: Routledge, 1998.

Rendell, Jane. *Art and Architecture: A Place Between*. London: I. B. Tauris, 2006.

_____. *Pursuit of Pleasure: Gender, Space and Architecture in Regency London*. London: The Althone Press, 2001.

_____. *Site-writing: The Architecture of Art Criticism*. London and New York: I. B. Tauris, 2010.

Rice, Charles. *The Emergence of the Interior: Architecture, Modernity, Domesticity*. London and New York: Routledge, 2007.

Robin Kinross, "The Rhetoric of Neutrality." *Design Issues* 2 (2) (1985): 18-30.

Rosenberg, John D. *The Genius of John Ruskin: Selections from his Writings*. Edited with an introduction by John D. Rosenberg. London: Allen and Unwin, 1964.

Rothschild, Joan and Victoria Rosner. "Feminisms and Design: Review Essay." In *Design and Feminism: Re-visioning Spaces, Places and Everyday Things*. Edited by Alethea Cheng, 7-34. New Brunswick, NJ: Rutgers University Press, 1999.

Ruskin, John. *The Storm-Cloud of the Nineteenth Century, Two Lectures Delivered at the London Institution*, 1884, Project Gutenberg. Accessed 29 June 2012. http://www.gutenberg.org/etext/20204.

Rykwert, Joseph. "Architecture is All on the Surface, Semper and Bekleidung." *Ressegna* 20 (93) (1998): 20-29.

_____. "Gottfried Semper: Architect and Historian." In *The Four Elements of Architecture and Other Writings*, Translated by H. F. M. a. W. Herrmann, New York: Cambridge University Press, 1993.

Sandin, Gunnar. "Modes of Transgression in Institutional Critique." In *Transgression, AHRA Critiques: Critical Studies in Architectural Humanities*. Routledge, Abingdon Oxon and New York, forthcoming.

Scher, George. *Beyond Neutrality: Perfectionism and Politics*. Cambridge: Cambridge University Press, 1997.

Schnapp, Jeffrey T. "The Fabric of Modern Times." *Critical Inquiry* 24(1) (1997): 191-245.

Semper, Gottfried. *The Four Elements of Architecture and Other Writings*. Translated by Harry Francis Mallgrave and Wolfgang Hermann. New York, Cambridge, Sydney: Cambridge University Press, 1993.

Serres, Michel and Bruno Latour. *Conversations on Science, Culture and Time*. Ann Arbor: University of Michigan Press, 1995.

Shaw, W. N. *Forecasting Weather*. London: Constable & Company Ltd, 1933.

Shonfield, Katherine. "Purity and Tolerance: How Building Construction Enacts Pollution Taboos." *AA Files, Annals of the Architectural Association School of Architecture*, 28 (Autumn 1994): 34-40.

Shultis, John. "Social and Ecological Manifestations in the Development of the Wilderness Area Concept in New Zealand." In *The State of Wilderness in New Zealand*. Edited by Gordon Cessford, 6-7. Wellington, New Zealand: Department of Conservation, 2001.

Solnit, Rebecca. *As Eve Said to the Serpent: On Landscape, Gender, Art*. Athens, GA: University of Georgia

Press, 2001.

Somerville, Margaret and David J. Rapport. *Transdisciplinarity: Recreating Integrated Knowledge.* Oxford, UK: EOLSS Publishers Co, 2000.

Sparke, Penny. "The Things which Surround One: The Domestic Aesthetic." In *As Long as it is Pink: The Sexual Politics of Taste*. London: Pandora, 1995.

_____. "Modern Interior: A Space, a Place or a Matter of Taste?" *Interiors: Design, Architecture and Culture* 1 (1-2) (2010): 7-17.

Stead, Naomi ed. "Special Issue: Women, Practice, Architecture" in *ATR* (Architectural Theory Review), 3 (2012): 2-3.

Stamelman, Richard. "The Object in Poetry and Painting: Ponge and Picasso." *Contemporary* Literature 19 (4) (1978): 409-428.

Stein, Gertrude. "Poetry and Grammar." In *Lectures in America*. Boston, MA: Beacon Press, 1985.

_____. "Patriarchal Poetry." In *The Yale Gertrude Stein*. Introduction by Richard Kostelanetz. New Haven, CT: Yale University Press: 1980.

_____. "Sacred Emily." In *Geography and Plays*. Boston: Four Seas, 1922, 178.

Stroll, Avrum. *Surfaces*. Minneapolis: University of Minnesota, 1988.

Surelius, Uuno Taavi and Alex Maeson. *The Ryijy-rugs of Finland: A Historical Study*. Helinski Finland: Otava Publishing Company, 1926.

Sutherland, David. "Wonderful Things." *Parnassus: Poetry in Review*, Spring/Summer (1973): 60-8.

Taylor, M. 'Surface-Talk.' *Architectural Design: Surface Consciousness*. Edited by Mark Taylor, 30-35, London: Wiley-Academy, 2003.

Taylor, Mark and Julieanna Preston, eds. *INTIMUS: Interior Design Theory Reader*. Chichester, UK: Wiley, 2006.

Taylor, Mark C. *Hiding*. London: The University of Chicago Press, 1997.

Teysott, George. "A Topology of Thresholds." *Home Cultures* 2 (1) (2005): 89-115.

_____. "Mapping the Threshold: A Theory of Design and Interface." *AA Files: Annals of the Architectural Association School of Architecture* 57 (2008): 3-12.

Thales of Miletus, Internet Enyclopedia of Philosophy. Accessed 22 June 2012. http://www.iep.utm.edu/thales/

Thoreau, Henry David. *Walden, or Life in the Woods*. New York: Thames & Hudson, 1854.

Thrift, Nigel. *Non-Representational Theory: Space, Politics, Affect*. London and New York: Routledge, 2008.

Tracy, James ed. *The Civil Disobedience Handbook: A Brief History and Practical Advice for the Politically Disenchanted*. San Francisco: Manic D Press, 2002.

Turnovský, Jan. *The Poetics of a Wall Projection*. Translated by Kent Kleinman. London: AA Publications, 2009.

Turpin, John. "Omitted, Devalued, Ignored: Reevaluating the Historical Interpretation of Women in the Interior Design Profession." *Journal of Interior Design* 27 (1) (2001): 1-11.

Vellacott, Jo. "Women, Peace and Power." In *Reweaving the Web of Life: Feminism and Nonviolence.* Edited by Pam McAllister, 30-35. Philadelphia: New Society Publishers, 1982.

Weisman, Leslie Kanes. *Discrimination by Design: A Feminist Critique of the Man-Made Environment*. Urbana and Chicago: University of Illinois Press, 1994.

Wharton, Edith and Ogden Codman Jr. *The Decoration of Houses*. London: Charles Scribner's Sons, 1897.

Wigley, Mark. *White Walls, Designer Dresses*. London and Cambridge, MA: MIT Press, 1995.

Wilkins, Craig L. *The Aesthetics of Equity: Notes on Race, Space, Architecture and Music*. Minneapolis and London: University of Minnesota Press, 2007.

Wilson, Elizabeth. *The Sphinx in the City: Urban Life, the Control of Disorder, and Women*. Virago: London, 1991.

Woolf, Virginia. *The Waves*. Edited with an introduction and notes by Gillian Beer. Oxford: Oxford University Press, 2008.

Yeneva, Albena. "When a Bus Met a Museum: Following Artists, Curators and Workers in Art Installation." *Museum and Society* 1 (3) (2003): 116-31.

Young, DJB. "The Material Value of Colour: The Estate Agent's Tale." *Home Cultures* 1 (1) (2004): 5-22.

Zeller, Thomas. *GHI BULLETIN 35* (FALL 2004). Accessed 1 July 2012. http://www.ghidc.org/publications/ghipubs/bu/035/35.123.pdf